ᵀᴴᴱ FUTURE ᴼᶠ
BUSINESS
JOURNALISM

Thank you for
appreciating good
business journalism.

Chris Roush

THE FUTURE OF BUSINESS JOURNALISM

WHY IT MATTERS FOR WALL STREET AND MAIN STREET

CHRIS ROUSH

Georgetown University Press / Washington, DC

The publisher is not responsible for third-party websites or their content. URL links were active at time of publication.

Library of Congress Cataloging-in-Publication Data

Names: Roush, Chris, author.
Title: The future of business journalism : why it matters for Wall Street and Main Street / Chris Roush.
Description: Washington, DC : Georgetown University Press, 2022. | Includes bibliographical references and index.
Identifiers: LCCN 2021038468 (print) | LCCN 2021038469 (ebook) | ISBN 9781647122560 (hardcover) | ISBN 9781647122577 (ebook other)
Subjects: LCSH: Journalism, Commercial--United States.
Classification: LCC PN4784.C7 R66 2022 (print) | LCC PN4784.C7 (ebook) | DDC 070.4/4965--dc23
LC record available at https://lccn.loc.gov/2021038468
LC ebook record available at https://lccn.loc.gov/2021038469

∞ This paper meets the requirements of ANSI/NISO Z39.48-1992 (Permanence of Paper).

23 22   9 8 7 6 5 4 3 2 First printing

Printed in the United States of America

Cover design by Amanda Hudson, Faceout Studio
Interior design by Paul Hotvedt

*To all the business journalists out there who simply want
to accurately and fairly report what is going on in
companies and economies. And to all the business owners, employees,
and consumers who simply want news
that will help them make good decisions.*

CONTENTS

FOREWORD

My first editor, Bill Castle, sat me down in October 1987 to go over the first story I turned in for the *Boston Herald* and wasted no time explaining the mission of business news.

"There are only two reasons people read business news," he said. "Either they work for the companies we write about or their competitors, or they are looking to invest in them."

That simple lesson, which I remember each time I get stuck writing, has carried with me for more than three decades. It has sustained me through a career in newspapers, wire services, electronic and digital media, television, radio, and now newsletters. Who are your readers?

During this time, business news and the way it is delivered went through a revolution. From the ticker tape of the old Dow Jones stock tickers, clacking away in newsrooms and brokerage houses, to the algorithmic delivery of real-time employment data to hedge funds. From the one-page business sections of city newspapers, with two staff tucked away in the dark corners of vast metro newsrooms, to the mighty armies of news services like Bloomberg and Reuters, with thousands of reporters across the globe. No other genre of journalism has changed so much, or created more opportunities for journalists.

Along the way, these changes in business news began to leave its readers—the reason it exists—behind. In *The Future of Business Journalism*, author and longtime journalism professor Chris Roush shows how money, influence, and, indeed, fame corrupted the process. From how business news was gathered to who it was sold to, Roush eloquently narrates a story of the rise and fall of business news in the last twenty years that left millions disenfranchised from valuable economic information in one of the "most misunderstood inequalities in twenty-first-century American civic life."

It started with the newspapers.

The late 1980s saw the rise of mutual funds and 401(k)s. Millions more people started to care about the stock market and investing strategies as well as changes to their industries. Tech, biotech, energy, financial services. All boomed.

Business news boomed with them, particularly in the big metro dailies, whose business sections exploded with local coverage and advertising from businesses small and large and from brokers such as Dean Witter Reynolds and E.F. Hutton.

The *Wall Street Journal* and the *Journal of Commerce*, the bibles of 1970s and 1980s business news, were joined by new services such as Bloomberg, CNBC, CBS MarketWatch, *The Street, The Business Insider,* Thomson Financial, and many more. All beefed up on journalists to chronicle the daily flow of trillions of dollars through global markets.

Then business news began to change. Perhaps it simply reflected the changing face of the industries it covered. But it became more focused on big money. The rise of the celebrity CEO, which started with Lee Iacocca at Chrysler and Jack Welch at General Electric, soon spread to the flashy tech sector and included Jim Manzi at Lotus Development as well as Steve Jobs and Bill Gates at Apple and Microsoft, respectively.

Investment bankers became superstars. And criminals. Or both. Deals became art forms. Donald Trump became famous for being rich, among other things.

Business news services did what they were told. Follow the money. In the process they left millions of readers behind—readers who cared nothing about private jet fleets or Davos but who wanted desperately to know what the job conditions were in their hometowns. Who was hiring? Was their company stable? Should they invest all their retirement savings in their own company's stock?

Without the guidance of focused journalism, the era of inequality— with its catchy 1 percent level of success—exploded. Roush details how advances in technology, the rise in financial markets, and the emergence of the celebrity CEO fed a system that ultimately created five major business news providers for elite Wall Street clients and very little for everybody else.

Roush then explores how we can get back to our roots of serving the masses, from a chapter on how new technologies that help journalists crunch data will invigorate local investigative stories to a chapter called "The Education Imperative," which provides a reasoned argument about why we need more business journalism majors.

My own story is instructive. Before I was hired in Boston, I spent a semester during college at the *Green Bay Press-Gazette*. For several weeks I wrote the police blotter, which I thought was the pinnacle of reporting excitement. I paid little attention to reporters Harry Maier and Tom Murphy over in the business section. I wasn't sure what they did. Except I noticed that, around town, they were the most popular people at the paper. The local businesses knew them and worked with them to craft the stories local readers needed.

As my career advanced from Wisconsin to Boston to London to San Francisco, I became part of the problem. When trying to explain the allure of business news to people who didn't follow it, I'd routinely compare it to sports. It's got big stars, big salaries, exciting events such as hostile takeovers, the Consumer Electronics Show in Vegas, and the Mobile World Congress in Barcelona. Bond yields were like batting averages, measuring the credibility of companies and countries.

All true to a business news junkie. But like sports journalists, business reporters had raised its importance to more than what it was. A glamorized game.

Business editors became minor celebrities themselves, as did the public relations executives who simultaneously built their empires helping companies manipulate business journalists to improve their own stories. The dance between journalists, bankers, CEOs, public relations reps, and lawyers took over, almost always leaving out the employees who all these big deals affected. At least until the layoffs were announced.

This is where Roush's analysis takes the invaluable form of historical narrative. He explains how business news created legends out of CEOs and investment bankers, only to see them turn on the press, aided by public relations executives, to not only restrict truth-telling but manufacture disinformation as well.

He explores how companies built elaborate networks and newsrooms of their own to push their agendas, bypassing the media. Or how they simply used social media networks like Twitter, as did Elon Musk and Trump, to skip journalists altogether.

As business news boomed, advertising sales and licensing sales did too. By 2000, news organizations were swimming in revenue, much of it from the dot-com bubble. As an editor, I tried to stay above it, and that further distanced me from our readers—the ones who might respond to the ads.

One of the biggest conundrums for editors back then was the demand for small business advertising. Clients wanted it, but editors never thought much of it. What was a small business after all? A software sales startup? Or a chain of laundromats? How could we produce editorial that appealed to both? Also, wasn't the collapse of the junk bond market more interesting?

Eventually, as in all markets, the bubble collapsed on itself. The stock market crash of 1987 and the dot-com market in 2001 were important warnings along the way. But the great financial crisis of 2007–8, which brought world economies to their knees, really was the catalyst. Countries thrown into recession. Millions without work. Business news covered it all, but it too had been exposed for focusing on the wrong stories. Why some bankers didn't go to jail was never really explained to the satisfaction of the average reader. The disconnect even contributed to the media's failure to identify the social conditions that gave rise to the Trump candidacy.

Social media soared in this vacuum, and Google and Facebook soaked up almost all of the advertising, putting newsrooms out of business far and wide. Companies and public relations executives blamed journalists for the trouble and began shutting them out rather than working with them to provide the most accurate information.

Today we still have a hierarchy of business news titles, celebrated at glitzy award ceremonies in New York and London. But underneath, business news is suffering with the rest of journalism, a victim of the rampant inequality it helped to fuel.

The pandemic has made it even worse. While sheltering in place recently at my home in the Bay Area, I picked up the local paper at a market. The front page had a photo of our family's favorite local Italian restaurant and a story saying it was moving to a smaller location. The news of the moving of Servino's—one of tens of thousands of businesses closed or affected by the pandemic—wouldn't shake global markets. But in our hometown, it was the big story. Neighbors went there. Friends worked there, and at competitors. What did the move mean? We were lucky to have our local paper to try to tell us. Millions of others no longer have a local paper.

Business news isn't sports. Or politics. Or show business. It really is all news. Reporting on how people and companies make, use, and invest money to build our societies is vital at every level.

Despite social media, and the collapse of media business models, the demand for news today is stronger than ever. Smartphones make us all news junkies, so the need for journalists to sift through the information to make sense of it for us is also greater than ever.

New business models will evolve, and journalism will live to fight another day. Perhaps thirty years from now someone will write about how these days were the glory days of journalism, when we found our way back to our audiences.

If we do, it will be by following guideposts set forth by Roush in *The Future of Business Journalism*, from business news schools and improved technology to adapting business models and, especially, news coverage to provide greater transparency and more accessibility to the millions of readers who need to know what's going on. Roush shows how the dilemma goes right to the heart of the media's current credibility crisis and instructs how we can fix it.

The challenges and responsibilities for business news journalists are more important than they've ever been. The basic mission remains the same. Follow the money but remember who your readers are. Books like this will help us find our way back. They have to. The public good demands it.

—David Callaway, former editor in chief of MarketWatch.com and
USA Today, and former chief executive officer of TheStreet.com.

ACKNOWLEDGMENTS

I'm like any book author. When I have an idea that I think people might be interested in, I run it by people that I respect in the field. In the case of *The Future of Business Journalism*, most of those people were individuals who have been in business journalism or currently are involved in the field. They provided valuable feedback on various topics and ideas in this book.

They include:

- Dean Starkman, a fellow-in-residence at the Center for Media, Data and Society and a visiting lecturer at the School of Public Policy at the Central European University in Budapest. He is also the author of *The Watchdog That Didn't Bark: The Financial Crisis and the Disappearance of Investigative Journalism* and a former *Wall Street Journal* reporter.
- Roddy Boyd, founder and editor in chief of the Foundation for Financial Journalism, the only nonprofit journalism outlet specifically dedicated to producing business journalism.
- Joseph Weber, a journalism professor at the University of Nebraska and a former colleague at *BusinessWeek* magazine who has written about business journalism education.
- Rob Wells, a journalism professor at the University of Arkansas and a former business journalist at Dow Jones, the Associated Press, and others. Wells has researched the impact of business publications and is one of the early business journalists.
- Angel Arrese, a professor at the University of Navarra in Pamplona, Spain, who has been researching business journalism for three decades.
- Dan Simon, a public relations executive in New York who specializes in handling financial communications. He agreed that the relationship between reporters and public relations people could be much better.
- Tom Herman, a longtime business journalist who now teaches at Yale University.

I should also note that Alexander Laskin, a public relations professor at Quinnipiac University, reviewed some of the chapters and provided feedback. Laskin is a noted expert in investor relations and corporate communications.

Jerry Brown, the former dean of the School of Journalism at the University of Montana and one of my mentors, read the first half of the book's first draft and provided some great feedback. Other experts such as Chris Martin at the University of Northern Iowa also gave important guidance.

Hilary Claggett, senior acquisitions editor of global business at Georgetown University Press, should also be thanked. Without her, this book would not have happened. She approached me after reading one of my previous books and liked my elevator pitch during our first meeting. She massaged the proposal and the manuscript with the help of the press's anonymous peer reviewers, to whom I'm also grateful for suggestions leading to key improvements.

Thank you for reading. I'm passionate about business journalism and its role in society. I think we—reporters, editors, business owners, public relations people, government officials, consumers—can do a lot better than what we've been doing.

INTRODUCTION

Juliann Francis is not your typical business owner. She and her husband, Kirk, own Captain Cookie and the Milkman, which has three locations in Washington, DC, and another in Raleigh, North Carolina, as well as three food trucks. They also operate a kitchen that makes food for similar companies. But before she joined the business, which her husband started, in 2015, she was a reporter for Bloomberg News for five years, covering all types of business and economics news.

She'd like to use business news outlets to obtain information to help make decisions on how to operate the company, like finding new locations. Instead she has come to rely on going directly to government agencies and talking to other business owners to find out what she needs. Her media consumption comes primarily from nonbusiness publications such as *Washington City Paper* and public radio.

"It's hard to find good, local business news," she said. "As a former reporter, I tend to go to the source on a lot of things I need to know about. But as a former reporter, I know the value of having someone distill that information skeptically so that I can trust it is valuable. As a business owner, I don't want to have to be searching."[1]

The lack of good, helpful, and aggressive business news—on topics ranging from local unemployment to consumer confidence—means that Captain Cookie delayed making critical decisions about its business during the COVID-19 pandemic, said Francis. She and her husband are relying on national news outlets and adjusting their business by extrapolating those stories to the local level.

"We should not have to be relying on government sources," said Francis. "We should have media looking at information skeptically. That would help us all from a business standpoint."[2]

Francis is not alone. Across the country, business owners and consumers on Main Street are searching for the business news and information that they need for their lives—everything from local real estate news to economic data to companies that are hiring or laying off workers. Most major metropolitan papers have dramatically cut their business news coverage or eliminated it altogether. In smaller towns and cities, a quarter of all newspapers—the major source of information in many communities—have closed, according to research from Penelope Muse Abernathy formerly with the University of North Carolina at Chapel Hill.[3] The media outlets that remain in most towns and cities, such as local radio, television, and online websites, barely report on business and economics news.

That is in stark contrast to the abundance of business news made available, for a price, to Wall Street and top corporate executives—news and information that can be used to make investments or major acquisitions. Bloomberg News, for example, has 2,700 journalists around the world that primarily cover business and economics topics. But the rate to rent a Bloomberg terminal is about $2,400 a month, a fee few business owners outside of Wall Street can afford. There are also plenty of other news outlets for those wanting specialty business news—for a price. A popular business news outlet for those wanting coverage about companies in trouble, Reorg Research, charges anywhere from $50,000 to $150,000 per year for its stories.

These outlets are primarily covering big, national companies and major economic trends, not business news happening in, say, Des Moines, Iowa.

Businesses such as Captain Cookie, which has about $1.8 million in revenue and about six dozen employees, couldn't afford business news from Bloomberg or niche business news publications such as Reorg, even if it was relevant to their needs. Francis said she and her husband recently bought a subscription to the *Triangle Business Journal* to get a better handle on the Raleigh market, but she questions, "Is there information in there that is going to pay off?"[4]

This shift in business news content away from many consumers and small business owners on Main Street and toward Wall Street investors, money managers, and Fortune 500 executives is one of the most misunderstood inequalities in twenty-first-century American civic life. There's a business and economic information gap that exists between most businesses and consumers in the country and those at the higher echelons of Corporate America and Wall Street. And the news media are part of the problem, according to recent research, because they focus too much on Wall Street and not enough on Main Street.[5]

If you work at an investment management company, venture capital firm, hedge fund, or mutual fund or are an executive at a major corporation and wish to understand the economic outlook for an asset (or even an industry), you have countless tools available to you. There is Bloomberg, Reuters, the *Wall Street Journal*, and other fee-based news enterprises. There are specialty news operations that examine and report on niche segments such as *Law360*, Distressed Debt Research, and Reorg.

To manage these many news streams, there is Nexis, which also allows you to search up to twenty years back. These high-end business news consumers can spend up to $500,000 a year to obtain business and economics news to deeply research something. And when they are betting $500 million or more on an acquisition or investment, it's a pretty easy purchase.

Then there is the news and information available to the so-called general interest business reader, probably a small- or mid-sized business owner interested in a topic or industry but who doesn't have much, if any, money to pay for such news. This reader's local or regional paper has sharply cut or eliminated all forms of business coverage, so her ability to get news (without committing to a subscription to a national paper, which, again, will primarily cover national topics) is limited to whatever a Google search index returns when she queries it. And what does Google search prioritize? Whatever is being discussed or debated in message boards, forums, and specialty blogs such as *Seeking Alpha*, which are heavily opinionated. So that query is going to return a massive amount of opinion, argument, and agenda, not reliable, factual information from a trusted source.

An educated news consumer is usually pretty good at quickly sifting informational wheat from chaff, but how many are educated, discerning news consumers like business owner Francis, a former business journalist?

As a result, the average business news consumer on Main Street staggers through a news desert. She doesn't care much about the capital markets because her investments are typically in a 401(k) plan or retirement account where she's not making investment decisions; instead, she wants to know more about some of the bigger employers or real estate developments in her area. But the paper she subscribes to doesn't cover the local university and hospital—in most small- and mid-sized cities, universities and hospitals are almost always the largest employer. And because there is no business coverage, there is likely to be nothing available to the average business news consumer on things like public subsidies and the practical import of rezoning.

Maybe she gets lucky: An enterprising editor assigns a story to a good reporter who looks deep into a challenge facing a local company—maybe even going so far as to explore whether the company's actions are as pure as they assert. Or a local company might litigate against another business or an executive, and a reporter picks up the court filing and writes a story about the brouhaha.

Business news that is valuable to consumers and business owners is an increasingly infrequent occurrence at most local media outlets. With no exposure to professionally edited and reported business journalism, other businesses and consumers are likely suffering as well.

The Future of Business Journalism concludes that Wall Street is getting the business news that it needs, but Main Street is not. Consider the news stories on July 31, 2020, as an example of how coverage for many business owners and consumers needs to be fixed: Most news organizations focused their top business news coverage on President Donald Trump ordering TikTok to sell its US operations by September 15, perhaps to Microsoft. It was a story that investors and those on Wall Street cared about. They wanted to know what banks would negotiate that deal and how it would affect Microsoft's stock price and that of its competitors. This was a story that may have been of interest to Microsoft employees as well.

But the bigger story that day—the one that affected millions of Main Street businesses and consumers around the country—was about the expiration of US government benefits for consumers who lost their jobs during the pandemic. Businesses needed to know whether the people who bought their goods and services would be coming back on August 1. Consumers needed to know whether they were going to have money to pay for what they needed. And yet that story did not receive as much coverage or as prominent play as the TikTok announcement.

Business journalism today primarily serves the 1 percent, not the 99 percent, with its focus on stories such as TikTok and reporting on the daily stock market. This situation needs to be exposed. It's not the fault of the reporters and editors, but it needs to be addressed.

For the future of business journalism, we must fix its problems so that it provides content for everyone, from consumers to small business owners to investors and big corporations. This book examines how we arrived at the current situation (Part I: Causes of the Information Gap), why it matters to both Wall Street and Main Street (Part II: Consequences and Their Impact), and how we can solve the problems (Part III: Solutions to the Problem).

WHERE IT ALL STARTED GOING WRONG

A series of business decisions, societal changes, and other factors contributed to the current situation, and we'll dissect these points in detail throughout the book. But here's a quick overview.

Many local business owners and employees and consumers used to have access to a lot of business news. Metropolitan dailies as recently as the 1990s published robust stand-alone business sections, full of advertising from companies that wanted to peddle their wares to other businesses and to consumers, although critics claim that such coverage was hardly critical. Many of them also published a tabloid business section on Mondays and special sections such as the top one hundred public companies in their regions. Those days are now long gone as the primary provider of news and information for many consumers in many cities has cut its printed business news to one page inside another section. Online business news "pages" on newspaper websites often include nonbusiness news.

The cutting of printed business news in daily newspapers started when *The Star-Ledger* in Newark, New Jersey, cut its printed stock listings from its business section during the first week of September 2001. During the next decade virtually every other metropolitan daily newspaper, and many smaller newspapers, would follow suit. That would lead to the cutting of stand-alone business sections, which had been supported by the stock agate. Newspaper editors and publishers argued that consumers could retrieve stock and mutual fund prices online.

Most of the cuts in business news coverage at metro dailies occurred in the first decade of the twenty-first century, but the trend has continued. For example, the *Omaha World-Herald*, at the time owned by billionaire Warren Buffett, cut two business reporters and the designer of its business section in early 2018. Before the layoffs the paper had a business news staff of nine. In addition, the paper cut its stand-alone business section to just two days, Saturday and Sunday.[6] In 2017 the *Milwaukee Journal-Sentinel* cut its stand-alone business section to where it remained a section front only on Wednesdays and Sundays. On other weekdays, business news is found inside the A section.[7]

To be sure, important business and economics news does appear regularly on the front page of metro daily newspapers. But the amount of space devoted to business and financial news in 2021 is less at every daily newspaper than it was at the turn of the century. And virtually every local newsroom has fewer business news staffers than it did in 2000. At the *News & Observer* in Raleigh, North Carolina, there are two business journalists, down from ten at the beginning of the century. With fewer stories covered, society is not as well informed about how businesses impact everyday lives.

A LACK OF NEEDED COVERAGE

Then there's what's being covered—or, more accurately, not being covered. There are more than 30 million businesses in the United States, but the majority of business news coverage is devoted to the larger companies that hold brand-name recognition with consumers. This is despite the fact that a majority of jobs in the country are at small businesses, and more than 99 percent of all businesses in the United States are considered small businesses. In addition, more than 40 percent of net new jobs between 1992 and 2013 were created by small businesses.[8]

As daily newspapers have cut back on their coverage, they're spending less time writing and reporting less on smaller businesses and the issues that they face; one of the issues is that this type of coverage requires time and effort that many business reporters don't have. Even magazines have cut back on small business coverage. *Fortune Small Business*, for example, closed in 2009. "There is so much going on with small business right now," said former-business-journalist-turned-small-business-owner Francis. "There is so much movement. You have businesses going under, and others surviving because they have been opportunistic."[9]

To be sure, the weekly business newspapers that exist in most major cities in the country such as the *Triangle Business Journal* do cover small businesses on a regular basis. Papers owned by American City Business Journals and Crain Communications have taken over covering many business and economics stories in their towns and cities. But it's impossible to cover all of the news that is occurring with these companies. And when news about companies goes uncovered, it hurts economies. In 2017 I wrote:

The decline of business news coverage in the main media outlets in the state is harming the economy. A lack of objective news and information about what's going on at businesses, particularly small, entrepreneurial companies that dominate the state, means that investors, consumers and executives often don't know what's going on. Lack of such coverage, I believe, has made it harder for some companies to find new investors and recruit employees and executives.[10]

There have been some recent efforts to focus business news on smaller companies. In 2018 *USA Today* launched a new online section called USA & Main aimed at helping small businesses. While the content focuses on small business owners, it also includes stories about how some small businesses were created and have grown. Another business news entity, Fit Small Business, was founded in 2014 and now has sixty employees. It focuses on being a resource for small business owners who seek news and information to help launch and grow their businesses. The Associated Press also started a small business newsletter in 2018.

Yes, many larger businesses are vital to the economic success of the towns and cities in which they operate. But the media organizations in those towns and cities often ignore them or write about them only when major news occurs. These companies employ hundreds and often thousands of workers in these areas, so ignoring them means that those consumers often look elsewhere to find news and information about their employer. Take the *Denver Post*, for example. Its business desk covers a metro area of 3 million people. It has one business reporter, alongside a consumer reporter and an economy / real estate reporter, covering the region. But there are eleven Fortune 500 companies in the area, along with thousands and thousands of smaller companies. The paper can't feasibly cover every important business news story coming out of these companies.

And when a media organization does cover local or state business news, it's also more likely to be political these days. Political polarization, and the "politicization" of everything in the United States, has made economic, financial, and business issues fade away amid demagogy and political battles. And if it hasn't faded away at most media, they are turning business, economic, and financial news into a political story. Some business stories may be political-related, but not certainly all business stories have a political angle.

There's also a knowledge issue. Despite gains in business journalism expertise in the last three decades, many business reporters and editors at smaller publications lack the skills and knowledge required to provide nuanced and analytical coverage. There is no formal business journalism training required, and many media organizations have cut their training budgets in the past decade.

Business journalism education at the undergraduate and graduate level is inconsistent across the country, and most journalism programs fail to offer a single course in business reporting. Only about a dozen journalism programs offer either an undergraduate or master's degree in business journalism, and those students often don't enter the field, choosing instead to go into public relations or a business-related job. The programs also are somewhat limited in output. The Knight-Bagehot business journalism program at the Columbia University Graduate School of Journalism accepts fewer than a dozen students a year.

Business journalism editors say the quality of people applying for jobs in the field is lacking. Mary Jane Pardue of Missouri State University found in 2012 that more than half of the editors still rated journalism graduates unprepared, "reflecting a call once again for academia to recognize that business journalism is a reporting area in high demand, requiring specialized skills that often are not taught at universities."[11] While business journalism students may take classes in their journalism departments, many of them are still not taking classes in accounting, management, and other business areas.

There's also a trust problem caused by social media and by those looking to use business news to make money on investments. In late June 2018 a tweet quoted Harley-Davidson CEO Matt Levatich as calling President Trump a "moron" and as criticizing the tariffs implemented on motorcycles. It was retweeted more than 25,000 times and covered in the business press before Levatich could respond to say that he had never made the comments. "It's shameful we live in a time when people create fake quotes," Levatich said in a tweet on June 27, 2018. "There's one attributed to me on Twitter. I have not, nor would I ever, speak about the President of the United States or anyone else in that way."

Fake news about companies and their leaders affects the trustworthiness of business journalism that is properly vetted and carefully written. Companies have been negatively affected by fake news releases being posted on the internet and then written about by reporters. In other cases, stories are written and placed on reputable websites by people whose sole intention is to profit off a rise in a company's stock price. In April 2017 the Securities and Exchange Commission charged twenty-seven firms and individuals with promoting stocks through articles placed on business news sites such as *Forbes, Yahoo Finance, Motley Fool,* and *Benzinga.*[12]

Fake news in business journalism is not new, but it has become more common due to technology and due to the increased focus—some would call it pressure—to produce higher stock prices and stronger financial performances. In the past it may have been sponsored content made to look like editorial stories written by an independent journalist or company-sponsored research released as an academic study. A company managing its earnings or sales higher or lower to be more in line with Wall Street analyst expectations could also be considered fake news in that the changed numbers don't accurately reflect the performance of the business. Publishing fake news can harm a company as well as the overall reputation of business journalism. A 2018 study by boutique public relations firm Bospar found that 28 percent of public relations professionals were willing to "manufacture news."[13] If they do that for a company and it's exposed, the public perception of that company may suffer.

Corporations, and the public relations professionals that they hire, are also hurting business journalism with a lack of interaction. *Washington Post* columnist Steven Pearlstein wrote that corporations are increasingly declining to comment to business journalists who call them while reporting a story, which can often hurt the quality of the content that is published. In other cases, the companies give "carefully scripted responses that are rarely satisfying, with no opportunity to follow-up," added Pearlstein.[14] He argued that such strategies have contributed to the decline in trust of companies by consumers.

Some companies also implement strategies to intentionally mislead business journalists or prevent reporters from doing their job. Matthew Herper of *Forbes* wrote about how Theranos CEO Elizabeth Holmes lied to him in an interview about its technology. Herper wrote, "But she managed, in a rushed interview that left me little time to write, to recast the way I thought about the story, and I wrote about those partners' confidence that her critics were wrong instead of the many red flags they raised. (One group had done no due diligence on Theranos machines!)."[15] Holmes was convicted in early 2022 of wire fraud. Goodyear Tire & Rubber asked an Arizona judge in 2018 to call a reporter for auto news site Jalopnik to ask them not to publish documents related to tire failure.[16] The judge declined. And Walt Disney Company prevented *Los Angeles Times* entertainment reporters from reviewing its holiday movies because it was not happy with the paper's business news coverage of its business dealings with the city of Anaheim.[17]

Companies also hurt business journalism when they criticize journalists for providing fair coverage when their operations struggle. Sears Holdings Corporation CEO Edward Lampert blasted the media at its 2017 annual meeting for "unfairly singling out" the company over the past decade and blamed "irresponsible" coverage for the retailer's woes. Tracy Rucinski of Reuters writes that Lampert said, "It's irresponsible and it's been irresponsible for too damn long. We're just looking for a fair chance. Excuse my rant, but a lot of what we're doing deserves a chance to see the light of day." Rucinski noted, however, that "five journalists in attendance were not allowed to speak with Lampert or ask questions."[18] Sears filed for Chapter 11 bankruptcy court protection a year later and closed locations.

Here's another way that businesses are hurting the media that report about them. Companies implement strategies to bypass traditional business media and create newsrooms that disseminate content about their operations or news related to their businesses. Broker TD Ameritrade hired Bloomberg Television reporter Oliver Renick in 2017 and launched the TD Ameritrade Network, which is now airing four hours of content every day about the markets. In 2021 venture capital firm Andreessen Horowitz, which invests primarily in technology companies, announced it was starting a media outlet to cover tech and business news. Companies have every right to take such strategies, but it hurts business journalism's goal of providing information to consumers.

Many companies and company executives are also bypassing the business news media and communicating directly with consumers through social media. Chief executive officers such as Tesla's Elon Musk regularly go on Twitter to talk about what's going on at the company or to reply to what's been reported about their business. In doing so, these companies and executives put the business news organizations in an unenviable spot of reporting what has already been disclosed in other media, giving consumers the perception that they are not needed anymore when in fact it's the media's work analyzing and distilling information—as Captain Cookie's Francis mentioned—that is vitally important.

It should be acknowledged that excellent, top-quality business journalism is produced every day. A business-related story has won a Pulitzer Prize almost every year during the past decade. An example is the work done by the Associated Press in uncovering how large seafood companies were using slaves to harvest fish. The problem is, this is primarily done at the upper levels of the media food chain at places such as Bloomberg, Reuters, the *New York Times*, and ProPublica, which most business owners and consumers don't read or ever hear about. This is not the coverage, unfortunately, that the average business owner or consumer needs for their everyday life to make decisions about how to spend money. Dean Starkman wrote in *Columbia Journalism Review* in 2012 that the bulk of business news coverage now catered to professional investors, not the public. He wrote, "It should at least be clear that investor-oriented news—no matter how well executed—is not the same as public-interest business reporting. If we do nothing else, let's get that straight."[19]

Society faces a crisis when it comes to business news and information. We need to recognize what the problems are, how they manifested themselves and grew, and how they can be solved. It's going to take a lot of work by everyone—journalists, companies that are covered and companies that own media outlets, consumers, public relations practitioners, and government officials—to return to a place where business journalism once again provides society with what it needs.

The future of business journalism—for both Main Street and Wall Street—depends on serious and smart changes being made.

Part I

CAUSES OF THE INFORMATION GAP

Going back in history can be illuminating in exploring how things change and seeing how parts of society have changed—for good or bad—and affected how we live.

In this case, looking at the history of business journalism shows that, decade after decade, news stories and other content helped all businesses and consumers. For example, in the mid-nineteenth century journalist Henry Varnum Poor helped expose railroad companies with questionable finances and business plans, weeding out the businesses that just wanted to scam investors. At the turn of the twentieth century journalist Ida Tarbell documented how the Standard Oil Company was forcing smaller operators out of business, leading the US Supreme Court to declare it a monopoly and order its breakup into smaller companies. At the same time, Upton Sinclair exposed the meatpacking industry for its unsafe working conditions and its unhealthy products, leading to reforms that benefited workers and meat eaters.

Fast forward to the 1960s, and Rachel Carson's *Silent Spring* detailed how chemical companies were releasing pesticides and other products into the environment that were killing animals and, sometimes, people. Ralph Nader's *Unsafe at Any Speed* led to changes in how the automobile industry made cars, improving safety for consumers and indirectly helping the auto industry better compete against foreign competitors.

These were all business stories that had broad effect on consumers, businesses, and customers. But in the past decade or so, business news has shifted. Yes, there are still stories that have broad appeal across the spectrum of small businesses, large businesses, their employees and customers. But increasingly the business news that dominates society today focuses on the big companies and the machinations of Wall Street, not Main Street.

As companies become bigger and bigger, and as many media organizations that serve towns and cities decrease their news content and their staffs, the business news—who's hiring, who's expanding, who's looking to move into a new product line—that's important to smaller businesses and consumers has been primarily ignored. The business news that they get is often not relevant because it's about bigger corporations and major economic factors that don't impact the operations of smaller companies or the wallets of customers and employees.

The first part of *The Future of Business Journalism* examines how this shift happened, looking at some external factors that have hurt business journalism. It's not just one or two changes but a combination of events—from the decline of daily newspapers to the more adversarial approach taken by many company executives and public relations professionals who have forgotten that the media have helped in many ways that have been quantified for decades—that have led us to this point. Social media and political polarization have also played a big role in the lack of business news that society needs to grow and thrive.

If you're a business owner, an employee, or a consumer, you're probably unaware that many of these changes have impacted your ability to make good, sound financial decisions. These changes have evolved over years and sometimes decades. Read on to realize how you're not getting the news you need.

1

A SYMBIOTIC RELATIONSHIP

To understand the importance of business journalism to businesses and consumers as well as why the field is so important, let's look at the history of how businesses used journalism and media to develop and grow, and how business news impacts what society thinks about companies and the economy. Both topics show how critical business news is to all types of readers, listeners, and watchers.

The importance of business news and information to companies and economies has been shown to be vitally important for centuries. We've seen time and time again that "news" has helped societies thrive and grow across the globe, and such information has allowed businesses and people to make decisions to improve themselves. Yet, in a dramatic shift from the past, specific businesses and executives have recently rebelled against news and information when it does not cater to their goals. This is despite research showing that coverage helps build companies' brand name recognition and could even help their performance when they have an initial public offering.

In addition, academic research has shown that business media play an important role in markets, providing details about what investments and companies might be good places to put money into or bad places to take money out of. Such news coverage, even if it is neutral, has been shown to help provide information to society, and a decline in pertinent business news is harmful to consumers. Business news and information also helps good companies because it exposes their unethical and illegal competitors.

A BRIEF HISTORY OF THE RELATIONSHIP BETWEEN JOURNALISM AND BUSINESS

The development of journalism and media—that is, communications—goes hand in hand with the development and growth of companies. At the beginning of civilization, man communicated about economic issues using cave drawings, argues David Forsyth.[1] The Code of Hammurabi of ancient Mesopotamia included interest rates and minimum wage laws among its guidelines for ancient society. In Greek civilization shortly before Christ's birth, business information was recorded on stone. After being conquered by the Romans, the Etruscans taught the Romans how to record business transactions.[2] In China, Emperor Wang Meng instituted an income tax—10 percent of revenue—on professionals that was widely documented during the first century. By the seventh century credit was produced on woodcuts in China due to a shortage of copper, which was used for coins.[3] In the first millennium, kingdoms in Ethiopia and Eritrea used trading routes to provide economic information in addition to various goods.[4] And by the thirteenth century, merchants had begun a basic bookkeeping system to keep track of transactions financed by loans.[5]

One of the first financial information advances occurred in the sixteenth century, when European banker Jacob Fugger began placing employees in important cities around the continent who would correspond with him to explain what was happening where they were. Historian George Matthews says these reports "represent the news as it might appear on the unedited, continuously moving tape of a press agency's teletype: true reports and false rumors, trivial occurrences and important events."[6] Writing more recently, author Greg Steinmetz argues that Fugger used this financial information, or news, to his advantage, becoming the richest man who ever lived, adjusted for inflation.[7] Similar systems of financial letters developed around Europe, particularly in London, which replaced Antwerp, Belgium, as the commercial center of the continent as a result. Business historian Alfred Chandler and James Cortada argue in *A Nation Transformed by Information* that information about business has been a vital building block in developing society and the economy since the 1600s.[8]

The early newspapers in both England and the American colonies were used primarily to disseminate business information. For example, an advertisement in a January 1727 issue of the *London Gazette* by a law firm offered a two-hundred-pound reward for a businessman who had gone bankrupt and disappeared.[9] Many early British newspapers provided a way for business owners to sell their wares, including the cargoes of ships that were arriving at port. The *London Post* of July 22–24, 1700, included the number of tea tables, chests, and pieces of china as well as various teas arriving from China on the ship *Sarah Galley*.[10]

In the colonies as well, newspapers were used for business purposes. The *Boston News-Letter* of 1704 noted that its purpose was to provide for "persons who have any lands, houses, tenements, farms, ships, vessels, goods, wares or merchandise to be sold or let."[11] Many early American newspapers used the word "Advertiser" in their name to convey that their primary purpose was aimed at helping businesses, not providing news. Seeing the growth of these newspapers, the British passed the Stamp Act of 1765, which levied a tax on the paper used by newspaper printers. The taxation of goods and services—from paper to tea—on businesses became the focal point of the American Revolution and of newspapers of that time.

The major newspapers in the eighteenth century and early nineteenth century throughout the Americas were called "price currents" for a reason. Their front pages gave detailed listings of the current prices, usually split between domestic goods and foreign goods. Most of the rest of these papers included shipping information and advertisements from merchants. The first daily newspaper in the United States, *Daily Items for Merchants*, also included information such as insurance premiums and prices of freight. Today, we'd consider these newspapers as early versions of wire services such as Reuters or Bloomberg, providing news and data about the economy to traders and business owners.

In the nineteenth century newspapers and magazines developed around specific industries. The most prominent of these was the *American Railroad Journal*. Think of nineteenth-century railroad companies as the internet and software companies of the twenty-first century. They revolutionized business and rapidly increased the speed at which goods could be delivered. The *American Railroad Journal*, under editor Henry Varnum Poor, analyzed railroad companies' financial performance, turning its focus away from the engineering and technical aspects of railroads. His publication is considered the first to help investors in determining whether a company was a sound investment.[12]

Other business newspapers thrived, although the advent of the penny press led to more mainstream newspapers that contained news about crime and government in most cities. The *Journal of Commerce* was started in 1827 and included business news from around the growing country. The *Wall Street Journal* started in 1889 and would expand in the twentieth century to be a national newspaper. Today it's the largest-circulation paper in the country, counting both print and online subscribers. Still, in the large city newspapers, business news was second only to politics during this time, with those papers allocating 22.9 percent of their coverage to business and labor, according to a study by Washington University professor Gerald Baldasty.[13] And advertising helped many businesses gain additional coverage. After a department store ran full-page ads for a year, a St. Louis newspaper called the store a "model advertiser" in an editorial.

Media coverage of businesses became more critical in the late nineteenth century and early twentieth century during the time of the muckrakers, demonstrating that business journalism could have an impact on society. Upton Sinclair's exposé of the meatpacking industry led to the creation of the US Food and Drug Administration. Ida Tarbell's extensive reporting of the monopolistic tactics of the Standard Oil Company in *McClure's* magazine led to the company being split up by the US Supreme Court. Other industries that received aggressive reporting included insurance and textile, and topics such as child labor were examined.

The creation of public relations or publicity managers occurred at around the same time. Westinghouse hired a journalist in 1889 to promote the company, and General Electric created a public relations department eight years later. The first public relations agency opened in 1900 in Boston. While initially these efforts led to additional information being released about companies, companies began using public relations to promote their positive actions and to thwart negative articles. The seeds of the issues between business journalists and companies had been planted.

It would not be until the 1960s and 1970s that the media would again aggressively and consistently take on corporations for the good of society. Post–World War II production led to a rapidly expanding economy. But companies were exposed by journalists for their wrongdoings. Rachel Carson wrote in *Silent Spring* in 1962 that pesticides from chemical companies were killing animals and people, for example. Still, the relationship between business media and corporations remained somewhat cordial and professional. For example, *Fortune* magazine placed the CEO of General Motors on its cover in the 1960s, giving him the platform to explain his managerial philosophy.[14]

The Arab oil embargo, inflation, and a stagnant stock market in the early 1970s caused an explosion of business and economics news as consumers began to see the importance of knowing about their companies and how they spent money. The demand for business journalism during the next two decades led to increased coverage and increased problems with the relationship with companies. Television channels and shows as well as magazines devoted to business news started during this time, and the percent of space in newspapers devoted to business news more than doubled in the 1990s, from 7 percent to 15 percent.[15] But a fair amount of that coverage was devoted to lists of the richest and the largest, and laudatory profiles about CEOs became commonplace. So did coverage of internet-based companies with little to no revenue. Companies began skillfully using their growing importance in society to use the business press to achieve a more positive perception with most people. "Top executives and shrewd investors are good bets to emerge as media heroes," wrote Norman Solomon.[16]

The chasm between businesses and business journalism began to grow. Despite such coverage, a poll conducted in 1992 by Louis Harris and Associates found that slightly more than half of executives have a positive view of business journalism in America, and only 27 percent believed that business journalism was fair, balanced, and accurate.[17] This was despite a study of business editors showing a more positive opinion about capitalism than the general public. A study by the First Amendment Center at the Freedom Forum Institute at Vanderbilt University found that 68 percent of executives believed that the news media are biased against management, and about half of the executives surveyed believed that they were not quoted accurately. Nearly three-fourths believed that journalists portrayed businesses in a negative light, despite the overall positive coverage that existed in the 1990s.[18]

When the stock market fell in 2001 and many internet-based companies went out of business, pundits argued that business journalism missed the story. A Selzer & Company survey for the American Press Institute in 2003 found that executives gave their local daily newspapers low marks for content and credibility. One in three was dissatisfied with the quality of business news in their local newspaper, and more than 60 percent gave reporters low marks for being able to ask intelligent questions about their businesses.[19] In the early part of the twenty-first century, business news coverage became more adversarial as reporters and editors became more aware of their failings. And during the recession that gripped the United States in 2007 and 2008, reporters pointed out many business wrongdoings, exacerbating the contentious relationship with companies, although much of their coverage simply reported on the problems that led to thousands losing their jobs and their investments. It was also at this time that the tide began to shift in journalism, and many media organizations cut the number of journalists devoted to business and economics news; at the same time, the number of working public relations professionals increased.

We'll examine in a later chapter the distrust between company executives and the journalists who cover them, but it's important to note that, despite the animosity, study after study shows that coverage of business, economics, and markets actually helps businesses and society. Failing to recognize this is a critical misstep. As distrust in business journalism grew within corporations, leading to an increasing lack of cooperation with the media, research was showing that businesses and the economy used that coverage to prosper.

COVERAGE HELPS BUSINESSES

Professors and researchers across the academic spectrum study relationships and effects. The bulk of the analysis of how business media impacts corporations and the economy has been done by those on the business side, not the media researchers. It's hard to argue that the research has a bias toward arguing the positive effects of media when the data is coming from business researchers, not the mass communication researchers.

That research also shows that the business community historically has played a negative role in business news, putting pressure on publications to ignore stories that might place them in a negative light with society despite the article's contribution to a better understanding of how that business works, according to Maha Rafi Atal of the University of Cambridge.[20] Many companies and executives view the business journalism field as an enemy rather than as a way to help society understand their impact. A report by the Freedom Forum Institute, written by Mike Haggerty and Wallace Rasmussen, concludes: "Executives perceive media people as liberal, adversarial, well-educated do-gooders—mal-informed and misinformed about business—who operate with little or no supervision. In their view, reporters come into interviews unprepared, ask arrogant and unfair questions, and see only one side of an issue, the side that is inevitably anti-business."[21]

Despite this adversarial perception in the business community, the importance of quality business journalism to consumers, to businesses, and to economies is well-established. Grant Hannis of the University of

Massey in New Zealand writes that "economic activity is, after all, how a society creates and distributes wealth, and a vigorous business journalism sector helps ensure this occurs efficiently, by, for instance, transmitting information between economic agents and exposing corporate malfeasance."[22] This interaction manifests itself in different ways. Paul Tetlock discovered that *Wall Street Journal* content predicts movements in broad economic indicators such as stock market activity.[23] Corporate reputation researcher Craig Carroll found that mentions of corporations in the news media had a stronger effect on their public perception than advertising spending or press releases. He writes: "There was a direct correspondence between the amount of media coverage devoted to executive performance and workplace environment and the use of these attributes by respondents for describing the firm's reputation."[24] A study presented at the 2018 International Conference on Advances in Social Sciences and Sustainable Development found that the business media help a company "disseminate brand value and employ more outstanding staff, and the assistance is more significant with local media." The same study also found that business media could increase the success of a company's initial public offering.[25]

Corporate executives, particularly those of public companies, should want media coverage, research has found. J. Felix Meschke, now a finance professor at the University of Kansas, examined how the market reacted when a chief executive officer was interviewed on financial news network CNBC and found an abnormally high return in the CEO's company stock price before the interview and after it ended.[26] And CEOs should want coverage from well-known business news organizations. Alexander Dyck of Harvard Business School and Luigi Zingales of the University of Chicago found that stock prices react more strongly to the release of a company earnings report when the media outlet reporting on its financial performance is more credible than other media.[27]

The impact of what is reported and the relationship between a business journalist and company executives have also been documented. Yi Jin, in a master's thesis at the University of Missouri in 2008, found a direct relationship between the tone of news coverage that a company receives on television news shows like NBC *Nightly News*, CBS *Evening News*, and ABC *World News* and the public perception of its corporate reputation. The more media coverage a company received, the worse its corporate reputation.[28] Journalists are "more reluctant to include highly negative performance information or make performance attributions that reflect poorly on the CEO's leadership" when the executive becomes friendly with reporters, according to a study in *Organization Science* by James D. Westphal of the Ross School of Business at the University of Michigan and David L. Deephouse at the Alberta School of Business at the University of Alberta.[29] Westphal and Deephouse also found that negative coverage in the media "has the potential to incite retaliatory behavior by the CEO. One possible form of retaliation is to limit or cut off communication with the offending journalist."[30]

The watchdog function of business journalism has also been quantified, helping the economy weed out the bad apples, so to speak. Gregory Miller discovered that one-third of accounting fraud cases brought by the Securities and Exchange Commission between 1987 and 2002 were first reported by business journalists. "In each of these articles, it is the reporter making the case for accounting impropriety based on analysis of public and private information," wrote Miller, a business school professor at Michigan. "No other information intermediaries (i.e. analysts, auditors, or the legal system) are cited."[31] The watchdog function of the media toward companies goes back nearly two hundred years, according to research from James Taylor of Lancaster University. He wrote for the Institute of Historical Research at the University of London that coverage in England of Ponzi schemes and disappearing executives was prevalent in the 1830s and 1840s.[32]

When news outlets cut back on providing such information, consumers and businesses suffer. A decline in business journalism content more than a decade ago came at a time when coverage was needed the most—during the economic crisis that gripped the United States in 2007 and 2008. Mass communication researchers Daniel Riffe and Bill Reader disclosed that most consumers relied on newspapers for local business news at a time when those newspapers were cutting back such coverage. "The findings of this study do provide evidence that increased coverage of state and, especially, local business news is a worthy investment for newspapers," wrote Riffe and Reader.[33] Their study came out just as most newspapers began cutting back on business news.

A 2020 study from the Dukas Linden Public Relations firm supports the idea that investors are clamoring for more information during times of economic crisis. This study found that 56 percent of respondents wanted to see and read more stories about how a business planned to recover from the pandemic. And nearly half—46 percent—said they are reading and watching more business news than before COVID-19 reached the United States.[34]

The importance of business news coverage to investors is also well documented. Writing in the *Journal of Economic Behavior and Organization*, Tomasz Piotr Wisniewski and Brendan Lambe of the University of Leicester discovered that business journalists help investors outperform the market. They found that journalists "not only report on the state of economic reality, but also play an active role in creating it. Investors acting upon sentiment in media reports would have been able to improve their investment performance."[35] More recently, Nicholas Guest, currently an accounting professor at Cornell University, found that *Wall Street Journal* articles with analysis of a company's financial performance increased trading volume in its stock and improved "price discovery."[36] And Samuel B. Bonsall and Karl A. Muller from Pennsylvania State University and Jeremiah Green from Texas A&M University found that greater media coverage of a company's financial performance leads to improvements in investor awareness and increased trading by retail and institutional investors.[37]

Some in the business media, ironically, should be ignored when it comes to providing investment advice, researchers have found. In 2009 two Northeastern University business school professors found that stock picks made by CNBC's Jim Cramer underperformed the overall market during a thirty-day period after the selections.[38] In 2016 Wharton professors at the University of Pennsylvania found that a portfolio that Cramer runs as part of a newsletter service underperformed the overall market.[39] Of course, there is a question whether Cramer is a business journalist or a Wall Street professional who happens to have a show on a business news channel. This literature review makes no decision on that argument but notes that the Society for Advancing Business Editing and Writing featured Cramer as its keynote speaker during its fiftieth anniversary conference. The distinction to draw here is that when the business media report financial news, it's helping, but when they're providing financial opinion, the opposite usually occurs.

Plenty of other research from business-related academics supports the positive benefits of business news coverage for companies. More coverage in the financial media meant higher stock prices for the companies covered, according to a 2015 study from a University of Cambridge professor.

Andrew Hill wrote in the *Financial Times* that the research shows "quantity was more important than quality: it did not seem to matter whether the news about the boss was good or bad as long as there was a lot of it. Alas, the study may encourage zealous PRs to push their leaders more aggressively into the media. It also gives corporate leaders a perverse personal incentive to court publicity."[40]

A study out in 2014 in the *Review of Financial Studies* found that mutual fund managers and other investors based their decisions on what stocks to invest in based on their access to business media coverage, unlike individual investors who do not have similar access.[41] In other words, professional investors used business media to help make investment decisions.

Other research supports that investors are helped when the business news media increase their coverage of company financial news. The media contribute to more informed and efficient financial markets. In 2016 researchers from Stanford University and the University of Washington found compelling evidence that earnings stories written using software and published by the Associated Press increase a company's trading volume and liquidity. "After the articles are published, we see an increase in trading volume that persists three to four days after the story comes out," explained Ed deHaan, an accounting professor at the University of Washington and one of the authors of the study.[42]

Similar research in the *Pacific-Basin Finance Journal* in 2017 found that when a company is recognized by investors through the mass media, it helps to increase its investor base and causes a stock price reaction. Trading activity was affected by the quantity and the quality of the news, the researchers found.[43] In the same year, research in the *International Journal of Strategic Communications* discovered that media coverage was crucial in helping publicly traded companies achieve a fair stock price.[44]

More recently, researchers at Pennsylvania State University and Texas A&M University reported in the *Journal of Accounting and Economics* that increased business media coverage of a company's financial performance helped improve investor information at both the professional and amateur level, and that the media serve an important role in capital markets during uncertain times. "We find that the greater coverage leads to improvements in trading and pricing," wrote the researchers.[45]

It is also possible for readers to estimate the state of the economy through business news stories, according to a study from a Yale University finance professor. In his paper, titled "The Structure of Economic News," he demonstrates that measures derived from textual analysis "accurately track a wide range of economic activity measures and that they have incremental forecasting power for macroeconomic outcomes, above and beyond standard numerical predictors." His model reviewed more than 800,000 articles published in the *Wall Street Journal* and Dow Jones News Archive between 1984 and 2017 and found that they helped quantify the economy for readers. He called the business media "a central information intermediary in society" that "continually transforms perceptions of economic events."[46]

A similar study in 2017 by the Federal Reserve Bank of San Francisco reached a similar conclusion. It analyzed tens of thousands of news articles from January 1980 to April 2015 about the economy to create a new sentiment index based on words used by reporters and their sources. The report concluded that the sentiment extruded from the articles "has predictive power for future economic activity."[47]

Finally, let's not forget about the continued role of business journalism as a watchdog for society. A Duke University public policy and economics professor found that naming a company that has violated workplace health and safety regulations can result in a 73 percent improvement in compliance by other businesses. Writing in the *American Economic Review*, Matthew Johnson discovered that when Occupational Safety and Health Administration press releases were sent to the local newspaper, compliance by other nearby facilities improved more as compared to if OSHA had inspected each of those facilities directly. "OSHA would have to conduct an additional 210 inspections to elicit the same improvement in compliance as sparked by a single press release about severe violations," wrote Johnson.[48]

You'd think that after reviewing these research results, company executives and the public relations and investor relations professions that work for them would be aggressively courting the business news media for stories. As I will show in later chapters, that hasn't been the case in the past decade. In example after example, companies have become adversarial toward the business media, even finding ways to deliver their communications using other outlets.

Of course, the rapid changes in journalism's business model haven't helped either. Let's examine those issues now before we get to the impact of company executives and the public relations professionals that they employ.

2

THE BUSINESS MODEL FAILURE

The *Atlanta Journal-Constitution* newspaper operated a robust business news desk in the late 1990s. In 1997 the business news operation had a staff of more than forty. One reporter covered just two companies—Coca-Cola and Home Depot. Another reporter covered another large employer in the city, Delta Air Lines, and the transportation industry. Yet another reporter followed UPS. All four companies employed tens of thousands of workers in the Atlanta area, and their ups and downs were followed closely. There was also a reporter who wrote about the stock market each day, particularly how Georgia-based companies rose or fell. One reporter wrote about commercial real estate while another journalist followed residential real estate. There was a technology reporter and a reporter who covered small business. Other reporters covered different beats.

That staff, along with more than a dozen editors, produced a full business news section each weekday and Saturday and a stand-alone Sunday business news section that provided deep takes and insights into the local business community. If you subscribed to the paper, you likely received several stories each week around a business or economic topic important to you as a consumer or as a business owner.

The newspaper was also thriving as a business. The morning *Constitution* and the afternoon *Journal* had daily circulation of nearly 410,000 in 1998. And it had more than 675,000 subscribers on Sunday, making it one of the top twenty newspapers in the United States.[1] Its reporters frequently traveled across the country to cover stories. The Home Depot reporter went to Davenport, Iowa, to examine Home Depot's rural store concept, and the Coca-Cola reporter traveled to Terre Haute, Indiana, to look at Coca-Cola's experimental contour twelve-ounce can. The Coca-Cola reporter also traveled to New York to cover its new ad campaign.

Those days are long gone. Parent company Cox Enterprises closed the sister *Journal* newspaper in 2001. By 2008, just a decade later, the number of subscribers during the week fell to just below 275,000, a decline of nearly one-third. At about the same time the newspaper began cutting jobs on both the editorial and the business side and cut its circulation area in Georgia. In 1996 it circulated the paper in 124 counties, but at the end of 2020 it circulated to 32 counties primarily around Atlanta, and the paper's circulation had dropped to just 111,000 copies.[2] That does not include readers who are getting their news from the paper's website. However, the metropolitan Atlanta population is now more than 6 million—double the population of 3 million in 1997.

And the paper's business news coverage? It cut its printed stock listings—the backbone of its stand-alone business news section—in 2006. Then the stand-alone section itself was cut in 2009, moving it inside the A section. "This was a difficult decision. After all, Atlanta is a business town," wrote editor-in-chief Julia Wallace when the decision was announced.[3] Its well-known business columnist Maria Saporta, who chronicled local business leaders for decades, took the paper's buyout offer in 2008, as did others from the business news desk. Its Coca-Cola reporter left for a job covering the same company for Bloomberg News. Its utilities, telecom, and media reporter left for Bloomberg in 2011. (Larger business news organizations can pay higher salaries and often pry away top reporters at smaller news outlets.) The business news desk is now one-eighth the size it was back in 1997, and there is no business editor. Four reporters cover business, but they also cover nonbusiness topics on occasion. A senior editor who also edits nonbusiness stories oversees the coverage.

The changes in business news coverage at the Atlanta daily are not uncommon. They've happened at virtually every metropolitan daily newspaper across the country in the past twenty years and are a prime example of the problem facing business journalism: Many small business owners and consumers no longer have a way to obtain the financial and economics news that they need to make important decisions.

The reasons are simple. Declining revenue from classified advertising and print advertising has not been recouped by increasing revenue from online advertising. Paid subscribers declined as papers started giving away its content online. (The Atlanta paper now charges for an online subscription and offers only a limited number of free stories, but many consumers still believe that news should be free or at least cheap.)

With fewer subscribers and fewer ads, the traditional print newspaper—the primary source of business news for many Americans, was cut in size. Business news was one of the first sections to go, and most metropolitan daily newspapers now include just one page of business news tucked inside another section, and that page is often full of wire service stories of national, not local, importance. Even the Sunday section, once a place to showcase in-depth local reporting, is sparse with local business news. The front page of the *Atlanta Journal-Constitution*'s Sunday business section on November 29, 2020, included no local news stories produced by its staff. It contained four Associated Press stories and one from the *New York Times*—all national stories.

Other factors have also changed business news. The rise of social media means that many consumers go to Twitter, Facebook, and other places to get their business news, even though that news may not be coming from a reliable source. While many websites now cover business news, for the most part they are specialized and cover only a certain industry; they also don't focus on geographic regions that are important to consumers and businesses. A recent example would be *Business Insider*, which does a great job of covering major business and economics news but not many local business and economics stories.

This decline in business news coverage from traditional media delivery systems such as daily newspapers has come at a time when businesses and consumers need business and economics news the most. Business news and the economy have become the dominant issues in people's lives during the past decade, with peaks during the financial crisis of 2007–8 and the pandemic-related recession. In February and March 2009 the Pew Research Center found that news about the economic situation in the country dominated news coverage, but that began to decline later in the year.[4] It also found that much less coverage was paid to the financial problems of average consumers. Mark Jurkowitz, an associate director at Pew, was quoted in the *New York Times* as saying that it was easier for media to cover the economy from a national perspective "than to fan out around the country and measure the impact on real lives."[5]

The past decade is also when most traditional local and regional media dramatically cut such coverage. The economic crisis in the media sector makes it necessary to prioritize content, and, except for exceptional moments, news about economy, business, and finance has never been a central priority in the newsrooms. Instead, most metropolitan newspapers still provide a full sports section and other news such as entertainment. Lucy Sutherland concludes in her Emerson College master's thesis, "Tiny business sections are often buried behind sports sections, and many business desks languish—even at some larger metropolitan dailies—with just a handful of reporters who struggle with shrinking news holes."[6]

To be sure, like other journalism fields, business journalism has undergone a rapid transformation in the past two decades that has helped dissemination. Spurred by technology advances, business news and information is no longer primarily found in the printed newspaper, placed alongside stock and mutual fund listings and commodities prices. Business news consumers now go to websites, podcasts, radio shows, blogs, and other delivery formats to obtain what they feel they need to know about the comings and goings of businesses. That content, as I will detail, is not necessarily what they're looking for or produced by people trained in journalism to provide factual information. The big news organizations on television, such as CNN and Fox News, pay little attention to business news throughout the day. Local television and radio news rarely devote time to a business news story unless it has national prominence.

And many new business news media now focus on delivering information to corporate executives and investors instead of the consumer and small business owner. "Business journalists approach their job mainly from the point of view of what investors want to know and hear about," said ProPublica's Jesse Eisinger. "That, of course, is often 180 degrees to what the public wants to know."[7]

The decline in business news coverage in traditional media formats also affects how stories are covered. Nadine Strauss of the University of Amsterdam discovered that business journalists think of themselves as watchdogs but act more like information disseminators. Part of the reason for this, she notes, is the recent cutback in editorial jobs covering business and economics news at many media organizations.[8] Craig Ey, former editor of the *Philadelphia Business Journal*, wrote that business journalists recently stopped asking the tough questions routinely asked by government and political reporters. "Life and business may be unfair at times, but an active press can certainly help level the landscape," argues Ey.[9] Other business journalists warn that the financial pressures on mainstream media may mean that boring topics that may have a big impact on businesses and the economy such as credit derivatives and subprime mortgages—two causes of the economic crisis of 2007 and 2008—could be ignored by the journalists who remain in the newsroom.[10]

The economic changes present an opportunity, according to former *Wall Street Journal* editor Gerard Baker. He notes that the diminishing revenue from traditional places such as subscriptions should cause media outlets to provide more business journalism. "The need of businesses, of investors, of consumers, of journalists, of governments, of everybody for . . . high-quality information they can trust is greater than ever," Baker said. "Good business journalism can thrive in that environment."[11]

THE BUSINESS MODEL

For more than one hundred years, daily newspapers acted as an intermediary between consumers, advertisers, and the journalists who produced them. The reporters and editors provided the content. Their counterparts on the business side of the newspaper sold ads that were placed around the content. And consumers read both the ads and the stories.

That model ended in the twenty-first century. Fewer and fewer businesses want to advertise in newspapers, either in print or online. They can now reach consumers through other delivery methods such as social media. Advertising revenue fell from $37.8 billion in 2008 to $14.3 billion in 2018, a 62 percent decline, according to the Pew Research Center.[12] With fewer ads, there are now fewer journalists to produce stories, including business news. Pew notes that the number of newspaper newsroom employees dropped by 51 percent between 2008 and 2019, from about 71,000 workers to 35,000.[13] The coronavirus pandemic accelerated that decline, according to the executive outplacement firm Challenger, Gray & Christmas, which estimated that more than 16,100 newsroom jobs were lost in 2020, the highest annual number since 2008.[14]

As you can imagine, that means fewer and fewer consumers are going to daily newspapers to get any form of news. US newspaper circulation fell in 2018 to its lowest level since 1940.[15] Other media have seen similar trends. Local and network television audiences have also declined, according to Comscore's StationView Essentials data.[16]

Research from Penelope Muse Abernathy when she was at the University of North Carolina at Chapel Hill shows the impact on society. In the fifteen years between 2005 and 2020, one-quarter of the newspapers in the United States disappeared. That leaves millions of consumers to live in what Abernathy termed "news deserts"—places around the country where there is no news, business or otherwise, about the community. Surviving media organizations are merely "ghosts," she notes, unable to report and provide news that they previously determined was important to their communities.[17] And many are now owned by public companies—90 percent of the US media organizations are controlled by five companies—influenced by investors such as hedge funds who want them to squeeze out as much in profits as possible. That means companies such as Gannett, which now controls a quarter of all US daily print newspaper circulation, deliver the same news to consumers in various cities without concern for localizing the content.

Despite these problems, which have been well documented as a business news story across the country, consumers don't understand the financial challenges facing local newsrooms that provided them business news coverage in the past. Seven out of every ten US adults believe local news media are doing well financially, according to the Pew Research Center.[18]

The pandemic exacerbated the problem with the business model. Most media are reliant on local advertisers such as car dealerships, restaurants, retailers, and real estate agents for revenue. But with people not leaving their houses to shop, these businesses are not advertising. According to FTI Consulting, newspaper ad revenue fell 20 percent to 30 percent in the early weeks of the pandemic.[19] To compound the issue, the Pew Research Center found that during the pandemic, many journalists faced issues around mental health, public safety, and widespread disinformation.[20]

However, a March 2020 poll by Gallup and the Knight Foundation found that nearly half of respondents said they were paying a "great deal of attention" to local news, up from 22 percent in December 2019. And more than eight out of ten people surveyed said that the news media were "critical" or "very important" to holding leaders in business accountable for their actions.[21] So consumers consider news important to society.

The disconnect is damaging. While most consumers receive their news from local media and believe that local news is important, local media have cut back on the news they provide because they can't afford to produce as much as they did in the past. So consumers stop subscribing or watching local news and don't get the news they need. It's a vicious cycle if not addressed.

THE LACK OF TRUST

If the failure of the business model and the impact of social media and the internet wasn't enough, the field has also been hurt by a decrease in trust. Journalism has never been one of the most trusted professions, usually ranking around the same level as politicians and car salesmen. In June 1976, 72 percent of Americans said they had a great deal or a fair amount of trust in the media, according to Gallup, but that number had fallen to 40 percent in 2019.[22] Part of that decline in trust is because consumers perceive the media as having "a great deal" or a "fair amount" of bias, according to another Gallup poll.[23] And business journalism has its fair share of critics who believe news about companies and the economy is too negative. James McCarthy, writing for the *National Review* in November 2020, says there's "obvious" bias in business coverage. "Few business writers display any understanding of the motivations or worldviews of the people who drive private enterprise," he wrote.[24]

Others would disagree. James Berger wrote in Salon in 2015 that the media have pro-business biases because they ignore coverage about labor and employment issues. "No newspaper I'm aware of has a 'Labor' section," he wrote. "There are no television networks or programs devoted primarily to labor issues. There is some coverage, of course, some in the news section, some in the business section."[25] Liz Ryan of the *Huffington Post* notes that there's not much coverage about the people who work at companies. She adds, "They power everything that happens in business, but we leave them out of the story and the equation. We don't send journalists looking for data to support the idea that paying executives tons of money is good for productivity. We take it as an article of faith."[26]

A 2017 study by two Finnish researchers discovered that shrinking or growing companies tend to receive less news coverage than stable or slow-growth companies, indicating a possible bias in what companies business reporters write about.[27] And former business journalist Dennis Kneale, who worked for the *Wall Street Journal* and Fox Business Network, has argued that there's an antibusiness bias in coverage and that companies should be more aggressive when responding to reporters.[28] (Two later chapters detail how company executives and public relations professionals have done just that.)

In 2007 *Investor's Business Daily* published a seven-part series on how the media's lack of understanding about the economy leads to ignorance from consumers. It stated, "Media bias has been detected in other studies, but this series raises an additional possibility—media incompetence in analyzing and explaining how the economy and financial markets work."[29] And a 2020 study found that the news media routinely paint a distorted picture of the economy, one attuned almost entirely to the fortunes of the most affluent while ignoring the economic conditions of the Americans who need coverage the most.[30]

A business publication, the *Wall Street Journal*, is the only media organization viewed favorably by both Democrats and Republicans, according to a 2018 Gallup and Knight Foundation survey. It received a "plus 2" rating from Republications and a "plus 24" rating from Democrats.[31] The *Wall Street Journal* was the only predominantly business news–oriented publication in the survey, and it's known for having an editorial page liked by conservatives.

Some news organizations participate in strategies that hurt their ability to appear as a fair and objective resource of business news and information. *Forbes* magazine, for example, publishes on its website content from companies that is often difficult to distinguish from the stories that its staff has produced. Jon Christian wrote for *BuzzFeed News* about how one marketer wrote articles for *Forbes, Entrepreneur,* and *Inc.* magazines where the marketer cited and linked to his clients without any disclosure. The editors at these business publications did not know such reputation-damaging content was on their sites until Christian alerted them.[32]

WHAT BUSINESS NEWS IS COVERED

Let's go back to how companies are covered and how mainstream publications are ignoring their audiences.

There are 31.7 million small businesses—typically, those with fewer than five hundred employees—in the United States, and those businesses account for 99.9 percent of all businesses in the country. They also account for nearly two-thirds of all newly created jobs and 47 percent of all private sector employees. They generated 44 percent of US economic activity in 2018, according to the US Small Business Administration, down from 48 percent in 1998.[33]

In comparison, there are approximately twenty thousand large businesses in the United States, with 53 percent of the employees in the country. About five thousand companies have issued stock that is traded on a public exchange, although some of those public companies qualify as a small company as well.

But if you go to any metropolitan newspaper's website, or any news organization's website, the companies covered will be large businesses in that community. On December 5, 2020, the business news page of the *Atlanta Journal-Constitution*'s website included multiple stories about Delta Air Lines and a story about UPS, two huge companies based in Atlanta. The stories also included one about Boston Consulting Group adding 331 jobs in Atlanta and automobile manufacturer Hyundai adding 678 jobs to a plant in the area. The one story that focused on small business, written by staff writer Andy Peters, was about how these businesses are targets of pandemic loan scams. News organizations have traditionally focused on covering the major employers in their region, and that's understandable. But if you look at the statistics, that usually means that they're providing a disproportionate amount of their "news hole," or space available, and their journalists' time and energy to big companies.

George McKerrow, the CEO of Ted's Montana Grill, an Atlanta-based restaurant chain with forty-one locations and $100 million in revenue, said, "*The Constitution* does not have much in the way of business news anymore. They really skew toward big giant companies, and in particular, public companies."[34] He argues that the business news coverage in the paper ignores topics that would be important to him and other similar-sized business, such as the debate over increasing the minimum wage.

Let's look at another example. The Raleigh, North Carolina, *News & Observer* on the same day, December 5, 2020, featured nine stories on the business news page of its website. The top story was a staff report about two people who were arrested for a shooting at a bar in the city. It's questionable whether that's "business news." The next two stories were business related and likely had some value to readers. One story reported the North Carolina labor commissioner saying that COVID-19 didn't require workplace safety rules, and the other story covered the federal government suing a New York investor for defrauding a local insurance company.

The other content on the *News & Observer*'s business news page that day included a story about local college students getting free meals,

Quicken Loans–sponsored content about real estate agents, a story about new restrictions in Southern California and San Joaquin Valley, and a story about a Japanese capsule with asteroid samples that had been retrieved in Australia.

The conclusion to be drawn here is that many local media organizations have gotten away from covering business and economics that's important to their readers and are simply filling their websites with content that they think might result in someone clicking out of curiosity. They're not looking at their local area to see what business and economics news might be of importance, or they simply don't have the manpower to cover what's important.

THE IMPACT OF BUSINESS WEEKLIES

There's some good news in all of this dreary assessment of the decline in business and economics news in mainstream media. Across the country weekly newspapers devoted to local business and economics news thrive both in print and online. They've been joined by some online-only business news outlets in some cities. Charlotte-based American City Business Journals (ACBJ) operates in 44 cities around the country, while Detroit-based Crain Communications operates in New York, Cleveland, Chicago, and Detroit. Smaller companies have business newspapers in markets such as Indianapolis, Los Angeles, and San Diego.

In many cases these news organizations have filled the void in providing business and economics news in their markets. They do a strong job of covering business news such as real estate transactions, fast-growing companies, and executives who are moving from one place to another. They also focus on smaller companies in their markets, compared to what the metropolitan newspapers covered and what the national business news organizations cover.

And for the most part, they're financially successful. Newhouse-owned ACBJ, the largest of these companies and owned by a big media conglomerate, has 1.3 million weekly print readers and 16.6 million monthly online visitors. It currently charges $135 a year for a digital subscription and $150 a year for a digital and print subscription to all ACBJ journals. The *Triangle Business Journal*, which is based in Raleigh, North Carolina, saw its paid subscriptions rise 13 percent in 2018 and another 17 percent in 2019.[35] The *Indianapolis Business Journal*, which is not owned by ACBJ, reported that its subscriptions rose 39 percent in 2019 and 2020 combined.[36]

According to ACBJ, its readers are savvy and busy. They view business news as a utility, not a luxury, meaning they want news that they can't find anywhere else. They want news and information that will allow them to make deals and that helps them run their businesses more creatively and efficiently. And they want a relationship with the business journalists. They expect business reporters and editors to understand their business as well as business in general. They want to interact with them at office parties and business journal events, where they can network with other people. And these media organizations cover the trial and tribulations of smaller businesses, not the big companies in their cities. For example, in 2020 all ACBJ papers examined how small businesses were coping with the pandemic.

Still, the average reader of a ACBJ business journal is not your typical consumer or small business owner. They have an average income of more than $200,000 and an average net worth of $1.8 million—much more than most small businesses owners. More than 60 percent of ACBJ readers are owners, partners, or top management in their companies.

ACBJ, Crain, and other business newspapers aren't in every city. In many smaller cities around the country where there's no business newspaper and no business news coverage from the daily newspaper, there is virtually no business and economics news for those who want it. An example is Macon, Georgia, which has a population of 150,000. Or El Paso, Texas, which has a population of more than 680,000. Or Montgomery, Alabama, which has a population of 200,000. Or Frisco, Texas, which has a population of 190,000.

ERECTING PAYWALLS

Media organizations that focus primarily on business news, such as the Wall Street Journal, weekly business newspapers, and Bloomberg News, have been successful in charging for their content and putting it behind a paywall. But that business model hasn't been as successful for mainstream business news organizations, where print advertising revenue and circulation revenue have both fallen in the past decade and online ad and subscription revenue have not been able to recoup those losses.

As far back as 2009, the Boston Consulting Group found that consumers would be willing to pay for online news, but only a modest amount—$5 per month, or $60 a year. Boston Consulting Group concluded this would not have much impact on the media organization's bottom line. And their subscribers' willingness to pay depended on whether the news was unique, timely, and accessible.[37]

Not much has changed in the past decade. Richard Fletcher of the Reuters Institute for the Study of Journalism found in 2019 that only 13 percent of US consumers were making an ongoing payment to receive news online. (The country with the highest percentage of paying consumers was Norway, where 26 percent of readers were making an ongoing payment.) Fletcher wrote that many news executives feared that the industry had already reached the upper limit on online subscribers. He added: "Others fear the emergence of 'subscription fatigue,' where people become frustrated by being asked to pay for multiple services separately. Will only the largest and most prominent news outlets survive, and how will they fare when forced to compete with entertainment services like Netflix and Spotify?"[38]

Those who are more willing to pay for news online happen to have higher household incomes and higher levels of education. As I explain in the next chapter, the top business news organizations have taken advantage of this knowledge, but they're generally not providing business and economics news for the masses, just for those who can afford their rates.

The Danish research group Audience Project found that Americans are not that keen on paying for financial news. Americans who pay for online content prefer other types of news instead, with 54 percent signing up for international news, 52 percent for domestic news, and just 37 percent for financial news. The American consumers surveyed by Audience Project, however, get their news from online sources more than from television, radio, and social media.[39]

It's clear that the business model for mainstream news publications, where most consumers and business owners get their business news, is broken not just from a financial standpoint but from a coverage standpoint and from a trust and bias standpoint. The internet, social media, and changing consumer habits have all had an effect, and the media haven't been able to come up with a working model that would also allow a return to the heady business news days of the 1990s, when the *Atlanta Journal-Constitution* could cover almost everything it needed to about the local economy.

There's plenty of blame to go around, though. Businesses, and the people that they hire to work with the business news media, shoulder some of the responsibility as well.

3

THE DOMINATORS

While it was the worst of times for metropolitan daily newspapers in terms of how they covered and delivered business news, it's been the best of times for some business news operators. Bloomberg News, Wall Street Journal, Reuters, Financial Times, and the television channel CNBC have grown and expanded their coverage and influence in the past decade. The big difference from the newspapers that cut business news? All five of these media operations are owned by deep-pocketed parent companies. And all five produce business news that traders, investors, and executives use to make a profit.

The difference shows the problem facing business journalism. While local business news has been cut, business news from these media focuses on a national and international level—the news that interests big company executives, bankers, and Wall Street traders. The coverage is about publicly traded companies, private companies backed by venture capitalists, the stock market, and broad economic movements—what people on Wall Street can use to make millions. Unfortunately, many consumers and business owners aren't interested in or need that type of coverage in their everyday lives and can't afford it either. "In the internet age, business journalism turned out to have a more robust business model than general news," notes Lionel Barber, former editor-in-chief of the *Financial Times*. "Readers are wealthier and will pay for information."[1]

This dominance in the realm of business journalism leads many to believe that these stories should be the focus of all business news. Few top editors—most of whom don't have experience in business journalism—of mainstream publications looking to expand their audience by offering business news coverage look to these news operations, see their success, and think they should be covering similar issues.

These business news outlets also, for the most part, charge much more than what businesses can afford. This has been great for these business news outlets, but not for many businesses and consumers.

Bloomberg News, which started in 1990, now has journalists around the world in more than 150 bureaus.[2] It produces more than five thousand stories daily and includes Bloomberg Television, Bloomberg Radio, and magazines. In 2009 it acquired *BusinessWeek* magazine from the McGraw-Hill Companies and renamed it *Bloomberg Businessweek*. As an indicator of the quality of its work, Bloomberg News won its first Pulitzer Prize in 2015. Its content is primarily available on the Bloomberg terminal, and Wall Street firms and companies pay $2,000 a month to rent one.[3] Its owner, Michael Bloomberg, is considered one of the richest men in the world, and his company primarily generates its revenue from the massive amount of financial data in its system.

The Wall Street Journal's parent company, Dow Jones & Company, was acquired by Rupert Murdoch's News Corporation in late 2007 for $5 billion and is considered to be one of the best, if not *the* best, media outlet in terms of covering big business and economics news. The *Wall Street Journal* now has more than 3.38 million subscribers in both print and online, making it the largest circulation newspaper in the United States. Unlike other newspapers, it charged for its content online from the very beginning—2.63 million, or three-fourths, of its subscribers are digital only, paying $36.99 a month, or more than $400 a year.[4] (In comparison, its sister publication, *Barron's*, charges $52 for an annual subscription.) Dow Jones has been seeing a revenue increase because of its online strength.

Reuters is considered the biggest competitor to Bloomberg News, and it has an estimated 2,500 journalists in more than two hundred locations. While Reuters is stronger in Europe and other international markets, it has placed an increasing emphasis on covering business and economics news in the United States. Like Bloomberg, Reuters provides its content to traders and bankers via a terminal that also provides voluminous financial data. The cost of its Eikon terminal is $22,000 a year, but a stripped-down version can cost as little as $3,600 a year—still a hefty sum that few business owners can afford.[5]

In 2012 Lucia Moses of *Adweek* predicted that Bloomberg and Reuters would dominate the future of business news. With their journalism paid for by non-advertising revenue, their business model can be sustained by rich subscribers. While print brands still struggle to adapt their content to digital platforms, these companies are churning out articles and sharing editorial costs across multiple outlets, from the internet to TV to print.[6]

The *Financial Times* topped 1 million subscribers in 2019, up from 780,000 in 2015, and—like the *Wall Street Journal*—more than three-fourths of its subscribers are online.[7] It has made a push to expand its US editorial staff in recent years. The *Financial Times* rolled out a paywall for its website back in 2002, and its revenues and profits have increased since it was acquired by the Japanese company Nikkei in 2015. It has struck deals to post stories on WhatsApp and has launched efforts in video to attract more consumers. Its online subscription costs $39.50 a month, and it offers a "premium" online subscription for $67 a month that includes analysis and research.[8]

And then there's CNBC, owned by cable television company Comcast. While its television channel is available on most cable systems in the country, CNBC has also launched a subscription service for its Web content called CNBC Pro that costs $29.99 per month.[9] CNBC Pro includes more than fifty exclusive articles per week, daily analyst notes about specific stocks released before the market opens, and monthly discussions with CNBC journalists and major investors. CNBC has reported a dramatic increase in its Web traffic in the past four years.

To subscribe to these five business news operations, it would cost nearly $4,500 a month to receive the content they produce. That's much higher than what the average consumer pays for journalism. The median weekly price of $2.31 for a newspaper subscription, according to the American Press Institute, is equivalent to $10 per month and $120 per year for a digital news subscription.[10] And just 53 percent of adults pay for news, according to the Media Insight Project, a collaboration of the American Press Institute and the Associated Press-NORC Center for Public Affairs Research.[11] Twenty percent of adults will pay for online news, according to the Reuters Institute for the Study of Journalism.[12]

These business news operations are highly successful in selling their content to people on Wall Street such as hedge fund, investment bank, and mutual fund managers. But the average consumer or business owner who wants and needs business and economics news and information to make decisions can't afford that price and wouldn't be helped that much by the content anyway because they're seeking more local business news. Those news consumers had relied on their daily newspaper, or perhaps another news source, to give them the news and information. So when those media cut or eliminated business news coverage, there wasn't much of an alternative because the five operators discussed here are catering to a different audience.

Business news has become a product for the upper echelon who can afford it, not the masses. And because these media operators dominate the field, it has hurt the ability of other business news organizations to break through and provide content that is needed.

Let's examine how these operations became so big and influential and what they're doing to maintain their position.

BLOOMBERG NEWS

Bloomberg News is a news service that in the past three decades has become a dominant name in business journalism. Although it is best known for providing business and economics news to investors, it also carries content in other areas, including the arts and politics. In 2020 Bloomberg News had more than 2,700 reporters and editors in 130 countries.[13] It has won dozens of awards and has become a well-known news-gathering organization that now includes television, radio, magazines, and book publishing divisions.

Former Salomon Brothers general partner Michael Bloomberg founded Bloomberg L.P. in 1981. Originally the company just sold to Wall Street investment banks' computer terminals that included financial data about stocks, bonds, and other investments. Those financial data still provide the bulk of the company's revenue.

The company began what was originally called Bloomberg Business News with a six-person editorial team. Bloomberg hired *Wall Street Journal* reporter Matthew Winkler, who had written a story about Bloomberg for the *Wall Street Journal*, to run the operation. The news service was—and still is—provided on the terminals. The first Bloomberg news story was published in June 1990.

By early 1995 the organization had grown to 325 reporters and editors in fifty-four bureaus and had started an investing magazine called *Bloomberg Personal* that was distributed as a Sunday newspaper supplement. Bloomberg Business News distributed its editorial content to other media organizations to improve its name recognition, giving terminals for free to newspapers in virtually every US city. Those newspapers then pulled Bloomberg stories off the wire and ran them in their business sections. In many cases Bloomberg helped the newspapers by creating an index of local stocks that could run each day in the business section. The reliance by newspapers on using outside sources for business news and information and not their own staffs had begun.

Bloomberg attracted business journalists from daily newspapers and other media organizations by offering them higher salaries—a common move among the big players in business journalism—and stock certificates that fluctuated in value based on the number of terminals sold by the company. In 2004 the company surpassed the 200,000 installed terminals mark. In 2020 it had more than 325,000 terminals.[14]

In 1997 *Time* magazine's Wall Street columnist Daniel Kadlec criticized Bloomberg in a *Columbia Journalism Review* article for putting pressure on newspapers and other media outlets to use more of the media organization's content. Kadlec noted that Bloomberg had pulled its terminals out of some newsrooms that weren't using or attributing Bloomberg editorial content in its publications.[15] By the end of the decade Bloomberg had stopped giving its terminals to other media organizations at no charge.

Bloomberg L.P. reached $10 billion in annual revenue in 2018, and it is the market share leader in financial market data, analysis, and news, with 32.5 percent, according to Burton-Taylor International Consulting. Reuters is number 2, with 22 percent market share.[16]

Bloomberg acquired the Arlington, Virginia–based Bureau of National Affairs, which provides news to business executives and government officials, in August 2011 for $990 million to bolster its existing Bloomberg Government and Bloomberg Law news services. These news topics are primarily of interest to higher-level business executives and white-collar professionals, not your typical consumer or small business owner. Although data about Bloomberg readers is hard to find, the average household income of readers of its *Pursuits* magazine, which goes to terminal users, is $575,000.[17]

Bloomberg expanded Bloomberg Radio in 2016, and in 2018 it launched TicToc by Bloomberg, a news service available on Twitter. Also in 2018 it began charging for access to its content on the internet, and it has greatly expanded its podcast strategy, showing that it's now trying to go after consumers with its coverage. As we'll examine later, consumers may not be all that interested in news that is primarily geared to investors, bankers, and traders.

THE WALL STREET JOURNAL

Dow Jones & Company operates the business news organizations Wall Street Journal, Barron's, MarketWatch, Mansion Global, Financial News, and the Dow Jones Newswire. The company also sells news and information to corporations through businesses such as Factiva, VentureSource, and Risk & Compliance. The *Wall Street Journal*, the largest and most influential operation within the company, has become the largest US newspaper in terms of paid circulation and has won thirty-seven Pulitzer Prizes during its 130-year history. The newspaper also now operates twelve different websites around the world in six different languages. The company is also credited with creating the first well-known stock market index.

The company has also explored new delivery formats and new consumer markets. It has launched Wall Street Journal Pro, which targets business professionals in specific fields such as accounting, bankruptcy, and artificial intelligence. In 2019 it struck a deal with Apple to provide news stories on Apple News. Its content is also now on Facebook's news page as well as through Bloomberg L.P.'s terminals.

The company has narrowed its editorial focus that often appealed to consumers, closing the Wall Street Journal Radio Network in 2014. That same year it also closed its operation that provided personal finance content to daily newspapers across the country for its Sunday editions. And in 2012 it stopped publishing the personal finance magazine *SmartMoney*, merging its content into *MarketWatch*, which until 2020 had been free. Now *MarketWatch*, which Dow Jones has billed as business news for the average consumer, is charging for access to its content.

The company has also expanded its video content and in 2019 partnered with the PBS show *Frontline* on a documentary. Baker is also now hosting a regular show called *WSJ at Large with Gerry Baker* on Fox Business Network.

The Wall Street Journal has focused on becoming a digital-first news organization, slowly moving away from its legacy print publications. In 2019 more than 50 percent of the company's revenue came from digital.

The company is also looking to expand internationally—only 12 percent of its current subscribers are outside the United States.[18]

The newspaper's audience trends toward an upper-income audience—executive management and millionaires are common readers. Its readers have an average household income of $242,000 and an average household net worth of $1.49 million.[19] (A net worth of $1.355 million means the household is in the top 9 percent of households in the country.) By comparison, the average US household income is $68,703, according to the US Census Bureau, and the average net worth of the average US household is $121,411, according to the Federal Reserve's Survey of Consumer Finances.[20]

In other words, typical American consumers and business owners are not typical *Journal* readers. The average business owner has a salary of $70,300, according to PayScale.[21] And many business owners eschew taking any pay during the first few years after starting their companies.

FINANCIAL TIMES

Nikkei, a Japanese holding company, acquired the Financial Times in July 2015 for about $1.3 billion from British-based Pearson PLC, but it's no stranger to financial journalism. It operates the *Nikkei*, a business newspaper with more than 3 million subscribers. It also operates other business news publications. The acquisition gave the London-based Financial Times a deep-pocketed owner, allowing it to expand its operations, particularly in the United States. It expanded its Chicago and New York bureaus and reopened a Houston bureau.[22] Former editor-in-chief Lionel Barber called the United States a "land of expansion" for the newspaper, which was founded in 1888.[23]

Although it didn't launch a US edition until 1997, the *Financial Times* is considered a rival to the *Wall Street Journal*, but it has previously focused on business news from a British and European perspective. Now 70 percent of its readers are outside of the United Kingdom.

In 2014, the year before the newspaper was acquired, it reported an operating profit of $37.3 million in revenue of about $519 million, so even with the decline in print advertising in the past decade, it's been able to maintain a strong business by catering to its readers.[24] According to the newspaper, 18 percent of its readers are millionaires, and its average reader has a net worth of $2 million. Thirty percent of its readers are C-suite executives, meaning they are top executives within a big company, and 42 percent work in a company with more than one thousand employees. One-third of the newspaper's readers work in the finance industry, while another 29 percent work in business services such as accounting.

The *FT*, as it is commonly called, has been experimenting with ways to expand its reach and increase its profits. In 2014 it began selling blocks of time to advertisers, charging them only for the time website users were exposed to the ads.[25] It brought on a special projects editor to experiment with how its content is delivered. For example, the *FT* has been posting stories on Facebook and live-streaming videos. With WhatsApp, the *FT* began posting one or two free stories a day to drive traffic to its main website.

Interestingly, the *FT* has also been looking for other sources of revenue and other types of business journalism to expand. In 2019 it led a group of investors who put money into the website *Business of Fashion*, which has 5 million readers around the world and more than 35,000 paying members.[26] The *FT*'s consulting arm provided it with subscription technology. Other clients of the newspaper's consulting firm include magazine publisher Bonnier and book publisher Penguin Random House. It also acquired a stake in the Next Web, whose annual conference draws 17,500 attendees from more than three thousand companies.[27]

The *Financial Times* also has developed strategies to keep its readers coming back. Its myFT product allows subscribers to follow specific topics. And in late 2018, it introduced a tool called Knowledge Builder that uses a point system so readers can keep track of how *FT* stories help them build knowledge about a topic. Knowledge Builder, of course, is available only to *FT* subscribers.[28]

The newspaper has maintained its profitability while changing how it generates revenue, according to published reports. It now generates 60 percent of its revenue from readers, and digital subscriptions now account for more than 75 percent of its circulation. Its 2018 financial results, the latest available, show profits of $33 million on revenues of $502 million— about where it was when it was acquired by Nikkei.[29] So it wasn't financially hurt like other daily newspapers in the United States by the decline in print advertising.

Subscriptions rose 11 percent in 2019. The coronavirus pandemic also drove readers to the newspaper. In March 2020 its website traffic grew by

250 percent, and a coronavirus business e-mail, which it also launched in March 2020, attracted more than seventy thousand subscribers in the first month.[30]

REUTERS

Financial news service Reuters has also benefited from new ownership in the twenty-first century. In 2008 it was acquired by Toronto-based Thomson Corporation, which is majority-owned by the Thomson family and was built early on through newspaper growth. Reuters started in 1851 as a service that transmitted stock market prices. The combined Thomson Reuters company has operations in legal, tax and accounting, and government, in addition to the news service. In 2018 private equity firm Blackstone Group L.P. bought its financial and risk business but also agreed to pay Reuters News at least $325 million a year for the next thirty years for its news and editorial content.[31]

Reuters doesn't disclose the average income and net worth of its subscribers, but because it's a rival to Bloomberg News and its Eikon terminal costs $22,000 a year, it's fair to assume that a Reuters News reader has a similar income and net worth to those who read Bloomberg content. In late 2020 Reuters announced that it was launching Reuters Professional, a new operation that will include news and events for "professionals." The executive leading the new initiative was quoted as saying that Reuters believes the market for Reuters Professional is $36 billion, and the new product would help advertisers reach more than 124 million professionals across the world.[32]

Reuters had been one of the last news services to offer its content for free, but in 2020 it told its employees that it would be putting its content behind a paywall in February 2021 but postponed that decision three months later. It also launched a video news channel on Roku aimed at subscribers in the United States and Canada.

The news service has also been able to maintain its revenue and profitability despite the pandemic and despite the shift in advertising. In the first quarter of 2020 Reuters News reported revenues of $155 million, essentially flat from the previous year and despite losing revenue when events were canceled because of COVID-19. Earnings were down $4 million to $19 million due to the cancellation of events.[33] Size for these business news companies—Bloomberg, the Wall Street Journal, the Financial Times—means that they're not affected as much when an operating segment is hurt, unlike smaller operations such as daily newspapers and local radio and television stations.

Indeed, Reuters is betting on the events business to respond. In October 2019 Thomson Reuters acquired FC Business Intelligence, an organizer of business conferences, and rebranded it as Reuters Events. The company says its event attendance is composed of 18 percent top executives, 32 percent directors and senior vice presidents, and 11 percent vice presidents of big companies.[34]

Reuters is also generating revenue from newspapers. It has more than one thousand newspaper clients, including thirteen of the top fifteen newspapers around the world.[35] So when newspapers cut their staffs because of a drop in print advertising and circulation revenue, they are able to fall back on content from wire services such as Reuters to plug into their news hole.

CNBC

CNBC is the oldest of the business news channels, starting in 1989 as a joint venture between NBC and Cablevision as the Consumer News and Business Channel. It is now owned by cable company Comcast, which acquired a 51 percent stake in NBC from General Electric in 2011 and the remaining stake in 2013.

The channel is known for focusing on what's happening each day in the stock market, from reporting on individual stocks rising or falling to interviewing chief executive officers whose companies are in the news. Its guests also frequently include investors and money managers. The median income for its viewers is $160,600, according to National Media Spots, which is more than double the average US household income of $68,703. Less than 20 percent of its viewers have a household income below $50,000.[36]

In the first six months of 2021 Comcast reported net income of $7.5 billion across its businesses. It does not break out CNBC's financial performance, but analysts believe the business news channel is highly profitable. NBCUniversal, which CNBC is a part of, reported revenue of $10.2 billion and a profit of $2.9 billion in the first six months of 2021.[37]

Fox Business Network has been a CNBC competitor since 2007. Fox

Business touts that its content is more geared toward a Main Street audience, but it has also focused on political coverage. Fox Business passed CNBC in total viewers, as measured by the Nielsen ratings company, for the first time in September 2016, but CNBC argues that its viewers are primarily watching at work, on trading floors, and in places such as hotel lobbies.[38]

In recent years, CNBC has emphasized growing the audience on its website, which has been part of MSN's MoneyCentral.com (now MSN Money) until splitting off in 2006. In January 2016 CNBC.com was the number 6 business news website, according to Comscore.[39] But in March 2020 it reached number 1, with 115 million unique visitors, with many of those readers coming from mobile phones.[40] Its primary competitors on the internet are *Yahoo Finance*, which provides data and news for free, and *Business Insider* and *Forbes*. *Business Insider* has begun charging more for its content, while *Forbes* has not. (Fox Business has not made a similarly strong effort in developing an audience for its website.)

To its credit, CNBC.com is going after viewers and readers who may not be interested in the stock market or big company deals. Its CNBC Make It section is aimed at millennials, while in 2019 CNBC struck a partnership deal with personal finance advice site Acorns for content around that topic. Still, most consumers associate CNBC's news content as being focused on Wall Street and major news around the stock market. And CNBC shut *Nightly Business Report*, the business news show that aired on PBS stations for forty years and provided content that appealed to average consumers, at the end of 2019 after acquiring it in 2013. The network attempted to shift more toward general news in 2020, with a nightly show hosted by former Fox News anchor Shepard Smith.

The success of these business news outlets is admirable. But that success has also changed how people in the field think about business news—as journalism for those who can afford it and who are interested in topics such as investing in the stock market, not as news for the average, everyday consumer, employer, or small business owner. And that hurts those readers and viewers.

The disconnect in who should be the primary audience for business news is also prevalent in other publications. *The Street*, cofounded by Jim Cramer, charges $29.99 a month for its "Action Alert Plus" service aimed at investors. Its "Chairman's Club" subscription is $299.99 a month.[41] *Seeking Alpha*, which is primarily written by other investors, charges $19.99 a month for its premium subscription and $199.99 per month for its pro subscription.[42] *Investor's Business Daily*, which was acquired by Dow Jones in 2021, offers a digital and print subscription rate of $349 a year, which is similar in price to *The Street*'s and *Seeking Alpha*'s base subscription rates.[43]

The prices can go higher. Reorg, which focuses on covering companies in trouble and was purchased by private equity firm Warburg Pincus in 2018, has more than five hundred subscribers who pay anywhere from $50,000 to $150,000 a year for its content.[44] The company says its clients include investment managers, investment banks, law firms, and corporations.

These publications are all involved in providing information to high-end readers such as corporate executives and investors who want to make money one way or another. Again, there's nothing wrong with that. But those readers are primarily in the stock market, not small business owners who are simply looking for better ways to run their company or consumers looking for a better place to work or smarter ways to spend their paycheck.

There's a much bigger audience for business news than what these media companies are targeting, but because daily newspapers have stopped covering many of the news stories that those consumers want, what's left is the content that these behemoths provide.

4

THE PUBLIC RELATIONS FACTOR

When Toronto *Globe and Mail* retail reporter Marina Strauss began reporting in October 2016 about strategy changes at restaurant chain Tim Hortons, she requested interviews with the company's chief executive officer
and other management. The public relations staff told her that interviews
would occur in late November. After interviewing a junior executive and
some franchise owners, however, Strauss was denied any further interviews by the company's public relations staff, who were upset with her asking about the executive's age and family. The PR people told the newspaper
that personal information was not allowed to be included in the story, according to Duncan Hood, the editor of the newspaper's *Report on Business*
magazine.[1]

Tim Hortons canceled all further interviews, including one with the
head of its store operations one hour before it was scheduled to start and
with Strauss in her car on the way to the meeting. Strauss and the *Globe
and Mail* published its story about the company anyway.[2]

This is just one example of the fractured relationship between business journalists and the public relations people who represent businesses
that often hurts coverage because a lack of cooperation can often lead to
incomplete information. While many PR professionals have good working
relationships with business reporters and editors and try to provide them
with accurate and timely information about their companies, an increase
in adversarial encounters has hurt what consumers, employees, and others
know about important employers in their towns and cities. And it's increasingly clear that public companies hire public relations staffers because
company news moves their stock price, and they don't want their price to
go down. For private companies, the hiring of public relations representatives helps them obtain a higher price when they sell to another company.

The battle between PR and business journalism is being won lately
by a rise in public relations staffers, making them more common than

the reporters who cover the companies they represent. According to the US Census Bureau, there were 6.4 public relations professionals for every journalist in the United States in 2018, up from 1.9 public relations staffers for every journalist just twenty years earlier.[3] And between 2008 and 2017, US newsrooms—newspapers, television stations, and radio stations—cut 26,000 jobs, according to the US Department of Labor.[4]

That disparity is likely to get worse—"employment of public relations specialists is projected to grow 7 percent from 2019 to 2029, faster than the [4 percent] average [growth] for all occupations," according to the US Bureau of Labor Statistics.[5] "Overall employment of reporters, correspondents, and broadcast news analysts is projected to decline 11 percent from 2019 to 2029."[6] Declining advertising revenue in radio, newspapers, and television will negatively affect the employment growth for these occupations.

The pay in public relations is also better than journalism, leading many reporters and editors to switch careers. According to the Pew Research Center, for every $1 in salary made by a public relations professional, a journalist makes just 65 cents.[7]

The result is that companies are increasingly hiding behind their public relations staff, ignoring requests from business reporters for information and interviews, or going on the offensive and attempting to change the focus of a story or issuing statements to reporters that don't answer the issues addressed in a reporter's questions. Public relations professionals are now recommending that the companies they represent stop inviting business reporters to events such as annual investor meetings or simply refuse to talk with them. In some cases a public relations person will lie or obfuscate the truth. And public relations strategies now go directly to consumers and others by using social media such as Twitter to deliver company messages. They argue that using social media eliminates the filter of journalism, where reporters will use only the part of the message that they believe is important.

To be sure, that's a reporter's prerogative. But, as noted in chapter 1, companies benefit in multiple ways from coverage in the media. By limiting interaction with the business news media, public relations professionals are, in the long run, hurting the companies who sign their paychecks. In the end, the truth about the company often comes out.

Take the case of KQED reporter Lily Jamali, who spent years covering

Pacific Gas and Electric Company, a San Francisco–based company that struggled to overcome the perception that it was ignoring its customers after its equipment causes wildfires that burned forests and people's homes. When the company offered some of its stock as part of a settlement and its public relations people said that was a common strategy, Jamali reviewed past cases and said, "It became clear to me that's simply not true." She also noted that the company was "reluctant" to have its executives talk to reporters. "The only opportunity to interview the CEO has been on the sidelines at regulatory or court hearings," said Jamali, noting that those instances were limited during the COVID-19 pandemic, when the hearings went online.[8]

Then there's the situation facing many business journalists. Write a negative article about a business, and its public relations people might cut off access to executives or its response to simple questions. In Virginia, the state's largest utility, Dominion Energy, declined to talk to reporters from the *Virginian-Pilot*. It issued a statement to the newspaper saying that it has been the recipient of "inaccurate, biased and unfair news coverage and opinion pieces" from the newspaper.[9]

Other public relations staffers will dangle exclusive interviews and stories in front of business reporters to get the journalist to drop another story that could portray their company in a negative light. When Fox Business News reporter Charles Gasparino was a reporter at the *Wall Street Journal*, he received a Merrill Lynch memo telling its brokers not to open accounts for less than $100,000, adding: "If you want to deal with poor people, you can get a nice job at the United Way." When Gasparino contacted the company for his story about the memo, the PR person responded by saying, "What can we trade you not to write this story? You want an interview with our CEO?"[10] Gasparino declined the request. But others may be swayed.

THE RELATIONSHIP

Public relations professionals who work for companies—whether in its internal corporate communications office or for an outside PR firm hired to work for the business—have several responsibilities. They write press releases about new products, financial results, management changes, and deals. In most cases, they're working with executives and managers, obtaining quotes and other information to include in the release. The executives, as well as a company's attorney, often have the final approval on news releases before they are sent out to reporters and editors.

In addition, public relations professionals field questions from reporters working on stories. They may then attempt to get the answer from an executive or manager and respond to the reporter. A veteran public relations person may advise the executive on whether the company should respond and, if it does respond, how it should respond. They may also provide information to the reporter on a background basis—meaning without attribution—or give a statement that can be attributed to a company spokesperson, not the executive. Or they may simply call or e-mail the reporter and decline to comment or provide additional information.

This relationship is part of the sphere in which public relations people try to influence and change how a business reporter reports and writes about a company. And most business journalists understand that is the job of a PR person. It's when the PR person uses tactics and strategies that constrain the ability of the reporter to accurately report on a business that society is prevented from understanding what's really going on.

Most business journalists have faced this problem: they wake up one morning to find that a competing publication has broken a story on their beat, one that they wish they'd gotten. In many cases, the competing reporter has been aggressive and reported the story. But in some cases, the story was published because the competing reporter was fed the story by the company's public relations staff and promised an exclusive. Or the company's public relations staff did not invite a business journalist to attend a news event because it was upset with past coverage.

Rod Meloni, a Local 4 business editor in Detroit, became angry when General Motors Company's public relations department chose to invite only print journalists to a news conference with CEO Mary Barra. He argued that the reporters who attended were "the usual gang that could be counted on to ask questions that would not shock or otherwise fluster the new CEO."[11] Yes, public relations people can invite who they want to attend their company's events, but cutting out journalists who routinely report on the business leads to a strained relationship and in many cases leads those reporters to become more aggressive.

When Renee Dudley was a reporter covering Walmart for Bloomberg News, she was banned from company media events. That did not prevent her from continuing to write Wal-Mart stories. The company's vice president of corporate communications, David Tovar, even went on CNBC and accused Dudley of "having an agenda," saying, "We've tried to speak with her editors, and it seems to fall on deaf ears."[12]

Dan Beyers, the former editor-in-chief of the *Washington Post's Capital Business* publication, said he noticed similar strategies. He said public relations staffers at companies his reporters covered would be uncooperative with requests for information or interviews until they wanted the journalists to write about what their CEO was doing or a new strategy, sometimes after years of stonewalling requests.[13] Beyers said the reason for the newfound chumminess was quickly apparent. "This shower of attention can be flattering, until you figure out the company in question is in trouble, or about to be sold or the CEO is fighting for survival," he wrote.[14]

The "embargoed" story is a significant strain between public relations people and business journalists. An embargo is used by public relations professionals to give news to reporters before it is officially released. This can commonly happen in mergers and acquisitions, or in technology when a company launches a new product and wants the reporter to test it. The understanding is that the publication can't publish their story until an agreed upon date and time.

Public relations people argue that embargoes give reporters more time to report and write a thorough story, increasing society's understanding. And the embargo helps build a relationship with the reporters. But journalists, especially those who do not receive the embargoed information, argue that this tactic is unfair and hurts coverage. In a TEDx talk at Queens University, Toronto *Globe and Mail* business editor Paul Waldie said embargoes "make us lazy. I'm fighting the embargo battle. I turned down two last week, and they were shocked."[15]

NO COMMENT AND ON BACKGROUND

One of the basics of business news reporting is that when you're working on a story about a company, you call the business to get a comment or a response. Depending on the size of the company, that call may go to its public relations person, or it may go to the head of the company. If the company has hired an outside public relations firm, the reporter may be directed to someone there.

Depending on what the business reporter is asking about, however, the company or its public relations staff may simply respond with "no comment." Or they may ask to give the business reporter information "on background," which means that the information can't be attributed to the company or the spokesperson in the story.

When noted media critic Jack Shafer wrote about Amazon's increasing use of "no comment" to media inquiries, he added, "Companies have every right to remain silent to their inquiries. Only the courts and the regulators can demand them to speak, and even then the lawyers act as mediators."[16] But the strategy, many business journalists note, hurts their attempts to provide balance in stories and eliminates what can be valuable context for consumers.

Harvey Radin of the *Times of San Diego* complained when a Wells Fargo & Company spokesperson declined to comment about reports that its executives had received millions in compensation during its fake accounts scandal.[17] He's not alone. In 2018 Pulitzer Prize–winning business columnist Steven Pearlstein of the *Washington Post*, with the help of *Post* researcher Magda Jean-Louis, searched the *New York Times* business section for instances when a company declined to comment of respond. The list included companies such as LVMH, First Data, Theranos, Dodge & Cox, Qualcomm, Warner Bros., Tiger Brands, Tesla, Google, Twitter, Toyota, ExxonMobil, and Lyft.[18] He noted that companies in banking, aerospace, and hospitality were better about responding than technology companies. In his column, Pearlstein quoted former IBM and Aetna public relations executive Roger Bolton, head of the Arthur W. Page Society of professional corporate communications people, as saying that responding with "no comment" "is not what we stand for as a profession. Media relations is a critical core responsibility, and companies should seek to build trusting relationships."[19]

And then there's the strategy where a public relations professional does respond to a reporter's inquiry, but only on background. Such was the case in 2020 when Amazon sent an e-mail to reporters defending its safety record after a report by the Center for Investigative Reporting about rising injury rates in its warehouses. The e-mail said its statement could be attributed to the company, but it also included an "on background" section where it slammed the Center for Investigative Reporting.[20]

Julia Angwin, the editor-in-chief of technology news site *The Markup* and a former reporter for the *New York Times* and ProPublica, blasted the

practice but noted it has become commonplace in the tech industry because reporters often comply with the request to go "on background." *The
Markup* insists on statements on the record and not on background, added
Angwin. "Anonymity isn't a standard; it is a privilege that should be borne
only out of necessity," wrote Angwin. "We reserve anonymity for people
who could face retaliation or undue hardship for the information that they
are providing us in the public interest."[21]

The sentiment of Herb Greenberg, a longtime business journalist, resonates with many business reporters. When he was working for *The Street*,
he wrote a commentary about the Michael Kors company and didn't bother
to ask for a response. The company replied that if he had taken the time
to contact them, they would have responded with a statement. Greenberg
said he didn't call because his writing was "observation" and "analysis" but
said in retrospect he wished he had called them. And, he added, if a company spokesperson had called him immediately after his commentary was
published, he would have added their comments.[22]

HURTING COVERAGE

Several strategies used by public relations officials at companies can only
be described as hurting coverage of their businesses. An increasingly common practice is the refusal by public companies to allow reporters to attend
the annual investor's meeting. In 2018, when motorcycle manufacturer
Harley-Davidson barred journalists from its annual meeting, a local business school professor noted that the tactic signaled, whether correct or not,
something was wrong at the company. "Keeping the press out could be
seen as a 'red flag' that a company is hiding something," Marquette University professor Matteo Arena told the *Milwaukee Journal Sentinel*. "It just
invites more media scrutiny after the meeting."[23]

M. G. Siegler, a reporter at tech news site *TechCrunch*, notes that he's
increasingly seeing public relations people downplay stories when the angle is not what they want. Or they will approach another business journalist
to cover the same story but take a different angle. While he didn't want to
suggest that all public relations professionals "are evil or have the wrong
intentions," he added, "Increasingly what they do is nothing more than
attempt to spin or grossly misrepresent what it is we do."[24]

Siegler's concern seems to be prevalent with larger companies, particularly those with brand names such as Facebook. When Jacob Silverman reported for *Columbia Journalism Review* about what it was like to cover the social media company, he found the results "troublesome" in that the company's communications department operated secretly. And many journalists that he contacted for his story declined to be interviewed because they feared hurting their relationship with Facebook's PR department. Others would talk only on the record, and other reporters who initially agreed to be interviewed then declined to speak after talking with their editors.[25]

Casey Newton, a former tech reporter at *The Verge* who left to start a subscription newsletter, attributes part of the problem with the relationship between journalists and public relations staffs to the current media business model.[26] Many reporters, particularly tech reporters, have an incentive to boost the clicks and likes of their articles, and losing access to the companies that they cover would cause those interactions to decline. Given the perilous state of many journalism jobs, that's a fair point. Business journalists would prefer to keep their jobs and their salaries rather than lose access.

There are other strategies used to stymie reporters. Jenny Gold of Kaiser Health News remembered how she was reporting a story for National Public Radio about blood-testing company Theranos and was in a Walgreens to interview customers using Theranos' tests. One customer after another was given a traditional blood test rather than the Theranos test, and Theranos representatives prevented Gold from questioning the pharmacist about why the Theranos tests were not being administered. When she attempted to question customers further, she was then told that the company's headquarters had received complaints from consumers that a reporter was bothering them. "I hadn't pressured anyone," wrote Gold. "The patients I'd interviewed had all been perfectly friendly and willing. I've also been a health reporter for 10 years, and never have I been told I was pushing patients to do something that made them uncomfortable." Finally, a fire alarm went off in the Walgreens—a sign she later took as trying to prevent her questioning of customers.[27]

Gold ended up killing the story. As we know now, Theranos was a sham company, and its blood tests did not perform. Its chief executive officer has now been convicted of fraud. "The PR tactics Theranos employed blocked journalists from providing the kind of scrutiny that might have revealed the fantasy the company was weaving for investors sooner," said Gold.[28]

Public relations professionals also engage in other tactics that make business reporters uncomfortable, which could also affect coverage. Many in public relations compile dossiers on the reporters who cover their companies. This commonly will include information about their dislikes and likes, and the questions they might ask an executive. Sophie Kleeman of *Gizmodo* wrote in 2016 that the dossier of *Fast Company* senior writer Mark Sullivan compiled by Microsoft detailed his writing style and his thoughts on Microsoft's competitors. While Sullivan was "remarkably chill" about the dossier, other journalists feel uncomfortable about this tactic.[29] Indeed, former *Wall Street Journal* reporter Dean Rotbart created a company that reported and wrote these dossiers for public relations clients, and many business reporters were taken aback when personal details were revealed. (I'm unaware of any service writing dossiers on public relations professionals for journalists.)

When business reporter Gretchen Morgenson left the *New York Times* for the *Wall Street Journal,* she recounted an instance when she wrote about an who investor brought an arbitration case against a major Wall Street firm. Although the firm won its case, Morgenson noted that she was later told by a representative of the company that, at a company dinner, her picture was featured on the menu, placed inside a red circle with a slash through her face.[30]

Such actions are bound to make a business reporter nervous about what might happen if they don't do what a public relations person wants them to do. Morgenson, however, shrugged it off, stating, "It wasn't my job to be part of a company's spin machine."[31]

ETHICS, LYING, AND THE FAKES

Many executives believe it's important for their corporate communications staff to gain the trust of journalists, and that requires honest and consistent communications between the company and the media, write researchers Ansgar Zerfass and Muschda Sherzada.[32] The executives also rank "press and media relations" highest among the instruments and platforms for mass communications.

So why is the relationship so strained? Many business journalists feel as if public relations staff serve as a hindrance to their jobs. David Carr wrote in the *New York Times*: "Business reporters have to work their way past background conversations with underlings, written statements that state nothing, and that increasingly hardy perennial: the 'no comment.' The modern chief executive lives behind a wall of communications operatives, many of whom ladle out slop meant to obscure rather than reveal."[33]

Carr is being polite with the word "slop." Public relations professionals are increasingly using lies and false and misleading information in their communications. In 2015 University of South Carolina professor Shannon Bowen, who researches public relations ethics, wrote that a study of public relations staffers discovered that a majority of them admitted to lying to the media on a regular basis. "And we wonder why journalists don't trust PR sources, rate their ethics lower than that of journalists, and go around digging for other sources, more dirt, or even simple confirmation of facts?" she wrote.[34] Let's look at some examples of how this happens. Sometimes the lies and fakes are obvious, and sometimes they are not.

Personal finance articles that appeared on CNBC's website and in columns written by a *Washington Post* personal finance columnist quoted an "expert" in student loan refinancing. But the person quoted was a creation of the public relations staff of a student loan refinancing company. The "expert" had conducted e-mail interviews with journalists but didn't exist.[35]

Allegations of "fake news," a popular term used by President Donald Trump, also plague business journalism. Dana Melius of the *St. Peter Herald* in southern Minnesota noted that companies that were subjects of stories in his newspaper made this accusation after publication. He noted that the stories are important to readers. "Prospective buyers or developers often don't want the news out early, in case other potential suitors get word and enter the market," he wrote. "Some like privacy in such business deals. And we respect that. But we still have a job. . . . If public dollars or policies are involved or affected, citizens have a right to know."[36]

In 2019 court documents exposed that the chemical manufacturer Monsanto used aggressive communications tactics to discredit a Reuters reporter covering the company. Carey Gillam, author of the 2017 book *Whitewash: The Story of a Weed Killer, Cancer, and the Corruption of Science*, said the records were "just one more example of how the company works behind the scenes to try to manipulate what the public knows about its products and practices."[37] A spokesman for Bayer AG, which bought Monsanto, said that the tactics were used to counteract "significant misinformation." Monsanto also had one of its communications firms hire a woman to pose as a BBC reporter at one of its Roundup cancer trials and suggest to real journalists story lines or points that favored the company.[38]

The lack of ethics is also significant when a public relations firm offers to pay a business journalist to write about their client or their company. That happened in 2014 when a freelancer for CNBC was approached by a PR firm specializing in image and reputation management; the freelancer refused the offer and disclosed the encounter to CNBC.[39] That same year *Fortune* senior editor-at-large Adam Lashinsky wrote about how a representative of a tech company, Arista Networks, offered him shares in its upcoming initial public offering. Lashinsky said he made it clear to the representative, with whom he worked on past stories, that such an offer was a "horrible idea."[40]

Sometimes public relations professionals are ordered to lie or to deny facts that are actually true. When a reporter from the *Memphis Commercial Appeal* called Schnuck Markets to ask whether the company was going to sell some of its stores to Cincinnati-based Kroger Company, the communications director responded by saying, "There is no truth in those rumors."[41] Nine days later, the company announced that it was selling its Memphis locations to Kroger. When the reporter went back to the PR person and asked why she had lied, the staffer responded that she was bound by an agreement to remain silent. But the PR person had done no such thing; instead she had denied anything was happening. When pressed, the public relations staffer said, "I did not lie to you."[42] The business editor of the *Commercial Appeal* later said that he felt as if the newspaper and its brand was damaged by Schnuck Markets' denials because it did not report on what it had heard about the potential sale. Readers complained that the newspaper was being derelict in its duties to local consumers by not reporting on the deal before it was announced.[43]

Again, to be sure, business reporters frequently turn to public relations professionals for help with stories. But, given the examples in this chapter and many others that were not included, it's obvious that the relationship has been severely damaged and hurts how businesses are portrayed in the media.

Corporate communications staff must do a better job of training executives to understand that they play an important role in today's society. That's harder than it sounds, given that many executives have egos. "They are required to represent and communicate, but they are usually neither trained nor primarily chosen because of these aspects," discovered Ansgar Zerfass and Markus Wiesenberg of the University of Leipzig and Dejan Verčič of the University of Ljubljana.[44]

If you're in public relations or believe that public relations staffers provide a valuable service to companies, don't worry. Later we're going to address what journalists do wrong when they cover business and economics. And we're going to tackle your bosses—the chief executive officers and others in management—and how they also hurt business news coverage.

5

THE CEO CAN DO BETTER

After reporter Amir Efrati of tech news site *The Information* wrote an article about Tesla, CEO Elon Musk replied with a tweet: "Can't believe you're even writing about this." Efrati, who noted that Tesla's public relations staff had confirmed the facts in his story, responded with "How about we set up an interview and you can tell me, among other things, what you think is worth writing about?" Musk tersely turned down the offer, saying, "Uhh, hello, I need to build cars."[1] This exchange shows the problem in the relationship between business journalists and company executives—both sides disagree about the role the other should play in communicating news and information.

Business reporters and editors often argue that corporate executives often fail to tell the truth about their businesses or hide behind corporate spokespersons, leaving society with an incomplete picture of the impact of their companies. These journalists simply want to be able to tell consumers as many facts as possible, whether good or bad, about a company. Corporate executives believe that business news media predominantly portray their operations in an unfavorable light and ignore the good that their businesses provide to society. This conflict often limits the news that journalists can present to consumers about what is going on at companies, which has hurt the quality of business journalism in the past decade.

Executives also use other tactics that are interpreted as being adversarial to the business news media. In 2018 Facebook CEO Mark Zuckerberg did not speak first to the media when it was disclosed his company had allowed another business to obtain data about its customers. Zuckerberg chose to make his initial comments in a Facebook post and in congressional testimony before speaking to the media.[2]

Business executives also complain that the reporters covering their companies lack an understanding of their operations and fail to cover good news, even when the reporters are in the audience to report the news, said former *Milwaukee Business Journal* reporter Olivia Barrow. "I am literally here," said Barrow. "What more do you want from me?"[3] She added:

> I write stories that aim to help businesses grow by giving them leads they can use to make sales, interviewing industry leaders, explaining touch issues, analyzing trends and helping them avoid huge pitfalls. That last part involves "negative" seeming stories—like reporting when a company is laying off hundreds of workers, or when their sales decreased for the third year in a row, or when they get sued, because other business owners need to know who NOT to do business with just as much as they need to know who TO do business with.[4]

Others note that corporate executives should court the business news media. Writing in *Harvard Business Review*, Rakesh Khurana argues that CEOs must have the "gift of tongues," which means having the ability to "inspire employees to work harder and gain the confidence of investors, analysts, and the ever skeptical business press."[5]

The business news media analyze and evaluate executives and companies for a wide audience, making interaction between journalists and corporate executives a necessity in society. "The CEO has become the personification of the corporation, and the changing environment has forced the corporation and the CEO into the public arena," wrote James E. Arnold in *Public Relations Quarterly*.[6] In addition, nearly every executive believes that media coverage influences the reputation of their corporation, according to a study by Ansgar Zerfass of the University of Leipzig and Muschda Sherzada, head of corporate communications at About You GmbH.[7]

For the sake of a better-informed society, corporate executives and business journalists would benefit from examining this relationship. Both sides can do better in developing a relationship with the other side and in understanding the needs and issues of the other. A study—compiled by a journalist and a retired CEO—by the First Amendment Center at the Freedom Forum argues for better relations between the two sides, concluding, "There is no doubt that the relationship between business and the news media would be improved if journalists would be fair and executives would tell the truth."[8] Despite this study, there has been no concentrated effort to address the situation. As one corporate executive said, "Considerable effort on both parts is required for them to attain tolerance, appreciation and understanding for one another."[9]

Developing a better relationship between business executives and business journalists would lead to better coverage. Reporters would be able to write with more expertise and knowledge about companies and issues if they understood more about what was going on inside the business, and executives and business owners would receive news and information that they need to make important decisions.

A HISTORY OF THE RELATIONSHIP

The most detailed reporting about a company and a corporate executive during the early twentieth century was the series of stories written by Ida Tarbell and published in *McClure's Magazine* about the Standard Oil Company and its leader, John D. Rockefeller. Tarbell used court records, sources within the company, congressional testimony, correspondence with other oil companies, and interviews from rivals forced out of business to explain how Rockefeller and his company had created a monopoly in the oil industry. Her series of articles began in *McClure's* in November 1902. Although Rockefeller never talked to Tarbell, he complained about her stories to another magazine, stating they were "without foundation. The idea of the Standard forcing anyone to sell his refinery to us is absurd."[10] Tarbell proceeded to uncover more about Standard Oil and turned her reporting into a best-selling book. After Tarbell wrote a biography of Rockefeller for *McClure's*, Standard Oil hired a prominent New York public relations executive who urged Rockefeller to respond to the articles, but Rockefeller never spoke publicly about Tarbell.

Rockefeller might have come off as a more sympathetic executive if Tarbell's stories had included some rationale from him. However, the impact of her coverage on the public's perception of a corporate executive and big business is irrefutable. In 1911 the US Supreme Court ordered the breakup of Standard Oil.

Other journalists wrote critically about companies and company executives during this time. Corporate executives were rarely quoted in business news stories during the early twentieth century, and when they felt their companies were being attacked, they reacted by hiring spokespersons or using money to exert influence. Sherman Morse wrote in the *American* magazine that public relations staff should have led to companies disclosing information that they had previously withheld but advised that public relations could also help companies obtain "greater publicity for such facts that are directly favorable to them."[11] John Dryden of Prudential Insurance Company ordered his advertising department to purchase $5,000 of additional advertising in the October 1906 issue of the *Cosmopolitan*, which then pulled an article critical of the company.[12]

Business journalist Bertie Charles Forbes changed the relationship with executives when he launched *Forbes* magazine in 1917. Forbes began a section titled "What Business Leaders Say," giving executives a voice. He also regularly wrote a feature called "How Forbes Gets Big Men to Talk," which recounted his strategy for obtaining interviews with executives. Among those he interviewed early on was John D. Rockefeller, with whom he had played a round of golf and had lunch. Before he published a profile of meatpacking executive Thomas Wilson, Forbes sent him a copy of the article. Wilson replied that he made "one or two slight changes. I am sure you will agree with me on them. Otherwise, I feel the article is fine."[13]

Forbes soon had competitors. *Fortune* magazine, launched in 1930, immediately began writing long corporate profile stories that included information about the company's executives. When Allied Chemicals president Orlando Webber refused to talk with a *Fortune* reporter, the magazine sent a reporter to Milwaukee to visit Webber's parents and obtain a photo of him as an overweight child. Magazine founder Henry Luce sent an enlarged version of the photo to Webber and threatened to run it unless he agreed to the interview. Webber acquiesced.[14]

The relationship between the business media and corporate executives softened in the 1950s and 1960s. For example, well-known General Motors head Alfred Sloan appeared on the cover of *Fortune* as part of a series of articles about his management philosophy. Some executives even took steps to improve the quality of business journalism. The Gerald Loeb Awards were established in 1957 by Gerald Loeb, a founding partner of stockbroker E. F. Hutton. His intention was to encourage reporting on business and finance that would inform and protect the private investor and the public. Today the awards are considered the most prestigious in business journalism.

The 1980s and 1990s brought about a new type of corporate executive being portrayed in the media. Executives such as General Electric's Jack Welch and Coca-Cola's Roberto Goizueta have graced the covers of business and general-interest magazines, lauded for their management. Reporters wrote about their personal lives as well, and executives became more willing to talk about their companies as the stock market boomed and the economy entered in a long period of prosperity. *Time* magazine argued in 1996 that seven of the ten most powerful people in the country were CEOs, and President Clinton was the only person more powerful than Microsoft CEO Bill Gates. The now-defunct *Brill's Content* wrote in 1998 how Gates had devoted time to maintain relationships with key journalists and had invited a dozen to stay with him at his family's vacation home.[15] That influenced what people thought about companies and their leaders.

Many corporate executives today interact with the business news media, but some bypass the news media and speak directly to their customers and investors using new formats such as social media. This hurts the reputation of their companies as the media are seen as being analyzers of good management and strategy. In addition, without the filter of an independent media, executives and companies are opening themselves to additional criticism and review.

HOW EXECUTIVES INTERACT WITH THE MEDIA

Interacting with the media "is one of the most important and often least desired duties of a CEO," write Virgil Scudder and Ken Scudder.[16] They add, "Both journalists and the general public put more trust in people whose voices and faces they know than in strangers. That factor alone demonstrates why CEOs need to have a media role."[17] Zerfass and Sherzada's study published in *Corporate Communications: An International Journal* found that 62 percent of executives surveyed believed it is important to give interviews and talk to journalists.[18]

Corporate executives use strategies and tactics to talk to the business news media, including press conferences, interviews, and conference calls, but those are often situations controlled by the company and the executive. In 2000 the Securities and Exchange Commission also adopted Regulation Fair Disclosure, which requires companies and their executives to disseminate materially important information about their operations to all interested parties at the same time. This has allowed the business news media to listen when an executive speaks at analyst and investor meetings.[19] Public relations professional Christopher D. Allen suggests that when executives are giving speeches or making presentations, they should do so in plain language that conveys the important messages. "Giving speeches is part of the role of a CEO," writes Allen.[20]

Virtually every company also handles requests from the business news media for interviews with executives. Whether those interview requests are granted usually depends on the media organization, the topics the journalist would like to cover, and what the company and the executives think can be accomplished by talking. For example, a company will have new executives give interviews to introduce them to the public. A company is more likely to give an interview if it is rolling out a new product than if it is facing a lawsuit from a competitor. However, Scudder and Scudder write, "It's also a good idea (sometimes) to go public in the face of bad news. The CEO can put the situation in perspective and give reassurance."[21] Interview requests are also decided on by the motives and personal style of the executives.

It's these interview requests where the relationship between executives and business journalists seems most troublesome and where a lack of interaction hurts coverage. Some executives are more at ease answering questions from reporters than others, and some feel the need to be the voice of the company more than others. Guy Shani and James Westphal of the University of Michigan discovered that a corporate executive did not want an interview with a specific journalist because the reporter had written about another company in his industry and included statements the executive thought were unfair.[22] A 2018 study by four business school professors—Andrew C. Call, Scott A. Emett, and Eldar Maksymov of Arizona State University and Nathan Y. Sharp of Texas A&M University—found that nearly one-fourth of business journalists said they are likely to lose access to company management after writing an unfavorable article about the company.[23]

Many companies also hold press conferences where they invite the media to hear their executives talk about developments in the organization. These events may be more controlled in terms of what executives are saying, but they also allow reporters to ask questions and to interact with the leaders of the business. Executives, however, may focus on talking only about the topic for the press conference and ignore other issues related to the company, which may frustrate some reporters. *New York Times* technology reporter Conor Dougherty notes that he tried to interview Google cofounder Larry Page at a press event, but Page simply shook his hand and headed in another direction.[24]

Annual meetings are another opportunity for executives and the business news media to interact. While annual meetings are held for the company's shareholders, most companies invite reporters and editors to attend as well, and some companies will also allocate a time—either before or after the meeting—for journalists to ask questions, either as a group or individually, of its executives. In a related matter, many business journalists will read the company's annual report, which includes a letter from the top executive outlining the company's performance and strategy. Gary Kohut of the University of North Carolina at Charlotte and Albert H. Segars of the University of South Carolina write that the letter can "provide meaningful information for appraising past performance and projecting future opportunities."[25] Most business reporters read the annual reports of the companies they follow; noted *Fortune* reporter Carol Loomis once disclosed she read fifty years of annual reports of one company while reporting on a story.[26]

That's still not direct access to executives. And many executives do not talk to the media, which hurts society's understanding of how they and their companies operate. *Wall Street Journal* reporter Rob Copeland, when profiling Google CEO Sundar Pichai, had to write the following in his story: "Mr. Pichai, along with Mr. Page and Google co-founder Sergey Brin, declined requests to be interviewed. Through a representative, Mr. Pichai suggested several current and former subordinates and colleagues to speak on his behalf. Though all were complimentary of his leadership, few appeared to know him well personally. One said he loved margaritas; another said Mr. Pichai preferred Italian wines."[27]

An executive declining an interview for a major story is, unfortunately, not unusual. And a lack of cooperation hurts anyone's ability to understand a company's strategy and how it operates. When Vivek Wadhwa was chief technology officer at Seer Technologies, he said the only time the company granted interviews was when it had good news. When the media asked about customer problems, "We went silent," he said. When the company went public, management took the advice from its investment bankers and declined all interviews, including one with a national technology publication. As a result, he said, "The coverage was negative all the way."[28]

Later, when Wadhwa was chief executive officer of Relativity Technologies, he took a different approach. "We opted for openness and full disclosure—of the good and the bad," said Wadhwa. "We were always in the news about our successes. And the coverage was sympathetic when things went wrong."[29]

DIRECT COMMUNICATION STRATEGIES

Top executives are "still geared towards traditional mass media and less convinced of social media," according to Zerfass and Sherzada.[30] However, some executives now use social media such as blogs, Twitter, and Facebook to communicate directly with consumers, investors, and other stakeholders, bypassing the business news media. Reporters follow executives on Twitter to ascertain their thoughts and write stories based on what the executive has posted. That's not direct access for the journalist but access for the masses.

Business reporters are increasingly using Twitter and other social media as part of their daily reporting about companies and executives, according to a 2016 study.[31] They look for newsworthy disclosures on social media by executives. They also use LinkedIn to help find sources either inside or outside of a company for their stories.

Social media allows executives to disseminate their messages without the filter of the media. Twitter has a length limit of 280 characters, but executives can string tweets together in a message stream. On other social media, such as blogs, executives are not constrained by length. Richard Vidgen of Hull University and Julian Mark Sims and Philip Powell of the University of London found that blogs from chief executives help build community around the company when they post seven to ten times per month.[32] Wan-Hsiu Sunny Tsai of the University of Miami and Linjuan Rita Men of the University of Florida found that executives "should actively respond to followers' posts and communicate in a responsive, friendly and empathetic manner to demonstrate their concerns for various stakeholders and willingness to listen."[33] If they are not responsive, then the executive's reputation may be harmed.

Social media communication can also hurt executives, particularly if they choose to interact with business reporters and editors in this public sphere. In one case an executive stepped over the line of decency in his interaction with a reporter on Twitter. After former Bloomberg reporter Gerrit De Vynck wrote about Hootsuite, a Canadian social media management company, CEO Ryan Holmes criticized the story on Twitter. When De Vynck responded with his phone number and asked the CEO to call him, Holmes responded with a phone number for a paid sex hotline, drawing criticism.[34]

Executives also use social media to bypass reporters. Chesapeake Energy bought promoted tweets on specific search terms to respond to an article from the *New York Times* that quoted company e-mails suggesting that executives were overstating productivity and profitability.[35] Pacific Investment Management Company tweeted about a forthcoming *Wall Street Journal* article detailing PIMCO's investments in Lehman Brothers bonds before it appeared in the business newspaper after a reporter contacted the company for comment.[36]

Lionel Barber, the former editor of the *Financial Times*, argues that the growth of companies producing their own content results in them "taking back control" and allows them to distribute their own "stories" on YouTube and Facebook. "This makes it much harder to secure quality time with the CEO," said Barber. "Why engage with real journalists when someone browsing the web is just as likely to find your 'story' when they Google your company's name?"[37]

THE TUG-OF-WAR

The relationship between corporate executives and business journalists is a never-ending tug-of-war in which each side is attempting to gain the upper hand. Many corporate executives feel they must use reporters and editors as independent analyzers to portray their company in the most favorable light, while the journalists distrust executives and question their motives. Both play important roles in society. Corporate executives lead companies that can build the economy and improve the lives of their workers and those who purchase their products. Journalists act as information conduits who provide valuable knowledge to consumers, investors, and employees.

Sometimes that coverage portrays companies negatively for good reason, and executives should realize that journalism plays an important role in society. Yet executives have threatened reporters when they perceived a story as negative even though the facts might be accurate. For example, the CEO of the blood-testing company Theranos, Elizabeth Holmes, sent high-priced attorneys to the *Wall Street Journal* to complain about coverage from reporter John Carreyrou. The reporter continued to publish stories about the company despite that meeting, and the coverage led to the company's demise as Carreyrou's reporting proved to be accurate. Holmes was later convicted of fraud; without Carreyrou's reporting, more investors, employees, and customers could have been misled.

Some executives lie when unfavorable stories are published about their companies. After a negative story in *The Information*, streaming service Quibi published a statement saying that it was "materially inaccurate." In a later interview with *Variety*, Quibi CEO Meg Whitman apologized for comparing the reporters to sexual predators and said the company was "mostly accurately portrayed" in the story.[38]

Both sides of the battle can do better in their interactions. Executives can be more responsive and respectful to journalists and understand that they are simply trying to do their jobs and present fair and balanced information to readers, who also happen to be consumers and investors of the companies that the executives lead. Executives should know that the media do not unduly blame them for economic declines, according to research from Gregor Halff in *Corporate Reputation Review*.[39]

And business journalists can do a better job of understanding that an executive's primary job is to run the business and not spend every day talking to the media. More business journalists should ask company executives and corporate communications staffers for help in understanding their business, and company executives and public relations professionals should often be more proactive in offering those tutorials.

James D. Westphal of the University of Michigan and David L. Deephouse of the University of Alberta discovered that reporters are less likely to write negatively about a company if they are treated with respect by its CEO. This may not necessarily be a good revelation for society. "In effect, CEO interpersonal influence behavior may weaken the power of the press as a corporate control mechanism," wrote Westphal and Deephouse.[40]

Many mainstream news organizations, particularly daily metropolitan newspapers, have cut their business news staff in the past decade. CEOs should also be concerned with a decline in business journalism. Fewer quality business news outlets give executives fewer opportunities to provide information about their company's strategies and to learn about other companies' operations by reading media reports.

Veteran business journalist William Holstein wrote, "If the shrinking business media loses its ability to raise these questions and provide in-depth news about them, then the workforce and the voting population will be more poorly informed. They'll lack the perspective, know-how, and appreciation for business that they otherwise would have had. And CEOs whose corporations suffer a damaged reputation will have themselves in part to blame."[41]

This conundrum remains: In the end, business journalists have few ways to influence or change their relationship with corporate executives other than by reporting honestly and fairly, even if executives disagree with the definition of what honest and fair means, and by being professional when interviewing executives.

Corporate executives often complain about the quality of business journalism they and their companies receive. Yet few of them in recent years have tried to find or fund a solution that would change that scenario. At a time when the media industry is undergoing rapid change and seeking new business models, executives can play a more prominent role by being more cooperative.

They, and their businesses, need the business media. And the business media need them.

6

SOCIETAL CHANGES AND ECONOMIC FORCES

When *Fortune* magazine published its first list of the five hundred largest US companies in 1955, General Motors was the largest, with $9.8 billion in revenue and $806 million in profits. Only the top twenty-one companies had more than $1 billion in revenue, and number 500, Copperweld Steel, had $49.7 million in revenue.[1]

How times have changed. In 2020 Walmart topped the list with $524 billion in revenue and $14.9 billion in profits, making more in profit than General Motors' total sales just sixty-five years earlier. And number 500 was Huntington Bancshares, with $5.6 billion in revenue—or more than one hundred times larger than Copperweld Steel. The 2020 Fortune 500 represented a whopping two-thirds of the US economy, with $14.2 trillion in revenue.

Shifts in society, primarily economic, have had an impact on business news. The economy is becoming much more concentrated among bigger companies, which means the business media are increasingly focused on those businesses and ignoring, for the most part, the smaller operations that are the key to many local economies. The spread is widening and is a contributing factor in the problem that business journalism faces.

In 2007, according to the US Census Bureau, there were more than 18,300 businesses in the United States with more than five hundred workers, and those businesses had $2.8 trillion in payroll.[2] A decade later, the latest statistics available, there were more than 20,100 such businesses, a gain of nearly 10 percent, and their payroll had risen to $4 trillion.[3] In contrast, the number of businesses with fewer than five hundred employees in the United States fell to just under 6 million in 2017, or a decline of about 1 percent from 2007.[4]

This means that bigger companies are garnering more coverage from the financial media, and they're also receiving coverage in mainstream media because of their size and importance, taking coverage away from smaller businesses and other business-related topics. (Remember what was pointed out in the introduction: A majority of jobs in the country are with small businesses, and more than 99 percent of all US businesses are considered small businesses. In addition, more than 40 percent of net new jobs between 1992 and 2013 were created by small businesses.[5]) An editor or media company operator would look at the size of these companies and argue that focusing coverage on the bigger companies is the right strategy for their often-depleted reporting staffs. With more employees and a bigger economic impact than ever before, they're vital to any economy in which they're located.

Such a strategy means that the smaller companies and their issues, which are also important to a town or city, will more than likely be ignored when it comes to news coverage. And that coverage often equates what's happening at big companies with what's happening at all businesses of any size, business owners and operators argue. George McKerrow, the CEO of Ted's Montana Grill in Atlanta, said big-company coverage is "information that really isn't pertinent to what we need to learn about or hear about. And it tends to skew too many small companies to think like a big company instead of a small company thinking like a small company."[6]

The growth of companies into bigger companies is not the only economic or societal change that mainstream business journalism has failed to keep up with. Fewer Americans are owning stocks or homes than they were before the 2007 recession. They're changing jobs more often, and changing how they're saving for retirement as well, but struggling to save. In addition, the population, including business ownership, has become much more diverse. Yet business and economics news often focuses on stories about the stock market—which we'll delve into in chapter 8—and about whether a consumer should purchase a home or, if they own a home, whether they should refinance their mortgage. Retirement-planning stories often focus on those who can afford it, and the coverage of women- and minority-owned businesses pales in comparison to stories about other companies.

SMALL BUSINESS VERSUS BIG BUSINESS

Look at the businesses in any town or city, even big cities such as New York or Los Angeles, and the overwhelming majority of businesses are small. There are some medium-sized businesses like McKerrow's, which has $100 million in revenue, too. The largest employer or company in most cities around the country is typically a hospital or a health care facility.

At the turn of the century, many newsrooms had what was called a "small business" reporter, or a reporter who covered issues that smaller businesses faced, such as rising workers' compensation insurance or finding employees with specific skills. Those stories have now all but disappeared in the mainstream media such as daily newspapers.

The media has covered how the big companies are getting bigger. Andrew Flowers of *FiveThirtyEight* wrote in 2015 that the revenues of the Fortune 500 companies grew from 58 percent of nominal gross domestic product in 1994 to 73 percent in 2013. And for companies in the Fortune 100, revenue rose from about 33 percent in 1994 to 46 percent in 2013.[7] You can argue this means the media should be spending more time focusing on these companies and how they impact society because of their increased size. But doing so downgrades, degrades, and ignores the impact of millions of smaller companies—the building blocks of a competitive economy.

Christopher Mims of the *Wall Street Journal* points out that the reason big companies keep getting bigger is because of their spending on technology. He notes that spending on proprietary information technology rose from an average of 7 percent of net investment by a company in 1985 to 24 percent in 2016. While smaller companies are also spending to build propriety IT systems, they can't copy the systems being built by the bigger companies, and they have to hire outside companies to build those systems, which prevents them from developing a unique way of competing.[8] A 2019 study in the *Harvard Business Review* confirms this, noting that the bigger the company, the increased amount of money that can be spent on research and development that fuels growth. That study concludes that the increased spending leads to a growing difference in the gap in how markets value companies.[9]

The gap is likely to continue growing, making it more important for the mainstream media to cover news about smaller companies. David McLaughlin writes in *Bloomberg News* that the COVID-19 pandemic has led to larger companies increasing their market share, forcing smaller companies to sell or close their doors, particularly retail, restaurant, entertainment, and travel-related businesses.[10] David Dayen notes in the *American Prospect* that mergers and acquisitions will "fuel corporate power" and that the private equity industry could benefit because it will be able to acquire companies in struggling industries at low prices and consolidate businesses.[11]

The number to watch is this: the US Small Business Administration reports that the small business share of the gross domestic product fell from 48 percent in 1998 to 43.5 percent in 2014, the latest figure available. While small business gross domestic product has grown by 1.4 percent annually during that time, large business GDP grew by 2.5 percent annually.[12] Yet small businesses are still more than 40 percent of the economy despite the growth of the big companies. But they are not anywhere close to being 40 percent of the mainstream business news coverage, even with the attention paid to small business struggles during the pandemic.

STOCK OWNERSHIP

Despite the thorough and extensive coverage of the stock market in the business media (see chapter 8 for details) stock ownership in the United States has declined in the twenty-first century. Gallup found that 55 percent of Americans owned stock in 2020, down from 62 percent in 2006 and 60 percent in 1998. Stock ownership has not fully rebounded after it fell beginning with the recession that started in 2007 and lasted until 2009.[13]

The pandemic has affected consumers' feelings about investing in stock. In the early part of 2020 Americans became less likely to view stocks or mutual funds as the best long-term investment. Just 21 percent named stocks as the best investment, down six percentage points from 2019, the lowest level since 2012.[14]

The stock market coverage in the mainstream media is aimed at higher-income US households. The wealthiest 10 percent of US households own an average of $1.7 million in stock while the bottom 50 percent of US households own an average of about $11,000, according to the Tax Policy Center.[15] The richest 1 percent of Americans now account for 56 percent of stocks owned by US households, up from 46 percent three decades earlier.[16]

What makes the stock market coverage so frustrating is that even with more than half of US households invested in the market, it's not close to being the biggest source of household wealth of middle-income families, according to the Federal Reserve Bank of St. Louis. For those families, home ownership accounts for 37 percent of household wealth, and vehicles account for 19 percent. Stocks account for just 11 percent of household wealth.[17]

Edward Wolff, an economist at New York University, has published research that shows swings in the stock market happen but are not being traded on by most Americans. Forty percent of US households with a stock investment are doing so through a pension fund in which they don't control the investments. Another 10 percent are investing in the stock market through mutual funds, again without any say in where the money is invested. Only about 15 percent of US households have direct stock holdings.[18]

The next time you see a daily stock market story in the mainstream media, wonder who's reading it and whether the average business owner or consumer is paying any attention.

HOME OWNERSHIP

Like stock ownership, home ownership in the United States peaked shortly before the 2007 recession, at 69.2 percent in the fourth quarter of 2004, and fell as low as 62.9 percent in the second quarter of 2016, according to the US Census Bureau. At the end of 2020 the home ownership rate had rebounded and was above 67 percent.[19]

As noted previously, a family's largest investment is in its residence. But residential real estate as a focus of mainstream media coverage of the economy downplays many of its issues, such as why minorities and younger consumers with higher amounts of debt have trouble purchasing homes. The Urban Institute notes that the US economy's increasing nonwhite population and decline of married couples with kids tends to decrease the home ownership rate over time.[20]

While owning a home is at about the same level as it was before the 2007 recession for those sixty-five and older, it's about seven to ten percentage points lower for people below the age of forty-four. And less than 50 percent of Black households own their home. For Hispanics, it's only slightly above 50 percent. The rate of white home ownership is above 75 percent.[21]

The Brookings Institution notes other factors affecting home ownership rates, including that new homeowners are older and less white than they used to be. A weaker labor market leads younger consumers to delay starting a family and purchasing homes. Younger adults also have a lower preference for owning a home versus renting. Jenny Schuetz of the Brookings Institution argues that delaying home ownership hurts consumers and the economy in the long run since it is the way most people build wealth.[22] But that's not what the business media covers when it focuses on buying and selling homes. Home prices rising or falling, not what home ownership means to consumers and to the economy, dominates the coverage.

RETIREMENT PLANS

Changes in how consumers save for retirement is also an issue. The shift from pensions funded by companies to individual savings accounts such as 401(k) plans means that retirement wealth has not grown fast enough to keep pace with the aging population, according to the Economic Policy Institute. That shift has negatively affected nonwhite consumers, noncollege educated workers, and single employees the most.[23]

In addition, consumer participation in retirement plans has declined since 2001. And nearly 40 million employees do not have access to a retirement plan through their employer.[24] One-quarter of Americans who are not yet retired have no retirement savings or pension, according to the Federal Reserve Board. And many consumers who have individual savings accounts are not comfortable managing these investments, meaning they aren't getting the information they need from the media. Nearly two out of ten consumers believe that housing prices can never go down, and nearly half of consumers weren't sure whether buying a single company's stock provides a safer or riskier return than a mutual fund.[25]

Understanding how to save for retirement became more acute during the 2020 pandemic, when workers lost their jobs and no longer had access to retirement plans that offered matches by employers, according to the Society of Human Resource Managers. In addition, consumers who are using contribution plans to fund their retirement delegate their wealth and power to the mutual fund companies, money managers, and financial institutions who make the investment decisions in those plans, meaning that the business media cater to the 1 percent, not average consumers, by writing stories about retirement plans.

MORE DIVERSE POPULATION

The US economy—business owners and consumers—has become more diverse across all races and will continue to become more diverse in the next few decades. In 2010 the US population was composed of 310.2 million consumers, with 65 percent of people classifying themselves as white, 18 percent classifying themselves as Hispanic, 12 percent classifying themselves as Black, and 5 percent classifying themselves as Asian. In 2000, just ten years earlier, the population was 75 percent white.[26] By 2050 it's expected that the US population will be 46 percent white, 30 percent Hispanic, 12 percent Black, and 8 percent Asian.[27]

Business journalism is dominated by white males in virtually every newsroom, which holds many newsrooms back from reporting on stories that affect other demographics.[28] A more diverse newsroom would help business news organizations find better stories in areas and with subjects where they never thought to look. Raju Narisetti, a former *Wall Street Journal* editor, cited the following reasons for a lack of newsroom diversity: "Weak leadership; Lack of real intent; Unwillingness to take risks by reaching deeper into the ranks when the top layers are not historically diverse; Not focusing enough on building a diverse starter pipeline; Being satisfied with tokenism in the masthead; . . . Poaching from each other [rather] than adding to the diversity pool."[29]

Hispanic, Black, and Asian women make up less than 5 percent of newsroom personnel at traditional print and online news publications, according to data from the American Society of News Editors.[30] The total minority workforce in the average newsroom is 17 percent. Without minorities in the newsroom, it's hard for business news organizations to understand economic and job-related stories that affect these populations.

The gender situation is slightly better. Female reporters composed 38 percent of journalists covering business and economics stories in 2014, according to data from the Women's Media Center.[31] That was up from 36 percent in 2013 but still below the American population (51 percent), and it's below other areas of journalism. Women cover 50 percent of lifestyle stories, 55 percent of education stories, and 49 percent of health stories.[32]

Some media organizations understand the significance of a diverse population in business journalism. Laura Zelenko, the senior executive editor of Bloomberg News, wondered whether American news organizations would have latched on to the subprime mortgage crisis of 2008 earlier if African American reporters covered the Federal Reserve.[33] Many banks targeted Blacks to sell their higher-risk home loans. Bloomberg has mandated that its reporters find more female sources to quote in its stories. It is also training female executives on how to gain media coverage.

Sherrell Dorsey, who runs a news site that focuses on Black-owned entrepreneurs, wrote for *Columbia Journalism Review* about how the mainstream business media have failed to cover Black-owned technology businesses. She notes:

> Today, there are roughly 2.6 million Black-owned businesses in the US. Of those, 8 percent operate within the technical and scientific services field, whose overall growth has brought with it an uptick in media outlets—TechCrunch, Mashable, Engadget, Gizmodo, DigitalTrends, and more—focused on covering the hottest startups, founders, and technologies. Insufficient coverage of Black business leadership—particularly in the technology space—furthers the trope that Black people are only successful in entertainment and athletic industries, argues Dr. Richard Craig, associate professor at George Mason University.[34]

There are 1.1 million businesses owned by women and another 1 million owned by minorities, according to the US Census Bureau. Health care is the industry that has the most women-owned businesses and the sector with the most Black-owned businesses.[35] The Brookings Institution notes that the percentage of women- and Black-owned businesses is less than their percentage in the population, meaning that they are underrepresented in entrepreneurship. But businesses owned by women and Blacks have seen strong growth since the recession that started in 2007.[36]

CHANGING JOBS

Feeding public interest in business news is the fact that fewer people in the twenty-first century remain with one company throughout their careers, which had been typical from the 1940s through the 1970s. Consumers today naturally have a higher interest in what's going on at companies that they might want to work for. The Bureau of Labor Statistics released a study in 2019 that determined that person holds twelve jobs on average between the ages of eighteen and fifty-two.[37] And a quarter of people held fifteen jobs or more.[38] The average length of time spent on a job has also declined, from 4.4 years in 2010 to 4.1 years in 2020. And the percent of workers who had 10 years or more with their current employer declined from 33.1 percent in 2010 to 32.2 percent in 2020.[39]

According to LinkedIn, the number of companies that people work for in the five years after college graduation nearly doubled in the past decade to nearly three. And the number of companies consumers worked at five to ten years after graduation increased as well, to nearly four. The turnover is higher in certain industries, such as media and entertainment and education.[40]

People are changing jobs because of decreasing loyalty to their employer and a desire to increase their pay. *HR Dive* reported that 43 percent of workers would leave their jobs for a 10 percent compensation increase, and that culture was the primary reason for leaving a company.[41] The Federal Reserve Bank of Atlanta found that income increased 4.5 percent for job switchers compared to workers who stayed in their position.[42] Job switchers in technology and construction are getting higher pay hikes, according to the ADP Research Institute.[43]

People are also waiting longer to retire, primarily because of the changes in how society funds retirement from company-funded pensions to employee contribution plans, according to the Bureau of Labor Statistics.[44]

SOCIAL MEDIA

There's another big societal change that's affecting business news and how consumers and business owners get information. Studies show that they're turning to social media and other unreliable sources where the content may not be vetted or even reported. The social media post may just be someone's opinion, and that someone may not be a journalist who has interviewed experts and other sources to determine the veracity of the information.

In 2005 just 5 percent of Americans were using social media to engage in news content and share information, according to the Pew Research Center. But that number grew to half of all Americans in 2011 and 72 percent in 2019.[45] The most common social media platforms were Facebook and YouTube.

Unfortunately, news consumers who get their information about current events from social media tend to be less knowledgeable about topics. Nearly half of consumers between the ages of eighteen and twenty-nine get their news from social media. They use news websites or apps only 21 percent of the time, and local television just 10 percent of the time.[46]

Here's how this impacts a consumer's knowledge of business and economics news: Of the consumers who were surveyed by the Pew Research Center in October–November 2019, just 40 percent of them who use social media as their primary news source were able to correctly answer questions about the federal deficit, and just 52 percent were able to correctly answer a question about unemployment.[47] That compares to 69 percent using a news website or app who correctly answered about the federal deficit, and 73 percent using a news website or app who correctly answered about unemployment.[48]

In another study, nearly half of US residents were unaware that the social media site Facebook does no original news reporting.[49]

There's another reason why the use of social media to obtain news that may be inaccurate about business and the economy should be concerning. Companies and the economy can be negatively impacted if that "fake news" is allowed to spread. Business investigations firm Kroll found that 84 percent of companies feel threatened by the risk of false rumors being spread by social media.[50] And that happens with regularity. In May 2019 a British bank was forced to post on Twitter that it was in good financial health after rumors circulated on WhatsApp and Twitter. In June 2018 the CEO of motorcycle manufacturer Harley-Davidson was forced to deny a tweet that alleged he had called President Donald Trump a "moron" about tariffs. The tweet with the fake quote was retweeted 25,000 times. The US Securities and Exchange Commission has warned investors as far back as 2015 that false rumors about companies could easily spread on social media.

It's not just social media. We now live in a society where people use the internet to find information, but many of them lack the knowledge to determine what is truthful and what is propaganda. While nearly three-quarters of Americans now have broadband internet service at home and 20 percent are using their smartphones for internet access, the News Literacy Project notes that two-thirds of people search, interpret, and recall information that supports what they already believe, even if what they believe is untrue.[51]

Personal finance site *Investopedia* gives an example of how this can impact consumers of business news: Suppose an investor hears a rumor that a company is about to seek protection in the US bankruptcy court system. Based on this information, she considered selling the stock and goes online, where she finds stories on social media and message boards that mention the possibility of bankruptcy. But she misses the stories that detail how the company has launched a new product that is expected to perform well and increase sales and profits. The investor sells her stock and misses out when it hits an all-time high.[52]

The same thing can happen in other instances. Let's say there's a consumer looking at a job at that same company and sees the same social media and message board posts. He decides to accept another job at another company, missing out on the first company's rise. Or maybe there's a small business owner thinking about striking a partnership with the company but backs away after seeing the same content on the internet.

The internet has another negative impact on business news, according to former *Financial Times* editor Lionel Barber. Once a business or economics news story that may be of interest to specific readers or business owners is posted on the internet, it is immediately copied, retweeted, and rewritten with scant or no attribution, meaning the consumer of that news story may not even know where it originated. "Once upon a time we would have called this plagiarism," said Barber. "Now, so long as there is acknowledgement or attribution, it's all about aggregation."[53] That has a negative impact on coverage, Barber says, because many journalists don't get out and do the legwork for "deep and original reporting."

Business news and information has been affected by how business and society has changed in the twenty-first century. Business news now makes big companies more of a focus of the coverage, and mainstream media continues to focus on stories such as the stock market to the detriment of other important news. Add these issues to the problems in the media industry and it's no surprise that business owners and consumers aren't getting what they need.

7

POLITICAL POLARIZATION

The problems facing business news have been exacerbated by increased political polarization, which has led to news coverage across all delivery formats to focus on the comings and goings of politicians and the political parties, to the detriment of other types of stories. With many mainstream print publications publishing fewer pages, a focus on politics and government means less coverage for business and economics news, even on media websites, where space is unlimited. "Political insider coverage serves a significant but narrow audience, at a cost," said Melanie Sill, former editor of the *Sacramento Bee* and former vice president of content at Southern California Public Radio. "The penalty: this approach pushes out other reporting, rooted in the needs of the public."[1]

Political polarization, along with the political focus of virtually every topic in the United States, has made important economic, financial, and business issues fade away in news cycles amid demagogy and political battles. And if it hasn't faded away at some news organizations, business, economics, and financial news has often become a political story. Media outlets have launched news operations devoted to the political and regulatory aspects of business news, often charging thousands of dollars for access, causing some business and economics coverage to focus on an angle that many small businesses and consumers don't need.

Business news has also been lost amid the increasing information overload facing consumers; the overload, fueled by political coverage, is no fault of the business media. In addition, political polarization has become a major issue in the overall media world, leading many consumers to distrust what they're reading or watching. The Pew Research Center found in 2020 that Republicans have become alienated from established news sources.[2] Frank Newport of Gallup noted in late 2019 that the polarization has harmful effects, leading to inaction on important societal issues.[3] One can assume that these important societal issues would include business-

related topics such as unemployment, the minimum wage, health care benefits, and other topics of great importance to businesses and consumers.

The emergence of more polarization can be seen in the media, with
news organizations considered liberal (CNN, the *New York Times*) or conservative (Fox News, which has been the highest-rated cable network for
most of the past decade). The media's credibility has also been hurt by their
tendency to exacerbate political divisions by pitting a liberal source against
a conservative source in stories, leading consumers to believe those are
the only two options.[4] There's also the increased tendency by consumers
to read or watch news only from media organizations that they favor, reinforcing their points of view and the polarization within society.[5] A Pew Research Center study in 2020 found that Republicans and Democrats trust
different media organizations and that the gap between the two groups is
widening in terms of what news coverage they trust and distrust. The only
media organization that both sides trusted more than they distrusted was
the Wall Street Journal.[6]

Social media isn't helping (see chapter 6). While logging off Facebook or Twitter reduces polarization, it leaves consumers disengaged and
disinterested on current events. For those who remain engaged with social media, the algorithms used by social media companies provide users with stories that make them more hardened in their beliefs.[7] Social
media also amplifies divergent interpretations of news, which exacerbates
polarization.[8]

This political polarization and the perception of political bias in the
media hurts the media. According to a Gallup poll, 41 percent of Americans
have a "great deal" or "fair amount" of trust in the media to report "full, accurately and fairly," no matter the topic.[9] This is a significant drop from the
high for "trust in the media," 72 percent in 1976. And research shows that
polarization has a widespread impact, including in the workplace, which is
an important topic where business news hasn't been able to break through
and adequately cover.[10]

That polarization has crept into business journalism. Researchers from
Indiana University and Michigan State University found strong evidence of
political polarization in business news, particularly as it relates to corporate
financial news.[11] The rise of partisan media changes how companies make
decisions as well, as research conducted when Fox News was just entering
the market has shown. Democratic-leaning companies in areas with Fox

News were less likely to report layoffs in an election year than Democratic-leaning companies where Fox News is not covering news.[12]

It's not just business and economics news. An analysis by Chartbeat shows that political ideology creeps into all kinds of news coverage, including entertainment. It found that even coverage of the Grammys and the Academy Awards were framed around political topics.[13]

It's safe to say that politics is now the main story that the media cover, even at downsized newsrooms at daily newspapers and television stations. Business stories that were once regularly covered at the turn of the century are now often ignored. And when business and economics news does make it into mainstream local media, it's now often presented through the lens of politics. For example, when a company decides to expand and add jobs in a location, the news is often announced by the governor of the state where the expansion is happening, and the story often focuses on what kind of deal the company was able to negotiate with a state agency in the form of tax breaks or other benefits and not what it might mean for other businesses in the region or whether the expansion will help a community with high unemployment.

To be sure, government- and political-focused business news is a growth market for many of the top business news organizations. Bloomberg started Bloomberg Government. *Politico* now has a burgeoning newsroom of reporters and editors focused on how federal government agencies are overseeing various businesses and the politics behind new regulations or laws being thrown out under new political leadership. The *New York Times* shifted coverage of its *DealBook* section of business news in 2017 to examine more the intersection between politics and business. Andrew Ross Sorkin, the founder of *DealBook*, said: "The business world is now inextricably linked with policy—in Washington, in Brussels, in Beijing—in a way that it has never been before. Corporate C.E.O.s and investors increasingly spend as much time in D.C. as they do on Wall Street. Business has become politics. And politics is business."[14]

That might be true for Fortune 500 companies. But for the average business owner who is simply interested in finding out from the media what's happening in his or her local economy, and where the company might be able to open a new location, such politically dominated news, particularly nationally focused political news, isn't much help. (Not that these media consumers are looking to the *New York Times* for the coverage that they need, but the local media aren't giving them anything.) And then there's the business's workers, and its customers, who might prefer to know more about competing companies entering the market or whether a freeze in south Florida might affect the price of orange juice at the grocery store.

Margaret Sullivan argues in *Ghosting the News: Local Journalism and the Crisis of American Democracy* that the overall decline in local news coverage has a negative effect on democracy because it "takes a toll" on civic engagement. Nowhere is this more true than in media coverage of business and economics news, where workers and small business owners are all but ignored because of the focus on political-based news. She found consumers across the country who were "disenchanted with their local news sources" and often complained of "political bias."[15]

BUSINESS MEDIA AND POLITICS

Business news has always had a fair amount of political focus. Government agencies regulate businesses, and the biggest political donors to politicians running for office are usually CEOs and corporations. Big companies and industry organizations hire lobbyists to influence legislation introduced by politicians. In *The Business of America Is Lobbying: How Corporations Became Politicized and Politics Became More Corporate*, Lee Drutman writes that bigger companies have invested "significant resources in politics" and are unlikely to cede "any political advantages to competitors," which stifles reform of important business issues such as US tax code reform.[16] He notes that of the one hundred organizations that spend the most on lobbying, ninety-five represent businesses.

Business and politics became more intertwined with the election of President Donald Trump as the country witnessed the first billionaire businessman as its leader. Businessmen often run for local and state political offices as well. It's been only in the twenty-first century, however, that business news coverage has been overwhelmed by political coverage. The national media focused extensively on what national politicians such as President Trump said or posted on Twitter, deeming it newsworthy, and wrote story after story. That coverage filtered down via wire services to local media, where newsrooms had been cut, and was posted on their websites or printed in their newspapers. In some cases, the local media followed the same coverage strategy with local and state politicians. Trump drove political media coverage with his claims of "fake news," according to a study of news content, leading to more coverage of "misinformation" or "disinformation" than of important topics such as climate change and immigration.[17]

Business news also covers political-related stories such as international trade, but primarily as a macro topic; rarely if ever does the local news media write about how small businesses in their community are being impacted by tariffs and trade imbalances. And let's not forget that other politically charged issues such as immigration and health care are of vital importance to businesses. Many companies, large and small, rely on being able to recruit and hire workers who just recently arrived in the United States, offering them benefits such as health insurance. But because of changes in how the media operate, they eschew these stories and instead "disseminate a tremendous amount of political content, but much of the material is trivial, unreliable, and polarizing," writes Diana Owen of Georgetown University.[18]

Businesses are also increasingly making decisions for political reasons, necessitating that reporters who cover them write about politics. A Nebraska bank dropped its National Rifle Association credit card after receiving customer complaints. Pizza chain Papa John's International dropped its National Football League partnership after players kneeled during the national anthem. Retailers DICK's Sporting Goods and Walmart ended sales for assault-style rifles. In many cases companies chose sides in political debates because they don't want to alienate customers, according to Barry Ritholtz, writing in *Bloomberg Opinion*.[19]

A 2019 study by analytics firm Parse.ly and news site *Axios* found an interesting divergence between what people read in the media and what they said they wanted to read. Consumers read the most about politics and government, followed by sports. But they said they wanted more news about health care, economics, technology, and business more than they actually read. The implication here is that people are consuming the news that the media are giving them—politics, government, and sports—but they really want news about other topics related to business.[20]

POLARIZATION AND THE MEDIA

The national media organizations have helped with the polarization, covering news from a particular political slant for most of the twenty-first century. In the past, network news—ABC, CBS, and NBC, for example—was considered neutral. But now they're competing with Fox News, which has a conservative angle toward many news items, and even MSNBC, which leans liberal in how it covers news. This divergence in how stories are covered leads to putting any business and economics news through the lens of politics. Economists at the Federal Reserve Bank in Dallas found the media fragmentation along political lines contributes more to polarization than does income inequality.[21] Another study found that people who consume news from media with an ideological slant are more likely to believe false information even when presented with the truth.[22]

How news is reported by the journalists also contributes to polarization. Jiyoung Han, writing in a 2016 dissertation for the University of Minnesota, found that when reporters frame their political stories around a conflict, consumers respond as members of a political party and not as individuals, which leads them to adopt more polarized attitudes.[23] Another study found that consuming online news typically leads to more polarization than when a consumer reads news not on the internet.[24]

Ezra Klein, a well-known political journalist and founder of news site *Vox*, wrote a book about why political media have led to polarization. In "Why We're Polarized—And How It Polarizes Us," he writes that the dramatic increase in political news has made it easier for people to find such content if they want it—specifically content that they already agree with. And he notes the effect of polarization on reporters and what they cover:

> Journalists are hardly immune to these forces. We become more polarized, and more polarizing, when we start spending our time in polarizing environments. I have seen it in myself, and I have watched it in others: When we're going for retweets, or when our main form of audience feedback is coming from highly partisan social media users, it subtly but importantly warps our news judgment. It changes who we cover and what stories we chase. And when we cover politics in a more polarized way, anticipating or absorbing the tastes of a more polarized audience, we create a more polarized political reality.[25]

Research shows that the best way for the media to reduce political polarization is for consumers to support local news media, which often have acted as an alternative to national news organizations. The increased trend of consuming news produced by big media organizations—like the ones covered in chapter 3—increased political polarization because consumers lost important information they were receiving from local media outlets that either closed or cut coverage.[26] Local media help keep a focus on the local communities, they found.

What's interesting about the increased political focus of news—and the criticism that news is often presented with a political slant—is that seven out of ten consumers still want the media to act as a watchdog against politicians.[27]

THE EFFECTS OF POLARIZATION

Political polarization has happened before in the United States, most recently in the late nineteenth century. And news coverage has been heavily involved in that polarization—in the late nineteenth century, when newspapers and magazines emphasized sensationalist stories, it was known as "yellow journalism." At that time, news about businesses such as Rockefeller's Standard Oil Company were primary targets for coverage because large companies were new in society, and their tactics drew attention. The result then was that the government and the courts took actions to regulate these businesses and to combat their monopolistic behavior. And these stories were widely covered in newspapers and magazines, the two primary media sources.

The twenty-first-century political polarization is different primarily because of the large amount of news coverage devoted to political-related news and because of how technology such as social media can disseminate content more widely and immediately.

The polarization is also having effects on large parts of society. Pierre Lemieux wrote for the Foundation for Economic Education that companies becoming more political has historically shown to be a negative strategy, often creating a vicious cycle that leads to more polarization and breeds conflict.[28] Todd Schaefer, a political science professor at Central Washington University, notes that the current political polarization requires businesses to be cognizant of who they're using as spokespersons. As an example, he referred to Nike's use of football player Colin Kaepernick in an ad campaign. While some consumers called for a boycott of the company because of Kaepernick's protests of how Blacks have been treated by police, the company also saw sales increase by 30 percent, and it also received $40 million in "free advertising" because of media coverage of the campaign.[29]

Social media has had a huge impact on political polarization, and the divide is currently at its height. One study found that exposing people to opposing points of view in social media makes them more likely to stick to their existing beliefs than to change the viewpoint. And another study showed that exposing people to views opposite of their own pushes them away from those views.[30] In other words, decreasing political polarization is not going to happen on social media.

Or can that be a solution? Research by Damon Centola, a professor at the University of Pennsylvania, shows that if people in social media groups are equal—they have the same number of friends and have equal influence—then the group members hold less bias and are more informed.[31] What needs to be eliminated are "influencers" who have a disproportionate impact and can force rumors and their opinion on a wide group.

What is being discussed on social media—and how it is discussed—has an impact on journalists, according to researchers at Northeastern University. Journalists use social media to find sources and to analyze content. And they tend to have followings on social media that correspond to the perceived political slant of their publication—a *New York Times* reporter is more likely to have left-leaning followers, for example. They discovered, with a few exceptions, a political correlation between how the reporters covered stories and who followed them.[32]

The increasing use of the term "fake news" and conspiracy theories have also contributed to the growing political polarization in the country and the decline in trust of the news media.[33] Those concepts spread and flow freely on social media. Both "fake news" and conspiracy theories tend to distort and decrease the legitimate, objective news that is prevalent in most news media. That doesn't help the news organizations that are legitimately trying to provide business and economics news to their readers—readers who have become skeptical of the news that they consume.

NEW POLITICAL-BASED PUBLICATIONS

The US media industry has also seen an influx of new operations that focus on political-related news; when these new operations cover business and economics news, they do so from a political angle. There's nothing wrong with this strategy. In many cases these news organizations satiate the desires of readers and viewers for any type of political news they can get, and those consumers are willing to pay for it.

But these new operations are also undermining the need and interest for nonpolitical business and economics news, the kind of news that simply provides the information for business owners, workers, and consumers who want to be able to use the information to make decisions about whether to expand their operations, where to look for another job, or what kind of products they should be purchasing. These news consumers are not interested in what political party is pushing for new regulations or deregulations. And they need that news explained to them in a way that shows how it affects them, not big companies.

Founded in 2007, *Politico* has a team of nearly six hundred who work across North America, more than half of whom are editorial staff. The publication has started a new subscription offering, AgencyIQ, focused on regulatory affairs of the pharmaceutical, biotechnology, and medical device industries. *Politico* expanded its policy offerings with new services on sustainability and cannabis. Its Politico Pro offering costs more than $1,000 per topic. In 2020 it acquired E&E News, which covers the energy industry. Again, this is all great content, but it's not what most business owners and workers want or need, and they can't afford to pay for the coverage.

Fox News started Fox Business Network in the same year, 2007, promising to provide content that caters to the average person and not Wall Street. But its coverage has been criticized for being too political, ignoring basic business stories that a mainstream audience would want.[34] In 2021 two of its anchors—Lou Dobbs and Maria Bartiromo—were sued by a voting technology company for making on-the-air comments that questioned the veracity of the 2020 presidential election. Dobbs's show was canceled shortly thereafter, and Fox Business has run content about another election systems company that countered claims made on its shows to thwart off another lawsuit. In 2020 Fox Business removed another anchor, Trish Regan, from the network after she claimed Democrats were creating "mass hysteria" over the coronavirus to "demonize and destroy" President Trump.[35]

Bloomberg L.P. launched Bloomberg Government in 2011 to cover news at the intersection between business and government. But as media critic Jack Shafer wrote, the news service was aimed at business executives willing to pay $5,700 a year for news that would "help them game the Washington system, especially in these days of endless quantitative easing and rampant government intervention."[36] Again, the emphasis is on political-related news that is too expensive for most business owners and consumers.

Former *Politico* staffers launched *Axios* in January 2017, arguing that readers needed smarter and more-efficient coverage of important topics. *Axios* publishes newsletters around topics such as business, technology, markets, health care, energy, and transportation—all big business news fields. It pledges to put its audience first, but it generates revenue from advertisements paid for by companies looking to improve their social responsibility and brand reputations. A large portion of its audience are the types of people already being served by other media: 41 percent of its readers have a household income of more than $150,000, and its readers are 3.5 times more likely to be executives or leaders than other media.[37]

CQ Roll Call was acquired in 2018 by Fiscal Note and is a combination of three previous publications—*Congressional Quarterly*, *Roll Call*, and Capitol Advantage. It tracks congressional news and legislation, which often focuses on how the government is regulating businesses. But think about the business-related content that has been the focus of congressional stories in the past few years. Those stories have been about huge companies such as Facebook and Google and their impact on society. While those companies are important and should be covered, they're not of particular interest to most business owners or consumers. *CQ Roll Call*'s audience—major corporations, industry associations, law and lobbying firms, and government agencies and departments—is evidence that this type of business news does not meet the needs of most business owners and consumers.[38]

Such news outlets have hundreds and hundreds of journalists on staff focused on politically related business news topics. That's a good thing and helps the readers who would like that information. But they're primarily covering news that is national in scope and not writing business and economics news with a local or regional focus. That model contributes to the inability of many consumers to receive the news that they need and want.

A Gallup poll found that the increase in information sources has made it harder for consumers to stay well-informed about the news that they care about, and 63 percent said that the increased number of news organizations that they can access due to technology contributes to making them feel overwhelmed. Gone are the days when people can simply read one newspaper and get all of the news they need, whether about business or not.[39] As a result, about one out of every six consumers simply opts out of consuming news.

Richard Tofel, the former president of ProPublica, suggests that readers would be better served by less coverage of politics and more coverage of how government affects people and businesses. He stated that such reporting is harder than writing about what a president writes on Twitter and harder than simply regurgitating the complaints of a politician or political group—and more expensive for smaller news organizations to perform. But these types of stories would bring journalism back to its goal of being a service to society and acting as a watchdog for those who can't afford—think of the small business owner or the worker—to protect themselves.[40]

The Brookings Institution recommends that news coverage needs to start ignoring "extreme viewpoints" that don't add to the public's understanding about a topic as a way to combat polarization. But it also recognizes that consumers need to take responsibility for their news consumption as well and steer away from content that provides a political slant to a story, focusing instead on news organizations that produce high-quality news and diverse information.[41]

Such changes in journalism and in news consumption habits could start reversing the political polarization trend that has gripped the media. And it would allow media organizations to perhaps turn back to the local business and economics news that it once covered.

Part II

CONSEQUENCES AND THEIR IMPACT

To be sure, the media outlets that provide business news and information must share some of the blame for the lack of content that many business owners, employees, and customers need. Business journalism has evolved to cover important topics that only a small fraction of society cares about, and they have also ignored or downplayed many stories that have a broad impact across all readers, listeners, and viewers.

The voluminous stock market coverage in daily business news is but one example. Monday through Friday, stock market journalists breathlessly report about the ups and downs of the markets and individual company stocks, and yet these stories are not relevant to huge parts of society. Stock ownership among households has gone down in the past decade-plus, and what happens in the stock markets is not a barometer to what is occurring in many local towns and cities. The readers who care about the stock market are usually those who have millions and sometimes billions invested in stocks, such as money managers and hedge funds, not the owner of a local restaurant who's more worried about making payroll next month. The millions of small business owners in the United States want to know more about how they can run their operation better and grow.

And when it comes to business news for employees, the coverage is minimal. Stories about workplace issues such as overtime, returning to the office after COVID-19, and benefits are in the minority when it comes to business journalism. Yet workers are the backbone of any business and of the economy. When working conditions are covered by the media, it's often from the perspective of how it impacts the consumer or the business, not how employees are being impacted.

Personal finance coverage is the same. There's plenty of stories in the business news realm discussing how to properly purchase life insurance or how to save for retirement. But this content focuses on those who can afford to spend or save money on such perks, not the huge portions of consumers who struggle to make ends meet every day and can't afford to purchase even a small term life insurance policy.

One of the fastest-growing expenses for any business or consumer is health care, and yet this topic is rarely covered from an economic perspective of how health care costs impact the profits of a company or whether a person has to file for bankruptcy protection because of medical bills. Health care is simply a business to many business news outlets, which often focus on health care company profits and whether stock prices for those companies are going up or down.

In part 2 of *The Future of Business Journalism*, I detail how business news has failed many businesses, employees, and consumers by focusing on topics that are of interest to only a few or focusing on these topics through a lens that doesn't help large portions of the population. And I make suggestions on how this coverage can change to help businesses, consumers, and employees be better informed financially.

8

THE STOCK MARKET IS OVERCOVERED

Consider the job of a stock market reporter in the United States for one of the major news outlets such as Bloomberg News, Reuters, and the Associated Press. He or she typically arrives in the newsroom by 7:00 a.m. and quickly churns out a story about what stocks might be moving up or down once the market begins trading at 9:30 a.m. After that story hits the wire, the reporter then begins working on a story about the market's opening moves.

The reporter might then update that story in the middle of the day and again before the market closes. Finally, a story wrapping up the day's action usually goes out by 5:00 p.m. Media operations around the country pick up those stories and post them on their websites and print them in their newspapers for readers.

On television, the stock market's moves are also detailed throughout the day on CNBC, Fox Business, and Bloomberg Television. (These media organizations also have reporters posting stock market stories on their websites.) On radio, there are also regular updates, particularly if a station partners with Bloomberg Radio.

After the US markets close for the day at 4:00 p.m., a markets reporter and editor may then write a story about what's happening in "after hours" trading, particularly if a major company such as Google or Facebook has reported earnings after the market closed and its stock price has reacted.

Monday through Friday, except for holidays, dozens of business reporters spend their days writing and talking about the stock market, trying to explain why the prices of some companies have gone up while others have gone down, and why the overall market may have risen or fallen. They're interviewing traders and analysts and hedge fund managers and mutual fund managers, trying to find general themes about what's going on in the market.

It's coverage that only those people with sizable stakes in the market really care about. To be sure, there are some people not invested in the stock market who like to read these stories. But business journalism has become overly focused on what the stock market does each day, and it's not a story that resonates with many business owners and consumers who don't have any holdings in publicly traded companies. And if they do, it's likely in a mutual fund or a retirement account that they don't actively, or even regularly, trade.

Stock market coverage is the classic story that shows the current problem with business journalism. It's content for only those with the financial means to invest and to spend on business news content.

Slightly more than half of Americans—55 percent—own stocks, according to an April 2020 poll by Gallup, down from 67 percent in 2002.[1] And according to the Federal Reserve, just 14 percent of American families have a direct investment in individual stocks, meaning most people invested in the market are doing so through a mutual fund or retirement account. And stock ownership rises based on how much money someone makes—the top 10 percent on the income scale own stocks about 90 percent of the time.[2] During the 2020 pandemic, when many households lost income and wealth, it was upper-income consumers—and white households—who benefited the most by the 16.3 percent rise during the year of the Standard & Poor's 500 index, a common barometer of stock market performance. Fifty-seven percent of white households own stocks, compared to 30 percent for Black households and 14 percent for Hispanic households.[3]

Jack Murtha notes in the *Columbia Journalism Review*, "Most Americans don't deal with stocks intimately enough to warrant a constant eye on financial news, just as most people don't need to check their 401(k) every day."[4] And only half of investors trust the media for information about markets, according to a survey for Natixis Investment Managers, while 41 percent said that the media are not trustworthy for markets information.[5]

The overemphasis on stock market coverage leads many to believe that the market rising or falling is a scoreboard for the economy, mimicking sports news coverage. The higher the market rises, then the better off the economy. Sean McElwee wrote in *Talking Points Memo*:

> While the stock market has been humming along and corporate profits rebounded quickly, unemployment remains stubbornly high and wages low.

At the same time, the recovery has been divided across racial lines, with the racial wealth gap in 2013 even larger than before the Great Recession. But news reports tend to downplay race gaps in unemployment, what Reniqua Allen calls the "permanent recession," focusing on the broad indicator. Newspapers and television anchors treat stock prices as though they are a symbol of broad prosperity, rather than a symbol that the rich are getting richer.[6]

Stock market stories and television segments about the markets are not good signals for what an investor should be following when deciding what to do with their money. Diego Garcia of Dartmouth College discovered that positive and negative words in market coverage in the *Wall Street Journal* and *New York Times* can affect the market.[7] But nobody uses those stories to buy and sell stocks.

And James Depore wrote in *Real Money* that stock market coverage assumes that all investors are betting on the market to rise. "It can be very disconcerting when all the folks on television are talking about how fantastic the action has been while you are still struggling to find more stocks to buy," he noted.[8]

Stefan Theil, writing for the Harvard University Shorenstein Center on Media, Politics and Public Policy, called daily markets coverage, even though it is often the most prominent business and economics news coverage for television and radio, "utterly meaningless to anyone but a day trader," primarily because it focuses on what has happened, and that past performance of an investment can't help anyone predict its future performance.[9] He added, "If Wall Street's smartest fund managers cannot, on average, outperform the market, the idea that journalists can do a better job predicting the future seems a little silly."[10]

In an ironic twist, CNBC's Jim Cramer blamed the media's negative coverage of the markets in 2019 for the lack of interest by consumers in investing. Cramer, who talks and writes about stocks to buy and sell on both CNBC and in *The Street* content, blamed stories about economic data. "Bad news gets better ratings than good news," Cramer said. "So I can't really blame people for failing to recognize how much money's being made in the stock market, especially in the best-performing individual stocks" on the market.[11]

Yet those stories about economic data were appearing on CNBC and in many other media outlets, helping business owners and consumers make important decisions that had nothing to do with investing in the stock market, such as whether to spend money to expand manufacturing or to delay purchasing a new car or house. Economic data in the media isn't just for stock investors, despite the impression in the media that everything revolves around stocks.

THE DAILY STOCK STORY

There's nothing obviously wrong with the daily stock market story that you may read online or from a wire service in your daily newspaper, or listen to on television or the radio. That story will likely mention what happened that particular day to the Dow Jones Industrial Average, or the NASDAQ, or the Standard & Poor's 500, or maybe even the Russell 3000. These are all indices that measure how specific parts of the stock market perform. The Dow, as it is commonly called, is a collection of thirty big company stocks, while the NASDAQ primarily focuses on technology companies, and the Russell 3000 is a barometer of small companies. The S&P 500, as you might have guessed, is five hundred stocks.

The story may then go on to mention individual stocks and why they rose or fell. If there was a major piece of economic data released that day, such as the first Friday of the month when the unemployment statistics come out, the story might mention that as well as a reason why stocks rose or fell. The story might also quote a trader or an investor giving his or her thoughts about the market's performance.

Now, to be sure, business journalism holds an important function in acting as an intermediary dispensing information that people want.[12] But this daily market coverage can often mislead people into thinking they can understand what's going on with stocks simply by reading these stories. Theil says reporters quote market analysts who "happily offer explanations when a simple 'I don't know' would be much more honest." That gives the stock market story of the day "drama, meaning and predictive power" that is often misleading.[13]

Most daily stock market stories simply breed confusion among consumers, noted Murtha. They become uncertain as to whether that day's performance should cause them to buy or sell because some stories caution investors against selling when the market falls while other stories tell consumers to sell when the market reached new heights. "How can lay readers be expected to judge one seasoned financial reporter's opinion over the other?" he asks.[14]

Here's another problem with daily markets stories: by the time an average consumer or investor reads, watches, or listens to the story, professional traders have already acted upon the news and likely used algorithms to trade almost instantaneously after the news is disclosed. That's even the case when market reporters are on the floor of the New York Stock Exchange and a network breaks in for a breathless report about big news.

Even some business journalists realize that the daily coverage of the stock market is not in the best interest of consumers or investors. Longtime business journalist Felix Salmon says the least informative form of stock market reporting is the daily story: "If any newscast tells you what the Dow did today, they're implicitly telling you that the Dow's movement today is important. Which, it isn't. If they tell you what the Dow did today *every* day, then they're implicitly telling you that daily movements in the Dow are *really* important, important enough to get reported day in and day out. Which is insane."[15]

During an interview on CNN's *Reliable Sources*, Salmon also noted that people who have their retirement invested in the stock market may want it to go down because if they aren't retiring tomorrow, or anytime soon, they can buy additional stocks more cheaply. "I think people concentrate far too much on what happens on any given day," he said. "And the fact is that if you're investing for a period of twenty or thirty years, what happens on any given day is completely irrelevant."[16]

NOT THE ECONOMY

There's also the misbelief that some consumers and business owners hold that a rising stock market means that the economy is also doing well. President Donald Trump often pointed to the stock market during his term as proof of a strong economy. The performance from 2020 shows just how wrong that can be. While the S&P 500 index rose 16 percent during the year, the gross domestic product, or the production and consumption of goods and services, fell 2.3 percent during the year. Millions of people also lost their jobs during the year and suffered financial distress.

Why did the stock market go up during such a year? Many investors look to the future when deciding whether to buy or sell. If they think that the economy is going to be better down the road and companies will be able to sell more of their goods and services, then they might buy stocks and wait for that to happen. With the economy, there are leading indicators and lagging indicators. A leading indicator is a data point that rises before the overall economy; the stock market is considered a leading indicator. When economic data such as the gross domestic product or unemployment figures released by the federal government shows that the economy is performing better than expected, then stocks may go up.

But the economy and the market are not moving in tandem. Nir Kaissar of Bloomberg News ran a comparison in 2020 between the gross domestic product and the stock market proving this argument. He wrote, "Economists and financial pundits can be more careful about using the market as a proxy for the economy and push back when politicians do it. But perhaps the best way is to just say it plainly: The stock market doesn't care about the economy."[17]

The problem, wrote Matt Phillips in the New York Times, is that many people associate stock market crashes with economic downturns. And in the case of the October 1929 stock market crash that led to the Great Depression, that correlation is correct. But it's also been a marketing ploy by the stock exchanges, said Phillips, noting that the New York Stock Exchange began a campaign to convince people to buy stocks so that they could "own your share of American business."[18] Back then it was easier to link stocks to the economy: The two largest companies—AT&T and General Motors— employed 1.2 million workers. Today, the two largest companies in the S&P 500 are Apple and Microsoft, and they employ just 280,000 people.[19]

Also remember that there are other "markets" out there that don't receive nearly as much media coverage when compared to the stock market. The value of all stocks in US markets is $36.3 trillion.[20] The value of the bond market—debt owed by companies and governments—is $40 trillion.[21] The value of the commodities market—everything from oil to gold and silver—is $20 trillion.[22] In currencies markets, trading is approximately $6.6 trillion each day, according to the Triennial Central Bank Survey by the Bank for International Settlements.[23] In many communities, such as the agricultural-focused Midwest, these markets are more important.

DAY TRADERS AND MONEY MANAGERS

Turn on one of the three primary business channels—CNBC, Fox Business Network, or Bloomberg Television—during trading hours and you're likely to see one of their journalists interviewing a professional money manager about specific stocks that he or she owns, or about what he or she thinks about the overall market. In some shows on these three networks, multiple professional investors may be on the screen at the same time debating, and sometimes yelling, about certain stocks or certain industries. Think of the Brady Bunch squares on steroids.

These are the people that fuel the breathless stock market coverage, and they go on television because it helps them and their firms develop reputations that attract clients. As Scott Wapner, host of CNBC's *Fast Money Halftime Report*, said in 2018, "Outlets like CNBC, we've certainly helped these people develop masters of the universe personas. We've helped make them into celebrities in their own right. They're certainly willing to come on to TV to talk."[24] In another interview, Wapner noted that he wants viewers of his show to have "actionable investment ideas in a fun and entertaining way" and wants to help people "understand why certain decisions are made by the group of experts we bring on."[25]

Stock market coverage on television is often aimed at day traders. Former *Financial Times* editor-in-chief Lionel Barber calls the coverage "a spectator sport, especially on cable news."[26] Others are more brutal in their assessment. Thiel calls coverage of stock market declines "'carnage' for the sake of news value."[27] Jana Schilder said in the *Toronto Star* that the active traders watching market coverage on television are being fed recommendations by analysts and fund managers "who, more often than not, may have a vested interest in seeing the price of that specific stock go up."[28]

Michael Hiltzik of the *Los Angeles Times* writes that CNBC learned from watching sports news shows. "Its impulse is to give even viewers with no stake in the outcome a rooting interest in the numbers snaking across the screen. They'll share the thrill of victory as the indexes climb back toward the green, and the agony of defeat as the effort falls short."[29] CNBC's *Trading Nation* program bills itself as providing investors and traders ways "to use the news of the day to their advantage."

And yet professional investors say that people should avoid what they see and hear about the markets on television. Vitaliy N. Katsenelson, the chief investment officer at Investment Management Associates, writes that investors should avoid financial television when deciding what stocks to buy and sell: "Business TV presents additional dangers to your rationality: It reprograms you to think about the stock market as a game. In encouraging you to play that game, it puts you at risk of nullifying all the research you've done, as you let your time horizon dwindle from years to minutes. It also threatens to strip from you the humility that is so needed in investing. Business TV guests who provide their opinions on stocks have to project an image of infallibility (the opposite of humility)."[30]

The advice that the average consumer needs when it comes to investing, such as whether to put money in index mutual funds, according to Harold Pollack, is too boring for television business news, and it wouldn't attract the advertisers that help fund the coverage. "People need a different financial media—one less focused on dispensing investment tips and what's happening on Wall Street, and more focused on dispensing realistic advice about how to make big financial decisions," he wrote in the *Atlantic*.[31]

There's been no bigger takedown of the money managers on business television than when Jon Stewart, host of *The Daily Show*, took Jim Cramer, himself a former money manager who now is more business journalist than anything, to task back in 2009 for recommending a bank that then went under. And yet Cramer remains as popular as ever, as do all of the other professional investors who appear on TV to talk about stocks.

As longtime business journalist Chuck Jaffe notes, people such as Cramer, on television talking about investments, should be judged by their record rather than how the stocks they're talking about on the air perform. He wrote, "If you like what you hear, the safer bet would be the fund, rather than the individual names discussed. Anyone making decisions based on what they heard or read somewhere needs to think of the expert as an oddsmaker and the investment as a wager, because they're speculating on both. That's almost always a bad bet."[32]

Just because a professional investor says he or she likes a stock on television should not be a reason to go buy it. In fact, the pro may not hold the stock in his or her portfolio.

THE OTHER MARKET PROS

There's plenty of market analysis and coverage on the internet as well. Business news sites such as *Seeking Alpha*, *ZeroHedge*, *Motley Fool*, *Yahoo Finance*, and *Benzinga* all tout the advice they provide for the average person. *Yahoo Finance* boasts the highest amount of page views and visits of any financial site on the Web, boosted by consumers being able to type on the stock ticker of any company and get basic financial information about the business.

Unfortunately, the content on these websites varies wildly, and many times the stories and advice are being written by people who have a vested interest, just like the professional investors on television channels.

Seeking Alpha says that its goal is to help consumers make better investment decisions.[33] And it's got more than 4 million registered users. But the nearly nine thousand contributors to its site are not journalists. Many of them are investors themselves, and some of them write under pseudonyms, making it nearly impossible to know their ulterior motives when writing about a stock.

ZeroHedge also has as its mission the goal of widening the scope of financial information available to investors, but its content contains only one fictional name as a byline, meaning that it's uncertain where the stories are coming from and whether they've been accurately reported. The site was launched by someone barred from working in the brokerage industry for insider trading. The site also republishes content from other business news providers, and its Twitter account was banned in early 2020 for publishing misinformation.[34]

Benzinga started in 2010, and it's also geared toward the individual investor, saying these people are "dissatisfied with the dinosaurs of financial media."[35] It does have a staff that covers news, but it also includes investment ideas, and it also charges for some of its content. It also includes a section that covers Wall Street analyst stock upgrades and downgrades and offers a pre-opening e-mail newsletter.

Motley Fool is perhaps the most sedate of the market websites, and it's been around the longest, starting in 1993 as a personal finance column syndicated in newspapers. In addition, *Motley Fool* doesn't allow anonymous writers, hiring its own staff to produce its content. Like *Seeking Alpha*, *Motley Fool* offers a service that provides stock recommendations, but it's more geared toward the long-term investor.[36]

With the hiring of former *Fortune* top editor Andy Serwer in 2015, *Yahoo Finance* has moved heavily into business news content. It has added editorial staffers who write for the website, and it has launched eight hours of video streaming shows as well. Again, the content is heavily geared toward individual investors and people who want to know more about the stock market.

To be sure, the goals of these websites are laudable. They're trying to even the playing field between professional and amateur investors. But that's impossible. Professional investors have computer programs that allow them to trade within milliseconds of market-moving news, meaning the news is already factored into an investment by the time an amateur hears about it and can make a trade online or call their broker. And they're simply feeding into the idea that watching the market and stocks throughout the day is something that can be valuable for everyone.

WHAT SHOULD BE COVERED

No one should be naive enough to believe that business media outlets are going to read this chapter and suddenly stop covering the stock market on a daily basis. But there are some simple steps that can be taken to dramatically improve the coverage.

Let's discuss first how market moves are described. Stefan Theil took business journalists who write about the stock market to task when he noted that they prefer to use words such as "soar" or "spike" or "crash" when writing about what has happened when it is often "no more than a market blip."[37]

More than a decade ago, the *SABEW Stylebook* for financial writers recommended that stock market coverage should adhere to using only certain verbs and adjectives to describe how averages and markets performed, which would lower the sports-fueled mentality of the coverage. Those recommendations still hold.

> The following guidelines should be applied when using verbs to describe how a broad market index has fluctuated:
> - **1 percent drop or less:** Use "fell" or "dropped," as well as "declined." And we're even OK with "moved downward."
> - **2 to 4 percent decline:** Any of the above, as well as "dipped" and "slumped," which are slightly more serious grades of a fall.
> - **5 to 10 percent decline:** "Sell-off" is appropriate here, as is "retreated." On Wednesday, October 15, 2008, the market "retreated" by 7.87 percent.
> - **Drop of 10 percent or more:** The term "rout" is correct. The stock market fell by 12.8 percent on October 28, 1929, the first day of the decline

that preceded the Great Depression. "Rout" needs to convey the suddenness of the move. On October 19, 1987, the market was "routed" when the Dow Jones Industrial Average fell 22.6 percent that day. And multiday drops that total more than 10 percent would also equal a "rout" as long as it's clear that the term refers to more than one day. Do *not* use "correction" in any instance. It is a euphemism.

Here are the verbs recommended when writing about increases:

- **Rise of up to 1 percent:** "Increased" and "advanced" are the most common accepted terms. "Gained" is good as well.
- **2 to 4 percent increase:** Again, "gained," "increased" or "advanced" is fine here, as are "rose" and "grew."
- **5 to 10 percent increase:** "Jump" and "soar" are appropriate here.
- **10 percent or more:** "Surge" seems to be the best antonym for "rout." When the Dow rose by 936 points on October 13, 2008, it rose by 11 percent, the fifth-largest one-day percentage gain in the market's history. The market has only had six one-day "surges" in its history.[38]

Stock prices and indexes are also discussed in the financial media with little to no context. For the average stock mentioned in a story, there's rarely if any reporting to let consumers know if it's a cheap or expensive stock compared to other stocks in the same industry or to the overall market. All the reporter would need to do is include the stock's price-to-book or price-to-earnings ratio—two measures used to assess the value of a stock—and then compare those numbers to other stocks or to an index. Theil adds that when stocks are written about after the company reports its financial results, there's usually no mention of its product pipeline or customer relationships or human relations, factors that can influence its future performance.[39]

Market coverage tends to emphasize how many points the Dow or the NASDAQ rose or fell on a certain day. With the Dow reaching 30,000 points in 2020, a drop of 1,000 points can seem huge, but that's just more than a 3 percent drop, which is not all that rare. Coverage should focus on the percentage change in an overall average, and in a specific stock, not by how much it rose or fell. Bloomberg News recommends that its stock stories should focus on "why" a market or a stock rose or fell and how that movement compares with what happened in the past. It also asks its market reporters to consider how many days in a row a stock or an average has been up or down, and to include in a story when was the last time a stock or an average rose or fell by as much as it did on the time that the story is covering. Again, it's all about the context.

Covering the stock market is one of the hardest jobs in business journalism. A reporter has to make sense of thousands of different reasons and stock movements, and what's causing one stock or average to rise may not be the same reason that another stock or average is rising. In fact, what may be causing one stock to rise could be the same reason causing another stock to fall. And then the reporter does it all over again the next day, finding what may be different reasons for why stocks and averages are moving.

That coverage may not always accurately reflect the core reasons why a stock or average is moving, and that coverage probably is not focused on what an average investor needs to know before buying or selling a stock. It's commonly accepted that most people should be investing for the long term, but most markets' coverage focuses simply on what happened that day, that week, or maybe that month. Some investors may be more interested in other factors not even included in markets coverage, such as a company's reputation, or its market capitalization, or its management team—topics that are rarely included in this type of coverage.

Josh Brown, a financial blogger and money manager at Ritholtz Wealth Management in New York who has regularly appeared on CNBC, summed up the situation nicely in a 2014 interview. He said, "People should not be relying on the financial media for advice at all. I think the financial media works better as a jumping off point for our own research, as inspiration, and as a fact or data-distribution mechanism."[40]

Most consumers and business owners would all be better off if they stopped reading and watching the media's daily coverage of the stock market and focused on something else. So would part-time investors, day traders, and everyone else looking at the market to make money.

9

FAILING EMPLOYEES AND CONSUMERS

The decline of unionization has been slow and steady. After reaching its height in 1955, when one out of every three Americans belonged to a union, unionized workers fell to 27.3 percent of the workforce in 1970 and to one out of every five Americans by 1983.[1] By 2019 the ratio had fallen to one out of every ten workers, with most of the union members working in government jobs.[2] During the same time, the rise in CEO compensation has been astronomical, rising by 940 percent between 1978 and 2018, according to the Economic Policy Institute, while wages for the typical worker grew just 11.9 percent.[3]

These trends have been documented by the top business media in the last forty years. Today, however, most mainstream media have cut or stopped covering stories around labor and the average worker, preferring instead to focus on what is happening with the people who can afford high-priced business journalism, such as CEOs. Once a common beat in the newsroom, the "labor" beat has been changed to the more nebulous "workplace" assignment, where reporters also cover topics such as ergonomics and dating coworkers.

"In its glamorization of the rich and powerful, the business press, I believe, has also begun to forget the American worker," writes Jeffrey Madrick, a former business journalist at *Money* and *BusinessWeek* magazines. "This tendency evolved since the 1970s. But what is most bothersome about it is that, if the press does not represent mid-level and low-level workers, who will?"[4]

Business and economics news coverage that focuses on consumers and how they should be spending their money has shifted as well, catering to those with the financial wherewithal to afford items such as life insurance, annuities, and long-term care insurance while ignoring stories that might be helpful to a wider audience. Researcher Nadine Strauss discovered that most business journalists "report for wealthy, male, well-educated business people or citizens with a strong interest in investments."[5]

The result is that many workers and consumers no longer look to the mainstream media for news and information about topics such as how much they should be paid, whether they should be renting an apartment or buying a home, or the effect of multiple credit cards on their ability to borrow money. While these topics are often covered by specialty news operations that have started online in the past decade, for the most part these journalists are targeting readers with a higher socioeconomic status, leaving workers and consumers in the lurch, scrambling to find bits and pieces without any coherence.

When these consumers do find help in the media, it's often misguided or comes from a personal finance "guru" whose advice is questionable, writes Helaine Olen in *Pound Foolish: Exposing the Dark Side of the Personal Finance Industry*: "These experts paint themselves as our financial saviors, while often neglecting to mention they are making a living (and a good living!) not just from their television appearances and books, but by their agreements with everyone and everything from mutual fund companies and credit reporting agencies—not to mention the host of 'products' they try to sell us."[6]

Indeed, the rise of free personal finance news sites and blogs in the past decade may seem like a positive step for consumers, but most are tied to a product such as a credit card, which calls into question the sites' objectivity. These ethical issues support the thesis that quality business and financial news is only for those who can afford it, and that most of the content that's available for free is not good for the consumer.

Editors and those who run newsrooms today would argue that there's no reason to devote a staffer to cover labor and employment issues because of the decline in union membership. And they've dropped their personal finance reporters or "helpline" reporters because they see an entire industry that's been built around helping consumers spend their money more wisely.

That rationale misses the point. While workers may not belong to a union, the Bureau of Labor Statistics estimates that there are 157.8 million people in the workforce—both union and nonunion members. Many are likely interested in understanding trends in the workplace, such as which companies are raising their minimum wage, which companies offer work-at-home options, and which companies offer job-swapping opportunities. Steve Greenhouse, the longtime labor reporter at the *New York Times*, explained the importance of such coverage in the media:

> A lot of people say it's a boring beat. I thought, there are 150 million workers and there are a lot of interesting stories about workers. It's not just about labor unions. It's about struggling farm workers, and struggling immigrant workers, and sex/race/religion discrimination at work, how workers are getting treated on the job, and public safety programs at work, and some companies that do a great job in how they treat their workers, like Costco.[7]

And in terms of personal finance, a 2019 study by GuideVine, a service that matches people with financial advisers, found that many Americans sorely lack knowledge when it comes to basic financial terms such as "interest" and "bankruptcy" and understanding how inflation works. Less than half of adults over thirty can explain a 401(k) retirement plan and how it works. By not helping consumers understand topics like these, the mainstream media is eschewing its responsibility to society.

The decline in relevant coverage for the working class and its impact has been well documented. In 2013 the Newspaper Guild and Communication Workers of America released a study that found the working class is not being covered in television news. In 2009, 2010, and 2011 just 0.3 percent of network television news content covered labor issues. And when there is coverage, the issues are often framed as being the fault of the workers, not the business or its executives. "It's a direct line from the decline of labor unions and collective bargaining to the decades-long economic slide of American workers, yet few journalists seem to be able to find the narrative thread," writes Christopher Martin, a professor at the University of Northern Iowa and an expert on the topic.[8]

In addition, labor news is now framed around how it affects consumers and rarely addresses the issues that workers face. Two Canadian professors argue that such reporting hurts society, which as a result lacks the knowledge about wages, working conditions, and changes in the workplace.[9] Martin adds that coverage of the working class focuses on white men and ignores women and people of color, and that stories about work-related topics have become political. He argued that the way for the news media to improve its work-related coverage is for reporters to unionize, which could "close the gap between journalists and the communities they cover," and to find and talk to workers, to "give them a voice, and include them in their audience."[10]

This last step might be difficult. Media outlets have primarily geared their coverage toward more affluent readers.

LABOR COVERAGE DECLINES

Few mainstream media organizations in the twenty-first century give a labor or workplace beat to a reporter. (Some notable exceptions include the *Sacramento Bee* and the *New York Times*.) This is in contrast to the early part of the twentieth century, when labor-focused newspapers were common in most cities; throughout most of the century the labor beat was common at newspapers. One of the last labor papers, the *Racine Labor* in Wisconsin, closed in 2002.

When there are stories today about labor and workers, they are fragmented, superficial, and lack context, focusing only on how labor issues affect consumers. For example, coverage of an increase in the minimum wage in the United States, a major issue for many workers, often focuses more on the harm a higher wage would mean for businesses and the effect on the economy, not how a higher wage would increase the standard of living for millions of workers and their families.[11]

In his book *Framed! Labor and the Corporate Media*, Martin argues that the decline in coverage of labor and workers coincided with an increase in corporate ownership of the media, which led to many media companies engaging in antilabor activities and focusing on a more affluent readership as opposed to a broader, more general readership that included the working class. And he notes that newspaper readership began declining when they de-emphasized worker content.[12] He also documents how media coverage of major labor stories, such as a General Motors plant closing and the major league baseball strike of 1994 and 1995, is framed from the perspective of a company upholding its values and the impact on fans, respectively, not from the perspective of the employees.

Timothy Noah, the former labor and employment editor at *Politico*, wrote in 2014 that stories that do focus on the labor beat often use the term "Big Labor" as a "cruel taunt." He says, "By the logic of media coverage, that means neither they nor the American working class that (not coincidentally) has declined along with them warrant much media attention."[13] That hurts the relationship between journalists and labor sources. Julie Ancel of *Labor Notes* writes that many union leaders are hesitant to talk to the media because they are often referred to as "labor bosses," and the media rarely cover peaceful negotiations that result in good contracts for both sides.[14]

Greenhouse has noted that there has been a slight uptick recently in media coverage of labor and worker stories. He states that stories about the issues facing temp workers and independent contractors have been important to society's understanding of what's going on in the workplace.[15] And David Uberti wrote in *Columbia Journalism Review* in 2015 that some mainstream media have made the beat a focus. *The Boston Globe* has a "workplace and income inequality" beat, and "the *Los Angeles Times* has produced stories on the West Coast ports labor dispute."[16] *Bloomberg News* reporter Josh Eidelson currently covers labor and has won national awards, and Bloomberg Government also has a labor reporter. The beat is also covered by Bloomberg Law. And in January 2021 tech news site *The Markup* hired a labor reporter. That follows a move by the *Financial Times*, which in November 2020 hired a labor and equality correspondent in the United States.

But those are major publications or media companies with deep financial pockets. And in the case of the Bloomberg newsrooms, the beat is primarily covered from a policy and regulatory perspective and available only with a premium subscription. In smaller cities, the beat is all but ignored. When the CEO of the arts and conference center in Pueblo, Colorado, which had laid off most of its staff in 2020 when the pandemic hit, contacted a journalist at the local paper to let him know about a story, the journalist replied that he had been laid off and the story wouldn't be covered.[17] A worker at a factory in the Midwest where a coronavirus outbreak had led to one death contacted a reporter for *HuffPost* about the story because he couldn't get a reporter for the local paper to cover the topic.[18]

The decline in reporting about labor and workers affected society during the coronavirus pandemic in 2020 and 2021, which resulted in millions of job losses and high unemployment, and at a time when an administration was implementing anti-worker policies.[19] Luke Ottenhof writes in *Columbia Journalism Review* that "this deficit means that new injustices might go unnoticed, while previous ones could reappear."[20]

Noam Scheiber, who covers workers and the workplace for the *New*

York Times, writes that labor coverage from the mainstream media should focus on how technology is changing jobs and employment. As an example, he cites how technology-based ride-sharing companies such as Uber and Lyft, and other tech businesses, have changed the average job for millions. "I often spend more time trying to figure out the machines than figuring out the humans," he wrote.[21]

WORKPLACE ISSUES

Andrew Stevens of the University of Regina and Charles Smith from St. Thomas More College, both in Canada, argue that one of the problems with labor and workplace stories is that when they are covered, the reporter is often someone with little to no knowledge of the beat. "Jumping from story to story, often overworked, and lacking experience with covering labour disputes, reporters can be forgiven for struggling to keep up with rapidly-changing developments in the world of labour relations," they write.[22]

There's another issue with coverage—mainstream media think that covering so-called workplace issues is the same as covering labor or worker-related stories. That's happened, writes Martin in his 2019 book, *No Longer Newsworthy: How the Mainstream Media Abandoned the Working Class*, because mainstream media are now focused on stories that upper-class readers want about offices and have "written working-class readers out of their business plan."[23] He cites the example of the *Chicago Tribune*, where a "workplace columnist" covered topics such as spotting the office jerk, connecting with your employees, and how to handle an office party.[24] These columns appeared after the newspaper's labor reporter retired and was not replaced.

What could a reporter for the local paper, any local paper, have covered that would be of interest to workers, particularly those in manufacturing jobs? In 2018 one now-retired labor reporter interviewed working-class people such as truck drivers and steelworkers and found that they wanted coverage from their local media outlets about plant closings; the negative effects of trade, layoffs, and automation; and how companies are changing their pension benefits, just to name a few story topics.[25]

Others have noted a shift in coverage resulting from a revenue loss from advertising. Liz Ryan wrote for the *Huffington Post* about how an editor at a daily newspaper wouldn't run her story about a large company lying to its workers about moving its headquarters because the business was a large advertiser for the newspaper. "People are meaty, earthy, milky, warm and wise," she wrote. "They power everything that happens in business, but we leave them out of the story."[26]

To give an example of how the major business media are not focused on workplace issues, in September 2020 Reuters announced a new editorial focus called "The Great Reboot" that focused on providing news to "corporate leaders and professionals" about how the pandemic has affected their businesses. The push, said then-editor-in-chief Stephen J. Adler, was to help Reuters' customers "make better, fact-based decisions on critical issues in their professional and personal lives."[27] The direction of the coverage is aimed at white-collar workers and not the working class.

Recent union movements in many newsrooms might swing coverage away from the workplace and back toward worker issues. Unionization efforts have occurred in local newsrooms such as the *Arizona Republic*, the *Fort Worth Star-Telegram*, and the *New York Daily News*. In the business news sector, recent union drives have taken place at public radio show *Marketplace*, tech news site *The Markup*, and *Wired* and *Fortune* magazines.

Journalists who are union members are more likely to understand and cover the workplace issues affecting other union workers, believes Martin, who argues that news organizations need to include working-class people as part of their audience—that they are "one of us" instead of an anthropological curiosity to visit only occasionally. But they'll need to regain the trust of workers who believe that reporters and editors are adversarial.

INCOME INEQUALITY

Labor and worker coverage also ignores the impact of compensation on how people live and their ability (or inability) to improve their socioeconomic status. This lack of news content around the topic, according to Martin, has helped create the increasing division in the country, where income inequality has seen an uninterrupted increase since 1980.[28] Working-class people feel as if they no longer have a voice in society through the media because news about working-class compensation isn't addressed.

The growing income inequality means that the upper income is now the fastest-growing segment in America. American adults who live in a middle-income household has fallen from 61 percent of the population in 1971 to 51 percent in 2019, according to the Pew Research Center. Middle-income households are now 43 percent of the US economy, down from 62 percent in 1970. In comparison, upper-income households are now 48 percent of the economy, up from 29 percent in 1970. And lower-income households have remained stagnant at 9 percent.[29]

To better explain these numbers, here's what you need to know: the wealth gap in America is increasing. And income inequality in the United States is the highest of the largest economies in the world, according to the Organization for Economic Cooperation and Development.[30]

In early 2020, about six in ten Americans said that there is too much income inequality in the country, and most believe that to fix that problem, the country's economic system needs to undergo significant changes. More than half of lower-income Americans say that reducing income inequality should be a top priority of the federal government.[31] Many people believe that the solution to income inequality is the American economic system that promotes economic mobility, but studies have shown that there's more downward mobility than upward mobility among workers.[32]

The COVID-19 outbreak made the income inequality situation even worse, according to studies, with women, Blacks, and other minorities being affected more than white males as these groups were less likely to be able to work from home.[33] And many of those affected hadn't fully recovered from the 2008 recession.

There's another impact of income inequality. The United States ranks last among industrialized nations when it comes to worker benefits such as health care, paid leave, vacation, and unemployment, according to Zenefits, a human resources firm.[34] The lower someone's income, the less likely they are to have such benefits.

Media coverage of income inequality has only recently reentered the societal discussion, but a 2017 study found that the media's focus on company and stock market coverage means that "the voices of employer's groups and political parties are relatively overrepresented compared with employee interests and disadvantaged groups." The study concluded that news coverage neglected the positive impacts of improving inequality such as a growing economy.[35]

This is not the first time that the United States has faced an income inequality issue. The early 1900s, known as the Gilded Age, produced vast sums of wealth for the richest. As a result, taxes were raised and unions grew in membership to protect workers. And the media coverage of worker issues was prevalent throughout mainstream publications.

ECONOMIC IMPACT

Income inequality and the workers who earn less should be a bigger story for the mainstream media. Income inequality slows economic growth, according to the Economic Policy Institute, by an annual average of 2 to 4 percent points of gross domestic product.[36] In 1979 the bottom 90 percent of US households had 70 percent of total US income. By 2016 that share had fallen to 60 percent.

Consider the impact this way: if lower-income workers don't see their compensation keep pace with inflation, they have less to spend on goods and services. While businesses, particularly smaller operations, argue that increasing wages would cut into their operating expenses, economists and others argue that they'd get that money back with increased spending by consumers.

This is where business journalism has failed workers. A 2013 study from the Pew Research Center found that poverty accounted for less than 1 percent of coverage every year from 2007 to 2012 in fifty-two major newsrooms. Dan Froomkin explained in *Nieman Reports* that the reasons are clear: "Journalists are drawn more to people making things happen than those struggling to pay bills; poverty is not considered a beat; neither advertisers nor readers are likely to demand more coverage, so neither will editors."[37]

Covering the issue of income inequality also takes more time than regular stories for most media organizations, and already overworked reporters in the mainstream media don't have that time. And it should be noted that businesses likely don't want to talk about the topic to the media. Many may simply be struggling to pay their workers a decent wage, particularly during the coronavirus pandemic.

Noted journalist Barbara Ehrenreich is trying to improve the coverage. In 2012 she created the Economic Hardship Reporting Project, whose goal is to change the national conversation about poverty and economic insecurity. It commissions journalism that aims to put a face on financial stability. It's also aiming to get stories into media that don't normally cover poverty, such as the *Mountain Outlaw* in Big Sky, Montana, and the *Clarion-Ledger* in Jackson, Mississippi. Its work has won an Emmy and been nominated for a National Magazine Award. The project also uses writers and photographers who have experienced income inequality.

Denise-Marie Ordway and Heather Bryant wrote for the Shorenstein Center on Media, Politics and Public Policy that coverage of the topic should be prioritized and avoid exploiting or dehumanizing, and that terms such as "low income" should be defined so that the readers know what they mean. They also note that stories should help audiences understand that people living in poverty are multidimensional, as are their experiences.[38]

However, as Sarah Jones notes in the *Columbia Journalism Review*, the media still frequently stumble over the issue, failing to accurately reflect the issues that people face and often reinforcing stereotypes such as that lower-income workers don't have the motivation to find a better-paying job. She also notes that journalists who aren't from low-income backgrounds have a hard time understanding how a lower income affects consumers— and because getting internships and jobs in journalism often requires taking an unpaid internship or a low-paying job in the beginning, the field is one that few people from lower-income households consider for a career. "Simple ignorance is much more common," she wrote. "It's more that certain experiences, like poverty, are opaque to people who have not lived them."[39] She added that the topic of income inequality is often only covered during an election year or through special investigations, not as a regular topic.

Income inequality is pervasive and should not be a hard story for mainstream media organizations to report if they are willing to get out and talk to those with lower incomes. According to the Brookings Institution, the number of metropolitan neighborhoods in which at least 30 percent of residents live in poverty has doubled since 1980, and almost two-thirds of high-poverty neighborhoods in 1980 are today still very poor.[40]

PERSONAL FINANCE REPORTING

Personal finance reporting has undergone dramatic changes in the twenty-first century. There's been a proliferation of websites covering the topic, including NerdWallet, Bankrate, Penny Hoarder, Wirecutter, Acorns, and Investopedia just to name a few. Investopedia, for example, now has an editorial staff, and its content operation is now run by a longtime business journalist. It uses data on heavily searched topics on the website to determine what to cover. Many of these personal finance websites have relationships with credit card companies or other businesses.

There's also been tremendous upheaval and a decline in personal finance in mainstream media. Personal finance columnist Gail MarksJarvis left the *Chicago Tribune,* and the *New York Times* retired its "Haggler" column from the Sunday business section, both in 2017. Personal finance columnist Scott Burns of the *Dallas Morning News* retired. Personal finance guru Helaine Olen was laid off from *Slate* in 2017 and became a general columnist for the *Washington Post.* Personal finance columnist Brian O'Connor left the *Detroit News* at the end of 2016. Noted personal finance expert Suze Orman left CNBC in 2015, and the *Wall Street Journal Sunday,* which ran in dozens of newspapers across the country and was full of personal finance stories, closed in early 2015.

Outside of the larger media operations, few media have a personal finance reporter or columnist. Some of the best are Sharon Epperson on CNBC, Quentin Fottrell of MarketWatch, Susan Tompor of the *Detroit Free Press,* and Erin Arvedlund of the *Philadelphia Inquirer.* But they write about personal finance and topics such as life insurance and investing that is geared toward the middle class and the upper class. Personal finance has a much different meaning to those who can't afford to put money into a retirement plan such as a 401(k) or buy shares in a mutual fund. Kate Bahn, director of labor market policy and an economist at the Washington Center for Equitable Growth, argues there's not enough emphasis on the issues that make personal finance more difficult for many workers.[41] And then there's the voluminous coverage of the stock market as a personal finance story (see chapter 8), despite the fact that just 55 percent of Americans own stock.

Many daily newspapers once included a personal finance reporter or columnist who answered or addressed personal finance questions from readers, ranging from how to handle finances well to purchasing a second mortgage. Most of those positions have now been eliminated. (MarketWatch's Fottrell is perhaps the last journalist to answer such questions on a regular basis.) And personal finance magazine *Smart Money* halted print publication in 2012, and another personal finance magazine, *Money,* cut its annual print issues to ten from twelve in 2018 and is now just an online publication after being sold.

Personal finance coverage, even aimed at the middle class and upper class, has had a negative ramification on the lower class as well. Bloggers, podcasters, and "quasi-independent financial sites," as personal finance expert Charles Jaffe calls them, have proliferated. Because they're online and free, they're often the only available resource for a low-income worker looking for personal finance information. As Jaffe notes, the people putting out this personal finance content about services they have never tried are promoted in return for a kickback when a consumer clicks on the link. There's no separation, Jaffe wrote, between advertising and editorial content "for the person who started blogging about their efforts to beat back debt and who grew into a media influencer."[42]

Noted consumer advocate Ralph Nader noted in 2018 that the media coverage of "very important consumer struggles" has "vastly shrunken." And he wondered why newspapers that cut printed stock listings didn't use that space for more coverage about consumer topics. "Instead, the business pages are filled with constant technology hype, as with the inflated promotions and data-starved claims by the companies working on the eminently hackable self-driving cars," he wrote.[43]

In addition, consumers who do rely on business journalists for financial advice are doing so at their own peril. Most reporters who cover personal finance lack the certification to give professional financial advice about investing or even topics such as insurance, mortgages, bank accounts, and retirement planning.

Low-income workers and those at the poverty level have a harder time making the correct personal finance decisions, according to research from experts at Harvard University, Princeton University, the University of British Columbia, and Warwick University.[44] And they often don't receive the correct personal finance advice when they seek it out, opting for products such as payday loans that charge huge interest rates.[45] Such moves can lead to stress and less productivity in the workplace.

This is where the mainstream media could have the biggest positive impact on society. Coverage of personal finance topics for low-income workers can help build up an audience for media that have lost readers and viewers and provide a needed service. Like business news coverage of metrics such as the consumer confidence index, there are numbers that the media can use to report on the state of workers, such as the standard of living, the strength of wages, and the value of benefits and retirement accounts—and whether those benefits exist at all. The media could also regain these workers as consumers by writing stories about the topics and issues that they face at their job, such as the safety of their work.

10

HEALTH CARE COVERAGE IS SICK

Business journalist Andy Miller covered health care for the *Atlanta Journal-Constitution* from 1992 until 2009, when he took the newspaper's third buyout offer when it began cutting costs and expenses. During his time in the newsroom he won numerous awards for his stories on hospitals and health insurers.

Miller freelanced for a while for publications such as WebMD, AOL's WalletPop, and *AARP Bulletin* before starting the nonprofit news organization Georgia Health News in 2010. It covers everything from prescription drugs to physicians, health costs and hospitals to health insurance—many of the same topics he reported about for the daily newspaper. He works a fifty-hour week, along with a copy editor and freelance reporters, covering health care news from around the state. "This is news that people need to have," said Miller. "We have done more health care coverage than anybody in the state over our ten years. Insurance company profits and CEO pay is totally ignored. Hospital profits are pretty much ignored, but not totally."[1]

One story that Miller wrote focused on two $26 and $35 copay bills he received from health insurance companies. Although Miller had paid one of them, the health insurance company threatened to send his account to a collection agency. "They didn't know me as a health care reporter," he said. "But I think Americans get these notices and wonder what the hell is going on. This is a kitchen table issue for most American families. We don't do enough coverage on this."[2]

The economics of health care is one of the most important topics that most mainstream media organizations have dropped or decreased in the twenty-first century, which limits valuable news and information for businesses and consumers and causes a further "dissemination divide."

In 2000 health care spending in the United States was $1.4 trillion. In 2019 US health care spending grew 4.6 percent, reaching $3.8 trillion, or $11,582 per person, so it's tripled in the first two decades of the twenty-first century. That's nearly 18 percent of the US gross domestic product, making it the largest segment of the economy.[3] Consumers spent $406.5 billion in out-of-pocket spending on health care, while private health insurance spent $1.2 trillion.[4]

In addition, health care spending is projected to grow at an average annual rate of 5.4 percent through 2028, a rate faster than the overall economy, and to reach $6.2 trillion, becoming 20 percent of the country's economic spending.[5] Prices of medical goods and services are expected to increase an average of 2.4 percent annually during the same time.[6] Studies also show that health care spending in the United States on a per capita basis is far more than other countries.[7]

Health care—from hospitals to pharmaceutical manufacturers—is a dominant and growing part of the economy. Yet coverage of these businesses, often the largest employer in a city, is lacking because of a drop in business-related health care coverage, and the stories that are written often focus on treatments and diseases and not the increasing cost of such care. And then there's who's paying for the health care—consumers and insurance companies—and the price increases that are regulated on a state-by-state basis. Few if any consumer media organizations are covering the cost of health care and how it impacts people and business owners on a regular and sustained basis, say health care experts.

"I see none of that reporting anymore," said health care coverage expert Wendell Potter, a former CIGNA public relations executive. "It's just gone by the wayside. We're completely uninformed about how businesses operate in the marketplace in terms of hospitals, health care facilities, and insurance companies."[8]

Potter cited the *Hartford Courant*, the country's oldest daily newspaper, as an example. In the 1990s it aggressively covered health care economics, particularly health insurance, with many stories from reporter Diane Levick. Her coverage led to changes in what health insurers covered. She left the paper in 2009 and has not been replaced.[9]

In 1992 former *Wall Street Journal* journalist Alan L. Otten wrote that medical advances and rising medical costs caused newspapers, as well as radio and television stations, to cover such stories, and universities offered programs to expand journalists' understanding of health care topics.[10] The economic realities of the media in the twenty-first century changed all of that. Look at any mainstream media organization's content today, and you'll be hard-pressed to find a local story about health care and its costs. A 2019 study of health care coverage at television stations found that industry consolidation has led to "more uniform content across geographic areas and duplicate rather than locally targeted content," including a paucity of coverage around health care disparities.[11]

To be sure, there are a handful of sites similar to Georgia Health News—which merged into Kaiser Health News in 2021—around the country. Health News Florida is a collaboration between WUSF Public Media in Tampa and public radio stations WLRN in Miami and WMFE in Orlando. California Healthline is a free news service of the California Health Care Foundation. And there are also websites and newsletters that cover specific health care business news, such as Industry Dive's Health Care Dive and FierceBiotech. The latter covers health care news primarily from an industry perspective. And there are many states where there's no health care-focused news service, leaving consumers and business owners with nowhere to find information about health care costs or developments.

Among mainstream media organizations, the *Milwaukee Journal Sentinel* is one of the few remaining newsrooms that focuses on important health care stories. In May 2021, for example, it won a National Headliner Award for stories that focus on hospital workers. It also has been recognized for its coverage that uncovered conflicts of interest that can compromise a doctor's judgment.

The nonprofit Physicians for a National Health Program believes that the lack of "vigilant and critical media" in covering health care costs is due to increased corporate ownership of the media, which are unwilling to fund reporting around the topic for fear of upsetting key advertisers such as health insurers.[12]

The decline in coverage also comes at a time when consumers have said that the cost of health care is an important issue for them. A January 2020 survey by the Pew Research Center found that two-thirds of the respondents wanted President Donald Trump to focus on health care costs.[13] Only terrorism and the economy ranked higher. Four years earlier, in 2016, 74 percent of people surveyed by Pew said that health care was important to their vote for the next president.[14]

There are some exceptions, such as George Health News; Kaiser Health News covers the business of health care across most of the nation. *STAT*, which is run by the *Boston Globe*, is an online news site that reports about health care issues and focuses on pharmaceutical companies and the cost of drugs and treatments. Some of the American City Business Journals newspapers have health care reporters. But there's no consistent or nuanced local coverage of the business and economics of health care for the average business owner and consumer.

FOCUS ON TREATMENT

Health care coverage at the local level is primarily focused on treatments and not the cost, which tells only part of the story. It's a huge debate in the United States—should consumers receive care, no matter the cost, or should the cost to provide that care factor into the decision?

To be sure, consumers receiving treatment for health care is vitally important. The COVID-19 pandemic and the vaccines that began to be distributed in 2021 to treat the illness were rightfully major stories that have been extensively covered in all media. But the stories, for the most part, also ignore major questions such as who is paying for the vaccine and whether that cost is being passed on to employers and consumers. Gary Schwitzer, the founder and publisher of HealthNewsReview, found that Pfizer's announcement in November 2020 about the development of its COVID-19 vaccine was covered without much scrutiny of the details of the data but did result in a jump in the company's stock price.[15]

Schwitzer, whose website grades health care news stories, found that only 20 percent of news stories adequately covered costs, and 63 percent of the stories relied on a news release, trusting the company's statements.[16] Health care journalist Maggie Mhar argues that journalists aren't more skeptical when writing about health care costs because many Americans want to believe that every new drug and health care procedure "must be the product of sound scientific evidence," and journalists ignore the waste in the medical system that often drives up cost.[17]

Part of the media focus on treatments is due to the health condition of many consumers. According to Living Facts, an initiative of the Pew Charitable Trusts, 60 percent of US adults have at least one chronic disease, ranging from cancer to diabetes.[18] So it's only natural for people to want news and information about health care treatments.

The increasing use of health care treatments, however, is not without an increase in cost. Health care spending totaled $74.1 billion in 1970 and doubled in the next thirty years to $1.4 trillion. On a per capita basis, such spending has increased over thirty-one-fold from $353 in 1970 to $11,582 in 2019.[19] Although health care spending has slowed and is now growing at near the pace of economic growth, it's still a large expenditure for many consumers and for the businesses that are often paying for the care. Medical care prices rose 1.8 percent in 2020, a smaller increase than the 4.6 percent advance in 2019. Prescription drug prices fell 2.4 percent in 2020 after rising 3.0 percent in 2019. Prices for hospital services rose 3.0 percent from 2019 to 2020, the same increase as the prior year, while prices for physicians' services increased 1.7 percent.[20] And a Brookings Institution study found that flaws in the health care system result in unnecessary care and higher prices.[21]

The rising cost is leading to another issue: nearly one-fourth of Americans say that they have skipped medical care because of the cost, according to a Bankrate survey.[22] And nearly a third of Americans failed to take their medications because of the cost.[23] It's easy to conclude that when consumers aren't focused on their health because of the cost, the situation is going to eventually lead to higher health care expenses because eventually they're going to have a major health care incident that will require immediate, and often expensive, care.

Some national media are covering this topic in a way that local business media could easily duplicate. Kaiser Health News and National Public Radio began a crowdsourced investigation called "Bill of the Month" where consumers share their medical bills and a journalist then explains the costs, with the goal of helping patients learn how to be more active in managing costs. Among the recent stories: a $207,455 bill for neonatal intensive care of a newborn, a $12,387 lab fee for sexually transmitted infections, and an $80,232 bill for an appendectomy.[24] These are not hard stories to uncover and report as long as the consumers are willing to share their bills. (In the early 1990s I wrote similar stories for the now-defunct *Tampa Tribune* when consumers began suing hospitals for high bills.)

Yet when you search for stories about health care expenses, they're primarily being covered by national media, ranging from nonprofit ProPublica to BuzzFeed News, and not the local media that many consumers rely on for news and information.[25]

POLITICS ARE INVOLVED

As noted in chapter 7, business and economics news has become overwhelmed by politics, and health care–related business news is no exception. The economics of health care—who will pay for the care and how much—has become a major political story in this country as costs have risen.

In the United States, consumers receive health insurance either through their employer, through a government-funded program such as Medicaid and Medicare, or through the Affordable Care Act. The split is even, with the private sector funding about half of all health care and the government paying the other half. And health insurance is regulated on a state-by-state basis, meaning there is no uniform health insurance across the country. Still, about 8 percent of the population, or 26.1 million consumers, do not have health insurance coverage, according to the US Census Bureau.[26]

This mixture of US health care coverage contrasts with many other countries, where the government provides a minimum amount of health care to anyone regardless of where they work or their economic status. Although presidents as far back as Theodore Roosevelt have tried to enact a universal health care system in the country, the health care industry—from doctors to hospitals and pharmaceutical companies—has vigorously lobbied against such a plan, arguing that they would lose revenue. (A 2017 study by the National Bureau of Economic Research showed that politicians who supported the health care legislation that benefited the industry received large increases in campaign contributions.[27]) Although President Barack Obama's Affordable Care Act, which expanded insurance coverage, was passed in 2010, it has faced attacks by Republican politicians who want to repeal it for a free-market system with less government involvement.[28] The Association of Health Care Journalists described the situation this way: "The U.S. system is a bizarre blend of undertreatment and overtreatment, a mélange of 'the best care in the world' and a system rife with quality control, infection, complications and error rates that would not be countenanced in other settings."[29]

It is interesting to note that most Americans—63 percent in 2020, up from 59 percent in 2019—continue to say that the federal government has a responsibility to make sure all consumers have health care coverage, according to the Pew Research Center.[30] And more than a third believe there should be a single national government system for health insurance. The Democrats, who have been pushing for more health care coverage, are divided on how such a plan should be implemented; 44 percent say that the government does not have that responsibility.[31]

What does all of this mean for businesses and consumers? Yale University researchers found that politics, particularly in the form of health care industry lobbying, increases health care costs in that it leads to treating more patients, hiring more staff, investing in new technology, and raising chief executive officer pay at hospitals. Their study concludes that politics raised hospital spending by more than $1 billion from 2005 to 2010.[32] But that's not a story that the mainstream media are focusing on in their business coverage.

HEALTH CARE PROFITS DOWNPLAYED

Most health care companies, from hospitals to health insurers to pharmaceutical companies, operate on a for-profit basis, meaning they're trying to make as much money as possible. The largest hospital companies reported large increases in profit in the first six months of 2020.[33] The Kaiser Family Foundation found higher profits for health insurers for the first nine months of 2020.[34] Pharmaceutical companies are typically more profitable than most companies in the Standard & Poor's 500 index.[35]

And there's nothing wrong with that. But the financial performance among health care companies, when it is reported by the media, is aimed at investors and not the business owners and consumers who are purchasing coverage or care.

Why is this important? If the customers of health care don't have the information that they need to make an informed decision about where to purchase care or coverage from, then they're making an uninformed decision that could be costing them money.

The business news coverage is particularly lacking with the financial performance of health insurance companies. They're regulated by state insurance departments, and that means they're reporting revenue and profits or losses for that specific state on a quarterly and annual basis. Those financial results can be important stories as they can tell whether the insurer is performing well in that market or whether it might need to raise its rates if it's paying more in claims than anticipated.

QuoteWizard, an online insurance marketplace, found that health insurance companies such as UnitedHealth Group, Humana, and Anthem reported profits during the second three months of 2020—during the COVID pandemic—that doubled from the previous year. UnitedHealth's net income rose to $6.7 billion from $3.4 billion. Despite these profits, the average cost of an employer health insurance plan continued to rise.[36] While health insurers are supposed to spend at least eighty cents of every dollar they collect in premiums on health care, some were spending only seventy cents per dollar.[37]

"I used to handle financial communications for CIGNA," said Wendell Potter. "Early on, the *New York Times* would frequently write stories based on their earnings reports. I haven't seen anything like that in a long time. And when they do, it's for a specific investor audience. So there's very little information about how these companies do business that affect regular folks."[38]

Hospitals and other health care providers, meanwhile, reported a decline in revenue and profits in 2020 because consumers were less willing to venture out during the pandemic for care, particularly if the treatment could be delayed. And hospitals stopped elective surgeries, which often lead to higher profits, to focus on COVID treatment. But the pandemic provided a financial boon to diagnostic companies such as Laboratory Corporation of America and Quest Diagnostics, which handled millions of COVID-19 tests. Quest, for example, saw its 2020 revenue to rise by nearly 50 percent as a result of testing.

Hospitals are required to file financial information with the government if they treat Medicaid and Medicare patients, and they must also file that information with state agencies. In California, for example, the agency is Office of Statewide Health Planning and Development. Even nonprofit hospitals are required to disclose their financial performance with the Internal Revenue Service. Reporters can obtain these financial statements and write stories that would be of interest to the businesses and consumers paying for treatments in the hospitals.

The situation is similar with health insurance companies, including health maintenance organizations and preferred provider organizations, which must file regular financial reports with the insurance departments in each state where they operate. This also includes nonprofit health insurance operations. These reports are valuable particularly for local businesses and consumers because if they're paying for coverage from a large public health insurance company, that business doesn't break down its financial performance by state in its Securities and Exchange Commission filings. It's these state regulators who also receive, review, and either approve or deny requests to raise or lower the rates that businesses and consumers pay. "Insurance departments conduct audits on a regular basis and also perform market conduct audits," said Potter. "I see none of that reporting any more. It's just gone by the wayside. We're completely uninformed about how businesses operate in the marketplace."

OTHER UNDERPLAYED STORIES

Here's another health care business story downplayed by the mainstream business media: When a hospital wants to expand by offering a new service or enlarging its facilities, it usually is required to file a request with a state government agency to receive approval. This "certificate of need" process is required in thirty-five states, primarily east of the Mississippi River. The hospital must prove there is a need for the new service, such as a neonatal intensive care unit or a cancer therapy. Other hospitals around the one that has filed to expand can respond to the request, arguing whether the new service would harm their business.

The primary purpose of certificate of need is to ensure that health care services are not being duplicated, thus keeping costs down. But critics of the process argue that the system eliminates competition because it allows hospitals that already have the service to maintain a monopoly, restricting competition and keeping prices high.

So such requests are business news and are information that businesses and consumers would want to know about, particularly if they used the hospital or a rival hospital. They'd want to know, for example, whether the cost of the expansion was going to be passed on to them in the form of higher health care costs.

But it's hard to find such stories in the local media. Here's an example: In early 2021 the Piedmont Athens Regional Medical Center in Athens, Georgia, where the University of Georgia is located, requested with the state to add sixty-eight inpatient beds at an estimated cost of $38 million. The only place where this proposed expansion was covered was in the *Atlanta Business Chronicle*.[39] The local paper, the *Athens Banner-Herald*, had not covered the story, nor had any of the local television or radio stations. And the *Atlanta Business Chronicle* covered only the initial filing, not whether Piedmont Athens' competitors, such as Athens Regional Medical Center or St. Mary's Health Care System, had objected to the request.

There's also a big health care business story at every state medical board, which licenses health care practitioners such as doctors and nurses. These boards can revoke or suspend the license of a doctor for performing an unnecessary surgery or prescribing the wrong drugs or, even worse, not treating an illness or sexually abusing a patient. While these stories do get covered on a regular basis, the news rarely goes into the financial impact for the consumers or businesses who now must find a new provider, sometimes at a higher cost.

A hospital is most likely the largest employer in a town or city, but rarely is it covered as a business by the local media. There are about 6.6 million hospital employees across the United States.[40] If a hospital is laying off or hiring workers, that's information that other businesses in the area will want to know. A loosening or tightening labor market may mean they'll have to adjust what they pay their own workers. Other stories, such as nursing shortages in many markets and drug store chains paying higher-than-normal salaries to recruit pharmacists to work in rural areas, are equally important.

The nuances of health insurance are often ignored as well. If the reimbursement of a procedure is being lowered by Medicare, Medicaid, or a private health insurance plan, what does that mean for the hospitals, doctors, and nurses? Will they now charge their patients more for other procedures to recoup the lost revenue?

It's these types of stories that aren't covered in the local media but have a huge impact on companies and citizens. Some of these stories may have been covered by daily newspapers before they began shrinking, but now there are not enough reporters and editors in the newsroom.

HOW BUSINESS IS AFFECTED

After Potter left CIGNA, he started an organization called Business Leaders for Health Care Transformation, a coalition of company executives, entrepreneurs, sole proprietors, and citizens from every state who believe the employer-based health insurance system is broken and hurts their competitiveness because it suppresses wages and creates a stagnant workforce.

Potter said there's not "any real reporting on how employer-based health coverage has changed, how it's skewed toward those who are well-to-do at the expense of those who are not. There's very little scrutiny for half the population."[41]

Rising health care costs make it more difficult for businesses, especially smaller companies, to pay for health insurance for their workers. Employers pay an average of $13,717 to provide health insurance for the family of a typical worker, according to the US Bureau of Labor Statistics, and pay more for workers with higher salaries.[42] A Harvard Business School study in late 2020 found that many consumers were struggling to pay premiums but did so before they paid rent. And just 5 percent said that they received premium cuts or refunds from health insurers.[43]

Many employees at small businesses have such high out-of-pocket expenses and deductibles in relation to their income that they're effectively underinsured, found the Commonwealth Fund.[44] (The average civilian worker in the United States paid $6,797 for premiums annually for their family in 2020, according to the US Bureau of Labor Statistics, up from $4,524 a decade earlier.[45]) The fund also found that as many as 7.7 million Americans could lose their employer-sponsored health insurance because of job losses.[46] Potter said this research rarely reaches consumers and small businesses so they can better understand how they're being affected.

Larger businesses are more likely than smaller companies to provide health care coverage, according to the Bureau of Labor Statistics.[47] As mentioned in chapter 6, business news coverage is already slanted toward larger corporations because of their growing size and influence in the economy. That means that when the media do cover the issue of health insurance from an employer perspective, it's more likely to focus on the issues surrounding big business.

The media, whether print, television, radio, or internet, shape what consumers and business owners think about health issues.[48] But with a decline in reporters and editors in the media focused on the business and economics of health care, the remaining coverage is clustered among higher-tier publications such as the *Wall Street Journal* or special health care sites such as *STAT* or Kaiser Health News that do a strong job but aren't typically read by business owners or consumers. Kaiser Health News, for example, says its coverage is for, in order, "policymakers, the media, the health policy community, and the public."[49] Note that the public is listed last, and business owners aren't mentioned at all. *STAT* does list "business

leaders" as part of its audience, as well as lab scientists, health professionals, and policymakers.[50]

What we need are more Andy Millers devoted to covering the business
and economics of health care in a way that helps business owners and their
employees.

Part III

SOLUTIONS TO THE PROBLEM

The last part of *The Future of Business Journalism* makes recommendations on how to improve business news so it provides useful and helpful content to everyone, from Wall Street to Main Street.

Some of the suggestions are for how business news organizations operate. For example, they can use software and other technology to provide news and information about topics such as unemployment, inflation, and real estate developments that many smaller businesses and consumers want from the media, allowing their reporters and editors to focus on bigger stories that take more time to research. Some news companies are already doing this, but many are not.

In terms of coverage, there are plenty of business stories that are important to many businesses, employees, and consumers that are simply ignored or rarely covered. News organizations need to refocus on these stories, such as local bankruptcy courts and zoning and planning decisions. The coverage for many local and regional news organizations should focus on what's important to consumers and smaller businesses, not Fortune 500 companies.

News organizations also need to look at the markets that they're serving and shift how and what business news gets covered. News about minority-owned businesses and female-owned businesses is scant even though these companies are valuable to local economies. The reason these stories often don't get covered is that business news staffs are primarily white and male. Hiring practices must change to provide different perspectives in the newsroom.

Business journalism training is also a huge issue, and *The Future of Business Journalism* makes two recommendations in this area. First, communications programs at universities and colleges must look at business journalism as an opportunity. There are plenty of jobs in the field for these students, but many college journalism majors graduate with little or no knowledge of how to write about business and the economy. College students need to be encouraged to consider the field, and they need to be encouraged to take classes in business journalism as well as business and economics classes. Media organizations can also help provide funding for such programs and beef up their training in this area.

The business model for business journalism must also change. Early indications are that e-mail newsletters are effective in helping spread business news and information. Other news organizations have found ways to generate revenue that have helped fund quality business news. These practices should be followed by others.

Making sure that business journalism serves businesses, consumers, and employees is not going to happen overnight. But the first step is to recognize the problem and look at ways to fix the problem. This is by no means a complete list of solutions, but it's a start, and businesses, consumers, and employees deserve coverage that helps them make more informed decisions. We can correct the financial illiteracy they struggle with.

11

USING TECHNOLOGY TO IMPROVE COVERAGE

The last few chapters have proposed ways to improve business journalism regarding specific coverage. Let's now look at some bigger and broader systemic changes that would improve the field.

Technology in journalism has dramatically changed how content is reported, written, and disseminated to its various audiences. The invention of the printing press led to the creation of newspapers, the first form of mass media. The telegraph in the nineteenth century helped deliver in an instant news that previously took weeks. More than one hundred years ago, stories were primarily written on typewriters and copyedited using pencils. Then the paper that those stories were produced on was sent to a typesetter, who then placed the text into metal type letter by letter, creating a block of text that was inked onto a page by a printing machine.

Now, stories are produced on laptops and desktop computers, and editors use those same computers—as well as software to check grammatical and style errors—to revise what a reporter has written. The stories are then uploaded into software used to lay out a newspaper page that is transmitted electronically to a faraway printing press or downloaded immediately onto a website for reading.

Reporters who previously needed to go to courthouses, police stations, and government agencies to obtain public records and interview officials can now receive those documents using the internet and can also communicate with interview subjects by e-mail, instant messaging, and other methods.

Technology's effect—both positive and negative—has been particularly dramatic in business journalism. As recently as thirty years ago, business reporters would send letters and checks to a Washington, DC, service, which would then find the Securities and Exchange Commission

documents that the journalist was seeking and mail them back to the reporter. The process would often take weeks, delaying the dissemination
of important information to employees, consumers, investors, and others
interested in the material. Today reporters can download those documents
from the Securities and Exchange Commission website, or from company
websites, immediately after companies file them with the government
agency. Business journalists can also obtain similar records about companies and industries from other state and government agencies by accessing
online databases.

Reporters can also now use websites to quickly determine who are the
largest investors in a public company. They can listen to a company's earnings conference call and watch the stock price react to what its executives
are telling analysts and investors. They can find sources using social media
such as LinkedIn and Twitter. They can use Excel spreadsheets to analyze a
company's historical performance. They can interview sources around the
world using Skype and texting applications. These are positive changes.

Then there's the negative impact. The increasing use of the internet by
consumers to find stock prices has led to the demise of the daily business
section in metropolitan newspapers, which has resulted in cuts in staff
and in the news hole for business news coverage. The declining attention
to business and economics news and information in many mainstream
media has also forced businesses and consumers to seek information
from nonmedia sources, which are not always reliable or may come with
a slanted opinion.

David Skerrett notes that technology has led to "a time of peak media"
where consumers can no longer spend enough time digesting all the news
and information that is being provided and can't spend the time to understand whether the news and information is accurate.[1]

Technological advances are extremely important to business journalism as reporters and editors increasingly face more complicated issues and
topics. The technology improvements are all in a bid to keep up with how
the companies they cover use technology, making their operations more
complicated. Many business news organizations are using some form of
technology to help them find and write important stories in minutes or
hours that previously would have taken weeks to uncover—or that they
would never have found at all without the software. But some of those basic
stories lack the nuance and analysis that many readers require.

Michael Casey, a former *Wall Street Journal* columnist and now the chief content officer at *CoinDesk*, wrote about how business journalism needs to use technology more than before to help it decipher complex business issues. Without this ability, additional financial crises such as the one that gripped most of the world in 2007 and 2008 might occur again. Casey writes:

> In this era of "big data," where high-tech analytical techniques can produce abundant, quantifiable information, we should all have been empowered to uncover the truth. But in reality, for the average investor, journalist, or even regulator, this new trove of data has been mostly out of reach and unintelligible.
>
> It should now be the duty of journalists to unlock it. And to do so, they need to harness the same tools that financial institutions and corporations use to sift, interpret and make sense of mass digital information. The value of human sources providing information on market players' activities hasn't gone away—think of the lasting impact of *The Wall Street Journal's* "London Whale" scoop on JPMorgan Chase's risky trading bets last year, a story that led to news that the bank had racked up $6 billion in losses and, later, $1 billion in regulatory fines. But those stories must now be complemented with computer-enhanced analysis and interpretation. To get at the truth will require crunching the numbers—billions of them.[2]

The need for additional technological applications in business journalism also comes at a time when the primary subjects of business news—companies, executives, and economies—increasingly use artificial intelligence to improve their operations and develop new products. As an example, Wall Street investment firms are using technology to make trades for clients immediately after important data such as the unemployment rate or the trade deficit is released. Since the beginning of 2015 business news organizations such as the Wall Street Journal, the New York Times business news desk, and tech news sites *Recode* and *The Information* have posted job openings seeking reporters to cover artificial intelligence and the future of technology. In May 2018 the *New York Times* began a series called "Fast Forward" examining how emerging technologies are shaping the future of business.

Indeed, one of the major ways that local news media can improve business news coverage is by using artificial intelligence, computer programs, and other technology. Investing and using technology can provide business owners and consumers with the information that they need and want.

Let's look at how four media organizations—two large entities known worldwide and two that have started in the past decade—use technological inventions. These media companies use technology to provide business news content in ways that helps consumers, investors, and other recipients better understand what's going on in economies and businesses. These are strategies that any media organization could easily emulate.

REUTERS

Global financial news wire Reuters first began producing stories written by a computer as far back as 2001, when it published computer-generated headlines from the American Petroleum Institute's weekly report on oil production. It is now producing an estimated eight thousand automated news items a day in multiple languages.

Executive editor Gina Chua was previously in charge of finding ways for Reuters to use computers and artificial intelligence to help it deliver news and information to its clients faster and with more depth. Her focus was on increasing the speed at which Reuters can tell stories and helping journalists tell stories that have deeper insights than what they would have been able to do by themselves. She said, "I think the big value will be in the marriage of humans and computers. Humans are good at some things and terrible at others. And computers are good at some things and terrible at others. We should marry the two of them. There are times when humans aren't fast enough, and that's when you want a machine. And there are times when a machine is not smart enough, and you will want a human."[3]

Reuters uses artificial information software to sift through press releases and financial disclosures to find what is important. That information is then presented to reporters in a template. Reuters also uses a tool called Reuters News Tracer that helps identify what Chua calls "clusters of newsworthy events" on Twitter. News Tracer ignores spam and non-newsworthy information and uses a language analysis to identify when multiple tweets mention the same event, such as a bomb exploding in Europe that might affect financial markets. Internal research showed that between 10 percent and 20 percent of news breaks first on Twitter.

Reuters developed a tool called Lynx Insight that takes financial data, runs it through a template, and generates simple sentences such as "The Dow Jones industrial average closed up 2 percent from yesterday." Lynx Insight then looks for trends and milestones around the data—such as the market has risen six days in a row, and it's the first time that has happened since January 2019—and presents that information to a reporter working on a markets story. The idea, said Chua, is to give reporters tips and ideas from analysis, data, and patterns that they typically don't have time to look at on a regular basis.

The company is also developing a once-a-day alert to Reuters reporters and editors who oversee company coverage to give them some ideas of what to focus stories on for that day. For example, if the price of beef is rising, then the reporter and editor involved in coverage of McDonald's may pay more attention to how its stock price reacts. Or Lynx Insight can analyze insider trading filings of a specific reporter and alert its beat reporter when insiders sell more than 10 percent of the stock during a certain time.

Chua also sees the potential for Reuters to be able to personalize stock markets stories for individual readers, where the first three paragraphs give a broad overview of how indexes performed during a day and the rest of the story is a personalized report based on stocks a reader has told Reuters it wants to know about on a regular basis. "Data analytics and language generation and, in effect, news on demand allows a whole new set of things to be done," said Chua. "We obviously can and do create tens of thousands of stories that are different in slight ways."[4]

There are other possibilities, said Chua. Reuters can use its technology when someone is nominated for the US Supreme Court, reviewing thousands of key cases and rulings the nominee was involved with using the Westlaw database. "That's a story that could only be done because AI tools exist," she said.[5] In 2016 Reuters partnered with semantic technology company Graphiq to produce data visualizations for its clients on everything from Apple's stock price to President Trump's approval rating.

Chua believes that these technologies mean that business journalism "is on the cusp of reimagining the kind of things it can do. There is potentially a brand-new age of machine-assisted, cybernetic-assisted reporting."[6]

Reuters has many more resources than other media outlets covering business news and therefore is able to do more with technology to help its business news coverage. But what if it started licensing some of this tech-nology to smaller news organizations that it doesn't compete with? That could help improve coverage.

ASSOCIATED PRESS

The Associated Press began working with Automated Insights in 2013 to develop a system where the North Carolina–based company's software would take data from Zack's Investment Research and the AP to produce thousands of quarterly earnings stories. That system rolled out in 2014. The AP went from producing 300 earnings stories each quarter to publish-ing more than 3,500 each quarter, also covering many smaller companies that are of interest to local economies. AP members are getting more earn-ings stories about companies in their markets.

Automated Insights' software is called Wordsmith, and it draws data from the AP on a company's formal name, its headquarters, and its main business. It then compares the earnings that a company releases to the an-alyst projections from Zack's. The computer-generated stories also include how much the company's stock price has changed since the beginning of the year and how that compares to the overall market.

Most of the AP earnings stories generated by Automated Insights go out on its wire without any changes from a reporter or editor. However, the AP has identified approximately 100 "top-tier" companies where reporters will still write their own story or incorporate the Automated Insights earn-ings story into a larger story about the company's strategy or performance. With another 250–300 companies, an AP reporter or editor will add con-text to the computer-generated stories. The AP stories without any human interaction include a tag line at the end notifying readers that the content was produced by Automated Insights.

The AP and Automated Insights believe that using the software to write basic earnings stories allows the wire service's reporters to focus on more important stories that require analysis, interviews, and understand-ing of complex topics. Philana Patterson, who was AP's assistant business editor at the time the system was introduced, estimated that it freed up about 20 percent of a reporter's time to work on other stories.

These stories have had another impact: researchers from Stanford University and the University of Washington have discovered that these stories increase a company's trading volume and liquidity. They wrote, "This study found a positive effect between the public dissemination of objective information and market efficiency, a major discovery for the implications of automated journalism on capital markets."[7]

However, there have been mistakes and omissions that the Automated Insights software misses when it produces its earnings stories. Business journalist Max Frumes writes that the story produced by the software about Under Armour's third-quarter 2017 earnings missed the fact that the company would restructure, costing it an estimated $110 million to $130 million, which caused its stock price to fall 10 percent. The AP / Automated Insights story reported simply that Under Armour's earnings exceeded Wall Street expectations.[8] In 2015 an AP / Automated Insights earnings story on Netflix missed that the company's stock had undergone a seven-for-one split. As a result, the story reported that the earnings fell 71 percent and missed analyst expectations. Other potential mistakes in these stories can occur when earnings include mergers and acquisitions or figures that do not follow generally accepted accounting principles, writes Ben Ashwell.[9]

The quality of the writing produced by the Automated Insights software has also been questioned. Allen Wastler, former managing editor of the CNBC website, wrote that the "copy is straightforward and on a par with most quick-turn human work." He also noted, "Earnings stories are boring to write. And they have to be done quickly, so there's no time to have fun or inject any art into them."[10] Joe Pinsker of the *Atlantic* argues that business news organizations should hand over earnings stories to computers because the earnings report "is already robotically formulaic."[11]

In 2015 National Public Radio reporter Scott Horsley went up against the Automated Insights software in writing earnings for restaurant chain Denny's. The Wordsmith software wrote its story in two minutes while Horsley took seven minutes. The AP / Automated Insights story's verbs were more mundane, using terms such as "reported" and "surveyed." Horsley's story noted in the first paragraph that the company "notched a grand slam of its own in the first quarter," referring to its popular breakfast menu.[12]

The opportunities for computer-generated stories, however, are endless. For example, American City Business Journals, which operates in forty-four markets in the United States, now uses Automated Insights to write stories about bankruptcy court filings. Similar computer-generated stories could be produced around data such as unemployment, housing transactions, consumer sentiment, and trade.

The AP collaboration with Automated Insights shows that a computer program could start generating the kinds of stories many business owners want from the local media. And that would allow overworked business reporters and editors to focus on more in-depth and important content. News organizations need to simply start spending the money to make this possible.

QUARTZ

Quartz is a financial news site started by the *Atlantic* magazine in 2013, first focusing on smartphones as its preferred delivery method although it also has a website. In 2020 it was sold to CEO Zach Seward and *Quartz* management.

In 2015 *Quartz* received a $240,000 grant from the John S. and James L. Knight Foundation to launch the Quartz Bot Studio to experiment with artificial intelligence and bots in providing news and information. Emily Withrow, a former professor at Northwestern University, was hired as editor of the studio, and she oversaw how it designs and builds conversational news experiences. For example, Quartz launched a bot on Facebook Messenger that asks users questions about experiences. Based on the user's answers, the bot then replies with answers in a "guided storytelling" format. Artificial intelligence is used to determine the responses, said Withrow. "What we found was that the [user] retention was outstanding," said Withrow.[13]

Tim Peterson reports that Quartz is continuing with its chatbot while other media organizations have discontinued similar operations. The studio makes chatbots for advertisers, and that income allows it to continue to experiment with delivery systems. Quartz Bot Studio worked with investigative journalism organization ProPublica on a messenger bot for the 2018 election.[14]

The studio's staff has also spent time in the Quartz newsroom, talking to reporters and editors to understand their needs. For example, the studio has automated software to scan a URL for a set of clichés or to take a screenshot of a website at any time and send notifications to a Quartz journalist when the website is changed or updated.

The studio has also added to the newsroom's functionality on Slack, a messaging system common in media organizations. After the studio heard that Quartz's data editor was receiving questions from reporters on where to find data for stories, it built an add-on that immediately responds to reporter queries with links to data from reputable websites such as government agencies. "We can do that with the bot," said Withrow. "A lot of it is making the reporting easier. We are really looking at tools to help our normal workflow, to free people up to spend time doing other things."[15]

Quartz has also used its technology in other ways. For example, it created a bot to answer common questions at one of its conferences, such as information on speakers and sessions and the Wi-Fi login. It also developed a way to send out its "Daily Brief" e-mail on Amazon Echo. Quartz is open sourcing the code for these technologies, sharing what has worked and what hasn't with other media organizations.

Quartz is much smaller than Reuters and the Associated Press. Yet it has made technological experimentation a priority in examining ways that it can improve its business news coverage, showing that such a strategy can be helpful to coverage if a media company is willing to commit the resources and time.

QUANT MEDIA

Max Frumes, a founding editor at Reorg Research, left the news organization in early 2017 after helping it build a business focused on selling news around distressed debt investing and corporate restructuring. Reorg used data and information from the federal court system to uncover news—with the help of financial analysts and lawyers—that was valuable to a niche audience of investors.

Several months after leaving Reorg, Frumes was introduced to a former executive at Credit Suisse Group who had a background in quantitative modeling for one of its investment groups. The executive had developed technology that looked for accounting irregularities and insolvency risks in company financial filings and then plugged that information into trading systems. Frumes pitched this executive on combining this technology with editorial content to create Quant Media, which launched in February 2018.

Frumes declined to disclose how the company's technology worked, but he explained it in general terms. He said algorithms place a value on certain information in a company's financial statements and conduct a series of tests, such as the amount of cash flow to operating income or whether a company's debt has increased to a level where the company can't pay the interest. He noted that sometimes with Quant Media's technology, one of its journalists would look into a company that the artificial intelligence has flagged and would find something the technology didn't uncover.[16]

The company began producing five to ten stories of various lengths and complexity per week for hedge fund and financial services clients. "The more work that you can get out of the way with a computer, reliably for technical subject matter, the better," said Frumes. "If you can filter out the discrepancies and warning signs in company financials with a machine, that does the work of one hundred reporters. And it's just a starting point. Then you're freed up to be more creative, to call up the CEOs and the employees, and to do that kind of work."[17]

Although Quant Media's clients were Wall Street investors with a vested interest in having the information first, Frumes believes that its stories quickly filtered into the market and mainstream publications. He says his competitors were sell-side research firms and short sellers who conduct similar research but have a vested interest in their reports because they typically hold a position in the companies they're writing reports about. Quant Media does not invest in the companies it researches.

Frumes wrote the following on LinkedIn in early 2018:

> Combining technology and investigative journalism creates a powerful third-party objective source of news focusing on those kinds of situations, ones that are too often front-run by short-seller research with an agenda. Add to this that business journalism is often a better source of independent information than sellside or buyside research, simply because the incentives for journalists are to get to the truth—while analysts at financial institutions have to wrestle with the conflicts inherent to their firms' business.[18]

At its height, Quant Media produced news stories on about thirty to forty companies on a regular basis, said Frumes, which he believed was less than 10 percent of the company's potential market. "With that, you try to get a good following and get some subscribers and get to break-even point, and then raise some more money and grow organically," he said.[19]

Quant Media raised an undisclosed amount of seed money and had four full-time editorial staffers and one full-time salesperson.

Frumes hoped the company would break even financially within two years. Unfortunately, the company faced legal difficulties and was forced to close. It also faced difficulties in coming to terms with its technology partner—it had an exclusive media license but not ownership.

Frumes believed that Quant Media was filling a niche in business journalism that many media organizations were ignoring. He believed that many companies have gone public in recent years with questionable financial results that will begin to sour once the market begins to fall and the economy slows. That's news that business owners, employees, and others value.

"When the market is down, that is when all of the interesting stuff happens, when the reporting on companies that we have already covered starts to happen," said Frumes. "We'll have an insight into them, and then you can start tackling them from all of the different process, those that lose financing, those that get handed off to reorganization and bankruptcy. We're getting a head start in pointing out all of the issues in these companies."[20]

CONCLUSION

These four media companies used technology such as artificial intelligence and computer programs to augment the work of their reporters and editors, showing that business journalism is attempting to keep up with the latest advances. And they're not the only ones exploring the limits of technology in business journalism.

The New York Times has been using technology to help its journalists create stories around the economy. In 2016 Bloomberg News expanded its team working on automation, and it continues to grow.

Bloomberg News developed a workflow tool called Cyborg, which publishes headlines and a short story within seconds of a company's earnings release. Through Cyborg, journalists decide which variables the system should capture and what order they should publish (for example, Facebook's monthly active users would be ranked higher than its earnings per share as that is a more accurate way to value the company). The moment an earnings statement appears on a company's website or via press release, Cyborg extracts predetermined information and adds relevant context—

pricing information or other data—from the Bloomberg Terminal. Using the tool, the story can be updated by a reporter with additional context or information as needed. Bloomberg also simultaneously publishes numerous stories in multiple languages.

"All this is in competition not just with Reuters but with specialist news-scraping sites that serve hedge funds looking for microseconds of advantage," wrote Bloomberg editor-in-chief John Micklethwait.[21] Bloomberg also has a product called Daybreak that allows readers to tailor their morning news to their portfolios, and it has a project that uses computers to tell it when a stock has risen or fallen a significant amount.

In a message to the editorial staff, Micklethwait wrote:

> Why do we need you, if the basic idea is to get computers to do more of the work? One irony of automation is that it is only as good as humans make it. That applies to both the main types of automated journalism. In the first, the computer will generate the story or headline by itself. But it needs humans to tell it what to look for, where to look for it, and to guarantee its independence and transparency to our readers. In the second sort, the computer spots a trend, delivers a portion of a story to you and in essence asks the question: Do you want to add or subtract something to this and publish it? And it will only count as Bloomberg journalism if you sign off on it.[22]

The problem with these technological advances is, as mentioned earlier, they are primarily being used by the media companies that dominate business news and who charge hefty sums for access, targeting the demographic that can afford to pay for this business news. In addition, many smaller media companies can't spend the money to develop the technology in order to keep up with how companies are using technology to advance their operations or tell their stories in a way that bypasses traditional media. But these examples also show that news media, no matter how small or big, can use technology to produce stories and help consumers and businesses.

To be sure, the use of technology and computers in business journalism is not going to solve all of the problems. Past attempts, albeit from startups and not established media organizations, have failed. A company called MarketBrief created software that read 10 million Securities and Exchange Commission filings per day and turned the information in those documents into stories. It lasted three years and had syndication agreements with news organizations such as CNN and StockTwits, but it closed in 2012, three years after it launched.

In addition, some business journalists have warned that the automation push results in fewer jobs for reporters and editors. Ron Day, a former *Bloomberg News* journalist, wrote that one former Bloomberg editor laid off from the company estimated that 25 percent of his job had been taken over by software.[23] The media organizations using computers and programs dispute this claim, saying that the technology allows their journalists to do bigger and more important stories.

The current technology has only scratched the surface of how it can help business news media. There are dozens of other routine business news stories such as economic data—unemployment, the trade deficit, consumer confidence, retail sales, new home sales, and so on—that can easily be written with the use of algorithms and computer programs.

If this trend continues, and if media organizations allow business journalists to spend more time digging for more important stories and give the routine stories such as earnings to the computers, then maybe some business journalism can catch up with how the rest of the world uses technology. But technology needs to be adopted by smaller operators who provide the bulk of business and economics news to most consumers.

12

THE EDUCATION IMPERATIVE

Business journalism education at the college and university level has expanded dramatically in the past fifty years since courses were first offered in the subject, but that expansion has stagnated in the past decade. An updating of the curriculum, changing the coursework required for students studying the subject, could go a long way in making business journalism more relevant and could help to produce the content that many businesses and consumers need. Programs should focus on teaching budding journalists how to provide stories that are actually needed by most business owners, employees, and consumers.

Fifty years ago there were no business journalism programs, and only a handful of classes were taught. About a dozen colleges and universities currently offer either an undergraduate or master's degree in business journalism. Some of the country's top universities, both public and private—Columbia University, Northwestern University, New York University, Arizona State University, University of North Carolina, and Washington & Lee University—are among those offering rigorous business journalism programs. In most cases these universities require business journalism students to take courses at their respective business schools as well as classes in their schools of journalism and mass communication. This gives students a basic understanding of how the corporate world works and the issues facing companies while also providing the groundwork for reporting on business and economic topics.

However, there have been few, if any, new business journalism programs or classes in American academia since the Great Recession of 2008, despite consumers' need for a greater understanding of how the business world impacts them. This lack of expansion comes when the biggest news stories of the past decade have included the changing nature of jobs, economic growth, the impact of technology companies on society, and international trade. In addition, many business journalists enter the field without proper educational training because of the lack of any business journalism courses at their university or college or the inability to take more than one course in the field. Mary Jane Pardue of Missouri State University found that many business editors find journalism program graduates unprepared to cover business and economics topics.[1]

To make the education situation worse, many businesses and industries attempt to discourage journalists from properly reporting on topics of interest or understanding their motives, according to Maha Rafi Atal of the University of Cambridge.[2] Media companies with big business journalism organizations have also done little to improve the quality of business journalism education at the college level. They may offer money for internships and occasionally have their reporters and editors teach a course at a university, but they are not involved in shaping the curriculum, nor do they provide funding for business journalism programs.

Even if media companies did fund business journalism education at colleges and universities, most programs in journalism and mass communication lack the faculty needed to teach business journalism and rarely encourage doctoral students—who often fill vacant faculty slots at other universities—to conduct research in and around business and economics news topics. Most of the current instructors teaching in the field worked in business journalism during their professional careers. Arizona State University's Donald W. Reynolds National Center for Business Journalism has previously funded short-term positions at universities across the country to teach business reporting classes, but that effort has not resulted in an expansion of courses and programs. In addition, faculty with business journalism experience are also often asked to teach courses outside of that specialty, limiting their ability to expand and create additional business journalism courses.

Universities with business journalism programs should consider a major overhaul of their current curricula, and universities without programs in the field should consider adding coursework to address the growing need for journalists who can understand and write about business and economics topics. Current programs should expand their curricula to include coursework in understanding data and in basic computer program coding, two areas increasingly used in business and economics reporting, without cutting other required courses.

In addition, corporations covered by the business media, and media organizations with a large presence in business journalism, should take a more active role in expanding and building academic programs in the field. As noted earlier, business news has been shown to help companies and expand the economy, even when the coverage is negative. And journalism and mass communication academic programs should focus on hiring faculty able to teach and expand their offerings of business and economics reporting classes.

Such efforts would come at a time when the status of innovation in programs of journalism and media are being evaluated. Allan Richards of Florida International University and Kathy R. Kirkpatrick of American University wrote that innovation in journalism education is helped by inspirational leadership, strategic focus, dedicated resources, collaborative spirit, and curricular currency.[3] Business journalism curriculum and education—and ultimately business journalism content—could benefit from all of these.

Kenneth R. Ahern of the University of Southern California and Denis Sosyura of the University of Michigan found that the quality of financial media stories improved with a journalist's experience, specialized education, and industry expertise, and that the quality of sources—from within the business world—for reporters covering mergers and acquisitions improves the quality of their articles.[4]

What follows are some reasonable ways that higher education can help improve business journalism education that would result in better coverage for businesses and consumers.

JOURNALISM COURSES

When a business journalism course is taught at a university, it is typical to offer it once a year and as an elective—not part of a student's required coursework. In addition, the course is commonly taught by an adjunct, typically a local business journalist who is not trained beforehand to teach such a course. This often limits the ability of a journalism and mass communication program to build and develop interest in business journalism because the temporary instructor relies on the program to drum up interest in the course with its students, and because the full-time faculty and administrators often don't understand the need for such a course.

If the course is successful, students will want to take an additional course in the area, sometimes as soon as the next semester, but the program is often not equipped—either financially or academically—to quickly add a class.

Recent changes by the Accrediting Council on Journalism and Mass Communication Education, which accredits 118 programs, have loosened the requirements for accreditation regarding the number of course hours taken, making this an opportune time for journalism programs to consider expanding their course offerings in business journalism.

A business journalism curriculum—whether undergraduate minor, major, or master's degree—should include the following courses, at a minimum:

- *A "Business Reporting" course that teaches students how to cover companies, both private and public.* This course should focus on finding information about businesses using public records such as Securities and Exchange Commission filings and state and federal government agency documents. Students should also receive an education in covering various types of business news stories, from hirings and layoffs to mergers and acquisitions. Reporting on these stories will help a student grasp the importance of businesses on the lives of everyday consumers.
- *An "Economics Reporting" course that provides instruction on covering major economic stories such as unemployment, consumer confidence, inflation, car and home sales, interest rates, and manufacturing data.* An overview of reporting on these stories helps potential business journalists understand how an economy works. This class should emphasize interviewing consumers about their spending habits as well as their attitudes about the economy. It should also give students an understanding of how company owners and executives look at economic data when making decisions.
- *A seminar class on the history and current issues surrounding business journalism.* It's important for students to know how business journalism has evolved, especially since the beginning of the twentieth century, when muckrakers were the first business journalists, writing about companies such as Standard Oil Company, and should know how books such as *Silent Spring* and *Unsafe at Any Speed* took on major corporations in the 1960s. Such a course could cover

topics such as how public relations can influence coverage and how companies have pulled advertising from media outlets when they have been upset with stories about their operations. A seminar class can cover topics such as whether business and economics news influences what consumers think about the stock market and how television business news is different from print business news.

- *An ethics course focusing on the unique challenges in business journalism.* This course should cover topics such as whether to buy stocks and other types of investments, and whether business journalists should take advice from Wall Street experts or special deals from businesses that they cover, such as mortgage banks. Other course topics should look at the influence of public relations and advertising on business news coverage.[5] Money permeates business reporting unlike any other field in journalism, so it's important for business journalist wannabes to have a solid ethical grounding in the dos and don'ts of the field. A review of business journalism ethics codes from organizations such as the Wall Street Journal, Bloomberg News, and the Society for Advancing Business Editing and Writing would lead to multiple classroom discussions. Most current mass communication ethics courses neglect to discuss business journalism topics, failing students interested in this topic.

- *A capstone course where students undertake the major production of business news content.* The content of this course could take on many different forms. At programs such as Arizona State University and the University of North Carolina, students report and write stories for a website that publishes content.[6] At UNC, the stories are edited by a business journalism professor for the North Carolina Business News Wire website. Those stories are then sent out to media in the state, helping them cover businesses and the economy. At other universities students spend an entire semester reporting and writing on a major business or economic topic, such as coal industry pollution. This course should provide a real-world experience for students that allows them to hit the ground running after graduation.

Journalism and mass communication programs often require students to take basic courses such as "Introductory Newswriting" and "Media

Law" as well, particularly at the graduate level. If the above five courses are each three hours credit, then two additional courses would total twenty-one course hours, giving both undergraduate and graduate students the ability to take business-related courses outside of journalism and mass communication to round out the curriculum.

Journalism and mass communication administrators should also work with local, state, and national business journalism organizations in developing these courses and determining the specific curricula, particularly if the program has no experience in teaching business journalism. Joseph Weber of the University of Nebraska says that teaching business and economics journalism "is especially challenging," but there has been "considerable pedagogical innovation. Teachers have found ingenious ways to make the topic engaging for students."[7] Such innovation could continue with additional classes, including some of the ones mentioned above.

There are few classes offered that teach the business of health care, even though health care spending is more than one-sixth of the economy. Longtime health care journalist Trudy Lieberman proposed a syllabus to teach journalism students for the Harvard University Shorenstein Center on Media, Politics and Public Policy. The class included a final assignment focusing on stories such as a hospital's prices or how a drug was developed and sold. One week of the course was devoted to how consumers and companies pay for health care, and two weeks covered the pharmaceutical industry.[8]

BUSINESS COURSES

While courses in a journalism program are intended to provide instruction on how to cover business and economic topics, courses in a business school should help provide knowledge and understanding of how companies and economies function. Combining journalism and business coursework into a program of study gives students a well-rounded education that prepares them to enter the professional world of business journalism. The *FACS/ FORD Study of Economic and Business Journalism for the Ford Foundation by the Foundation for American Communications* recommended that students interested in business journalism should double major in business or economics.[9]

An introductory accounting course should be a requirement for all business journalism students. It will help them understand how a company makes or looses money as well as what it does with the money that it makes or raises. Being able to read an income statement, a cash flow statement, and a balance sheet allows a business reporter to find stories in a company report that might not otherwise be disclosed in press releases or Securities and Exchange Commission filings. A classic example is the financial collapse of energy company Enron in the early twenty-first century. Its negative cash flow was not a topic discussed in the company's earnings press releases or its earnings conferences calls, yet it was one of the primary causes of its demise.

A corporate finance course should also be a required course for a business journalism major. This class typically covers topics such as how a company raises money for expansions, such as building a new warehouse or stores, and for mergers and acquisitions. It often covers selling stocks and bonds to investors as well as how loan agreements are structured with banks and lenders. These are all topics that would help a business journalist do a better job in covering the companies on their beat.

A business management course is also a necessary course because it goes over the internal structure of a company and explains different jobs within an executive suite and who reports to whom. Business journalists need to understand the role and function of a president versus a chief executive officer and how both interact with the company's board of directors. It's often in these roles where big business news stories are found.

These are only three courses in the business school; business journalism students should consider enrolling in others. The more they understand the mindset, strategies, and inner workings of companies, the better job they will do in covering these businesses. Corporate communications, marketing, organizational behavior, and business law and ethics are other business school courses that might be helpful for a business journalism student. In addition, taking business school classes exposes journalism students to the people who will be running and working for companies.

I won't go as far as recommending that business journalists earn a master's in business administration. But many business journalists do hold that degree. Business journalist Louise Story, formerly with the *Wall Street Journal*, earned an MBA from the Yale University School of Management and wrote that her B-school education helped her as a business journalist, particularly when it came to using the tools that are used by companies. "As for Excel, if you gain confidence with it, as B-school forces you to, then functions like pivot tables and filters will become your secret weapon in journalism, helping you spot stories that other people miss," she wrote.[10]

Menachem Wecker argues in *US News & World Report* that journalists with an MBA can make them more attractive in finding jobs. But he notes that universities that offer an MBA to journalism students have few takers.[11]

DATA AND CODING COURSES

Today's business journalist is increasingly using advanced techniques to find and report stories. These can be skills such as manipulating data in a Microsoft Excel spreadsheet to look for anomalies in a company's financial performance to setting up software that scans corporate websites and press releases to look for stories. Some business journalism organizations are also using computer coding skills to report and write stories and to find stories their reporters may not be discovering, as noted in chapter II. The Associated Press uses software to write basic earnings stories, for example, while Reuters uses software to alert reporters and editors when a change in a commodity price might be the cause of a company's stock price drop.

Many journalism schools are beginning to teach courses in these areas. The curriculum should be expanded in journalism schools to provide more skills that are easily transferable to reporting. However, Neil Reisner of Florida International University warned that teaching journalism students how to code risks "creating journalists who know coding, but don't know how to cover news."[12] Business journalism students could be taught coding in a way that helps them uncover news and find stories that may not be found otherwise. For example, a coding course focused on business journalism could download data about companies from many federal and state government websites into simple programs that display stories unseen to the naked eye—such as what type of injuries are occurring most commonly in the workplace or what companies in a state are seeing the largest amounts of insider buying and selling of stock.

In addition, journalism schools are woefully inadequate when it comes to teaching math and data skills like using a Microsoft Excel spreadsheet, which can be a valuable tool for any reporter, whether they cover business or not. And there are opportunities for business journalism students to learn how to put data into programs to build simple charts and graphics that go along with their stories—often telling the story to a reader better than words can. Grant Hannis argues that data journalism should be taught in all journalism programs. "Whether data journalism is taught as part of the business journalism course or the program's investigative journalism course remains to be decided, but it needs to appear somewhere," he argues.[13]

Too often, business journalism is taught by having students simply read a company's earnings press release or other statement and having them explain in their story what is going on without analyzing the numbers that lurk behind the story. Teaching business journalism students how to look at numbers—and use advanced techniques that can be picked up quickly—to look deeper into a company will make business journalism better and serve society.

Tech journalist David Cohn argues that one way for journalism schools to improve in this area is to offer technology reporting classes. "Students can learn about technology because it will be their beat and they want to be good reporters," he wrote for The Poynter Institute for Media Studies. "When students aren't even paying attention, they'll begin to understand the power of technology, the richness of the industry, and the culture of the community."[14]

PARTNERS

More than anything, colleges and universities need to reach out to potential partners in the corporate world to aid in creating business journalism programs and to improve existing business journalism curricula. Corporations once were vital in launching some of the country's first business journalism programs. The Independent Natural Gas Association of America gave money to the University of Missouri in the 1960s to help start its business reporting program.[15] And a master's-level business journalism program at Columbia University was started in the 1970s with the backing of companies such as IBM and Prudential Insurance.[16]

In recent years such partnerships have been lacking and virtually nonexistent. Journalism program chairs, directors, and deans need to approach companies about helping fund business journalism education, making the argument that improving the quality of business reporting will boost the economy and the fortunes of these companies. Research from journalism and business school researchers support this statement. Kenneth Ahern and Denis Sosyura of the University of Michigan found that the quality of business news improves when a journalist has specialized education and industry experience.[17] Other research has discovered, as we saw in chapter 1, that business journalism helps investors outperform the market.

Companies that operate business news media organizations would be prime targets for such collaborations. For example, American City Business Journals operates more than forty business newspapers across the country and has seen its circulation and advertising revenue grow in recent years, bucking the downturn seen by most of the rest of the media. It is owned by the Newhouse family, which has given generously to the journalism school at Syracuse University, but it has not funded any business journalism education initiatives. Another candidate would be Dow Jones & Company, the parent of the Wall Street Journal, Barron's, and Market-Watch.com. It is owned by News Corporation, which is controlled by billionaire Rupert Murdoch.

One business news organization that has been funding business journalism education initiatives has been Bloomberg L.P., which is owned by billionaire Michael Bloomberg. It has funded professorships and classes focused on business reporting in the United States in the past, but in recent years it has channeled a large portion of its business journalism education funding to programs in Africa, where it believes improved business reporting can have the biggest positive impact on society and the economy.

Such prospects should not be confined simply to US media companies. Executives from other industries have recently purchased business publications such as Fortune and Forbes. These executives and corporations can be approached about supporting business journalism under the guise that a quality education in the field would also help the publications they own.

Business journalism programs have been created at universities without corporate or foundation funding. But at a time when many universities are budget-constrained, particularly state-run institutes of higher education, funding from the business world would facilitate the process.

CONCLUSIONS

While the proposal for a full-blown business journalism curriculum that incorporates classes from across a university or college is ideal, many journalism and mass communication programs lack the bandwidth to implement such an offering. However, the proposed curriculum provides suggestions and ideas for how other programs—particularly those with a large faculty and large student population—can provide business journalism education in a way that would help the profession and at a minimum cost. At most universities, the business school classes are already on the schedule and would simply require a mass communication faculty negotiating with its business school colleagues to provide a handful of open seats in those courses to add them to a business journalism curriculum.

In addition, adding or expanding a business journalism education offers an opportunity for journalism programs to focus on a field of study where job prospects for students have remained steady in the past decade despite a downturn in positions at outlets such as newspapers. They could attract students by noting that business journalism pays better salaries than other reporting and editing jobs. In addition, business journalism programs address a growing need from the industry—their desire to hire journalists who understand how to report and write about business and economics topics, whether for a business news audience or a general news reader. The skill of reading documents such as budgets and financial statements is one that cuts across all types of reporting, not just for business.

Despite the demand and interest, a majority of journalism and mass communication programs in the United States have no business journalism curriculum, not even a single course. Some may offer one class sporadically, when they can find an adjunct instructor with expertise in the area. Other programs may teach a regular course in the field if someone on their permanent faculty has the interest and desire. However, one of the reasons that journalism programs don't teach business journalism is the lack of available faculty focused on the subject. Many business journalism courses are taught by faculty who do not hold a doctorate or advanced degree. The University of South Carolina's School of Journalism and Mass Communication has offered funding to graduate students interested in business journalism, but so far it has produced just two potential faculty members, and only one who teaches full time.

Journalism programs could also actively recruit instructors from the business journalism industry. David Cuillier and Carol Schwalbe discovered that the winners of a teaching competition by the Association for Education in Journalism and Mass Communication with bachelor's and master's degrees were more likely to have higher ratings in teaching effectiveness than those with a doctorate.[18]

It is in the interest of every party involved—corporations, media organizations, and journalists themselves—that academia take the lead and focus on improving the quality of business journalism. The first step would be for programs to understand the impact that a lack of understanding about business, markets, and the economy has on society and to make business journalism education an important initiative.

Focusing on business journalism education would also serve as a counterbalance to the growing number of public relations and marketing students at many journalism and mass communication programs. And it would make business journalism more nuanced and more valuable to consumers.

This history of some of the major business journalism education efforts in academia shows that two types of business journalism academic programs have emerged over the past fifty years—one that serves experienced journalists and offers a master's degree, and another that primarily trains undergraduate journalism students. Both types of curricula have had moderate success in attracting interest from foundations, businesses, and executives and involving them in improving the quality of business journalism, but those efforts have been inconsistent.

In examining the creation and evolution of business journalism academic programs, one can see that funding from corporations, their foundations, and executives has helped many of these efforts get off the ground. However, these funding efforts are minimal when compared to the funding received for university programs in business and other fields. For example, the School of Pharmacy at UNC–Chapel Hill has received a $100 million gift from pharmaceutical company executive Fred Eshelman but no corporate funding for its business journalism program.

The dearth of corporate and foundation funding at most business journalism programs comes at a time when the field—at least among its top entrants—is thriving compared to other media. The *Wall Street Journal* is the only one among the top one hundred daily newspapers in the United

States that has seen an increase in circulation in the past decade.[19] The *Economist* and *Financial Times* have also seen an increase in circulation—combined print and digital—during this period.[20] Even smaller business publications such as those owned by American City Business Journals have seen increases in circulation and advertising revenue in the past decade.[21] As noted in the beginning of this book, improving the quality of business journalism has shown to be beneficial to businesses and economies. These larger media organizations could help the field—and could help the smaller media organizations—by providing funding to higher education efforts.

The programs at Missouri, Columbia, and Arizona State show that corporations and foundations can successfully fund and build business journalism curriculum. While Columbia University lost funding when one corporation dropped its sponsorship due to its distaste for coverage produced by the program director, it remained one of the top, if not *the* top, business journalism programs in the country. This shows that academic units can survive pressure that businesses may put on them.

Additional corporate involvement in business journalism education would be beneficial to both universities and colleges as well as corporations. As the demand for journalists who can write about business and the economy intensifies due to changes in society, journalism programs could look to corporations and executives, who have a vested interest in the quality of business journalism, for support and guidance on how these programs can be added, expand, and proliferate across college campuses.

13

FIXING BUSINESS JOURNALISM

At the higher end of business journalism, individual reporters have left their news organizations and started newsletters where they're charging consumers to read about national topics. With niche newsletters that focus on specific regions or specific topics, many media companies believe they have found the future of providing news and information that an audience wants—and in a way that can be produced profitably. They include news in short, digestible nuggets and can also collect pertinent stories from other news organizations. The newsletters are usually delivered to readers by e-mail, meaning they can be opened and read at any time.

Newsletters are just one of many examples for how to rethink business journalism, how it is delivered, and what is covered—in other words, how to provide a brighter future for business journalism. These newsletters are not just for investors and bankers and CEOs. They're for consumers, for small business owners, and for employees. "Newsletters are the workhorse of media companies . . . they provide flexibility and optionality," wrote Sean Griffey, CEO of Industry Dive, which publishes two dozen business news-letters about a variety of topics.[1] And they're for people who have been underrepresented in past coverage such as business owners of color and female business owners.

Without changes such as converting to writing and delivering newslet-ters, business journalism will continue to focus on what only a small per-centage of consumers want, and journalism overall will suffer. Journalism is intended to serve society, but as it exists today business journalism is failing that purpose because it's serving only a fraction of society.

Change is difficult, but it can be achieved, and it can result in readers coming back to local business news if the content is made available to them in a format that they find appealing. The focus needs to be on the content that business owners and consumers want and need, not what Wall Street bankers and investors desire. Let's look at what business journalism can borrow from other forms of news and examine what journalism can change to be valuable for both Main Street and Wall Street.

Three former Politico staffers founded news website *Axios* in 2017 and designed it as a mix between the *Economist* and Twitter, with brief stories that have bulleted points of why the news is important. It generates revenue from advertising and sponsored newsletters. In late 2020 *Axios* acquired the *Charlotte Agenda*, a newsletter started in 2015 to cover news around the North Carolina city with 55,000 newsletter subscribers and a profit margin of 30 percent.[2]

The *Charlotte Agenda* was started by former *Charlotte Observer* staffers who felt the daily newspaper was ignoring local news. In 2020 it covered the rise of homelessness during the pandemic and business closings. For many Charlotte residents, the *Agenda* is now the preferred source of news over the daily newspaper, which is now owned by a hedge fund and has 68,000 daily subscribers.[3] (The *Observer* says its website has 4.7 million monthly visitors compared to 650,000 for the *Agenda*.) *Axios* is also launching local news operations in other cities such as Tampa, Denver, Minneapolis, and Des Moines.

In another part of Charlotte, former *Observer* business journalist Tony Mecia has launched the *Charlotte Ledger*, perhaps the first business news e-mail newsletter in the country not backed by a larger publication or website, aimed at consumers and business owners starving for local business news. "The idea is to try to serve the demand for local business news in a way that is smart, engaging and entertaining," said Mecia. "There's a lot of innovation going on at the national level, particularly on newsletters (The Hustle, Axios, etc.), but I'm not aware of much being done along those lines in local journalism."[4]

The *Ledger* has a total e-mail distribution list of more than 6,200. In February 2020 it switched to a partially paid, partially free model and does not publicly disclose how many subscribers pay. But in the industry, the standard is to expect to convert 10 percent of your free list to paying subscribers, and the *Ledger* is comfortably above that.[5] "We are a local publication and people feel more of a connection than they do to a national newsletter," said Mecia. "We also sell a limited number of sponsorships on our free editions, but that accounts for only about 10–15% of our revenue this year (that's by design)."[6] A subscription is $9 a month, or $99 a year, something that is affordable to a small business owner or consumer. About thirty companies and individuals pay $379 a year to be sponsors.

The *Ledger* sends out four newsletters per week, and the newsletter typically has a lead story that is usually five hundred to one thousand words long. In addition, there are two to three shorter articles and some curated items from other publications. The *Ledger* is written and produced by free-lancers, typically former *Observer* reporters, and an intern from Queens University. "It's still early, but I am happy to report that subscription growth is steady, and that the Charlotte Ledger is already more profitable than Uber and Lyft combined," said Mecia. "As far as why I am doing this, I love business journalism."[7]

The world of business journalism needs more people such as Mecia who produce quality news and understand what readers want to help them make decisions. Produce quality content at an affordable price, and people will pay for it. Business journalism needs to follow what media business model expert Ken Doctor calls "one of the most refreshing trends into the 2020s"—the rise of single-subject journalism.[8] He writes: "In topic after topic, the focus on expertise—in reporting, writing and increasingly presentation and storytelling—have produced their own revolution. In health, we see Kaiser Health News excelling and expanding. In education, Chalkbeat (with its new five-year plan) and the Hechinger Report drill into the real issues of the field."[9]

The chapters in part 3 provide changes in specific areas that could improve business news for many consumers. This chapter includes some broader ways to fix business journalism, including focusing on hiring reporters and editors who represent the equality and diversity of the community, changing coverage to emphasize topics of interest to smaller business owners and consumers, working on a better relationship between business journalists and corporate executives, providing more training for journalists about how businesses and the economy operate, examining new ways to fund business journalism, sharing strategies and business models that work, and focusing more coverage on the needs of consumers.

EQUALITY AND DIVERSITY

There are nearly 8 million minority-owned businesses in the United States, with $1.4 trillion in revenue, according to the Minority Business Development Agency of the US Department of Commerce. That's about 29 percent of all businesses in the country (people of color are about 40 percent of the US population).[10] In addition, there are 9.9 million women-owned firms, and another 2.5 million businesses co-owned by men and women, according to the US Small Business Association.[11] That's more than one-third of all businesses in the country (women are 51 percent of the US population).

Look at what any mainstream news organization covers, however, and it's not devoting its content to minority- and women-owned businesses by anything close to the percentages these groups represent in the population or as business owners. So it should not be a surprise that the news media are failing to attract readers from these demographics. The Brookings Institution reports that minority- and women-owned businesses added 1.8 million jobs between 2007 and 2012, during the last economic recession and recovery, while businesses owned by white males lost 800,000 jobs.[12] In another study, the Donald W. Reynolds National Center for Business Journalism found that 83 percent of minority and independent business owners said reporters must improve their understanding of business.[13]

Look at the demographics of business newsrooms. Rarely, if ever, do they correlate with society, even at the highest levels of business journalism. At the *Wall Street Journal* female bylines fell to 34.3 percent in 2016, down from 39.2 percent in 2015, according to the Women's Media Center.[14] The *Wall Street Journal* also pays its female staffers less than its male journalists.

There is a growing effort in business news to provide content that better reflects these important readers, but more work needs to be done, especially in making newsrooms more diverse. The *Economist* disclosed in 2019 that less than 1 percent of its staff is Black.[15] In 2020 American City Business Journals announced that it was making its minority internships in business reporting a year-round program.[16] The *Wall Street Journal* has developed relationships with historically Black colleges and universities such as Morgan State University where their reporters and editors will mentor students. *Forbes* has started a fellowship program for journalism students at historically Black colleges and universities, and Reuters has struck a deal for a similar program with the National Association of Black Journalists.

Most of the bigger media organizations in business news understand the importance of diverse voices and stories in their coverage. *Bloomberg News* senior executive editor Laura Zelenko says maintaining a diverse workforce helps it tell better and more nuanced stories.[17] Bloomberg has begun a program to provide media training to Black and female businesspeople. The percentage of women guests on Bloomberg Television rose to

18 percent at the end of 2018, up from 10 percent at the beginning of the year.[18]

The *Financial Times* created a dashboard that monitors what female subscribers are reading and what they are not reading as well as the percentage of female readers for each section. It has also taken a step to improve diversity among sources: after the newspaper found that only 21 percent of people quoted in its stories were women, it created a software program that tells editors and reporters when they're quoting too many men.[19]

Some business journalists have taken it upon themselves to track the diversity of their sources. For example, in 2018 *Bloomberg News* emerging markets reporter Ben Bartenstein tracked his sources and increased his percentage of female sources to 50 percent, up from 13 percent in 2017. "There's some initial legwork in finding new sources," Bartenstein concluded. "But that is, after all, our job. Diverse sourcing is about far more than numbers. It gives you a competitive advantage over your competition & leads to more interesting and higher impact stories."[20]

New York Times economics reporter Ben Casselman tracked his sources in 2019 and found that 42 percent of them were women and 15 percent were minorities.[21] It was the first year he tracked the demographics, and he discovered that his sources were more diverse on stories that were not written on deadline. "This exercise forced me really to think about whom I was calling and to seek out new voices," he wrote on Twitter. "Even when I ended up quoting a white guy, it was often a different (and more appropriate) white guy than the ones I'd called in the past."[22]

Sarah Paynter, who covered real estate for *Yahoo Finance*, disclosed that she increased the people of color quoted in her stories in 2020 to 29 percent from 21 percent, and the women quoted to 39 percent from 27 percent.[23]

The takeaway here: business journalism should hire more diverse newsrooms, and it should focus more on telling the stories of minority and women businesses as well as quoting more sources that show a more reflective diversity.

CHANGE COVERAGE EMPHASIS

If changing the demographics of the business newsroom is the first step, then focusing on reporting and writing stories in a way that businesses and consumers will understand their significance is the second.

With the decline in local business reporters, many good business stories that would draw readers and revenue are going unreported. Here are some practical ways that business reporters and editors can improve their coverage in ways that will help consumers, employees, and business owners understand better what's going on in their areas:

- **Bankruptcy court:** Most major US cities have a bankruptcy court, or there's one nearby. This is where important stories of companies and individuals are told, and those stories can provide great insights into what's going on in a local economy. Yes, they're often stories of failure and trouble, but they're stories that will help others understand what pressures businesses and individuals face. In 2020, there were 7,129 Chapter 11 bankruptcy court protection filings, the common filing for businesses in financial trouble, the highest level since 2012.[24]

- **Unemployment data:** Again, most cities in the United States belong to a metropolitan statistical area that produces monthly unemployment data. While the monthly unemployment number can be news, dig deeper. These statistics often show what industries are gaining or losing jobs, which is important to businesses looking to hire workers and people looking for employment. Business journalist David Lieberman encourages more local economics reporting, adding that communities built on agriculture have different news priorities than those depending on manufacturing or technology.[25]

- **Zoning and planning:** When a company or a contractor wants to construct a building, whether a high rise or a strip mall with a grocery store, the building plans have to be approved by a city or county zoning and planning office. And other businesses and consumers want to know what's being built and where. Remember Juliann Francis, the co-owner of Captain Cookie from the start of the book? She's looking for new locations for her store, and she's interested in what's being built and where. Locating her store where other retailers will help draw traffic will be good for her business.

- **Health care:** This book devotes a whole chapter to the importance of health care news coverage. The business of health care is one-sixth of the US economy, and it's usually the largest employer in a town or a city. Look for news around the hospitals and the surgical centers, such as expansion plans. And reporters should question whether consumers really need those additional health care services.

- **Price changes:** Consumers care about how much they're paying for goods and services, and these stories can easily be done. Why are gas prices rising faster in one city than the next city over? GasBuddy and the American Automobile Association have those statistics.[26] Regularly check with the state insurance department for price hike requests on car, homeowner's, and health insurance rates. Those prices affect tens of thousands of consumers in every state.
- **The courthouse:** The court system is a big business story, but it is rarely covered that way. Businesses sue other businesses all the time, and businesses also sue former executives and employees when they leave to go to a competitor. Those are stories that other companies, and people considering jobs at those businesses, will want to read.
- **Trends and issues:** The December 21, 2020, newsletter of the *Charlotte Ledger* examined the financial toll of the pandemic on Blacks and Hispanics, a story that every business in the North Carolina city would want to read if it has customers struggling to pay for products and services. Find out what's affecting customers and start talking to them. Many of them want to share their stories. And ask them if they know anyone else who might also be affected.

Harold Meyerson of the *American Prospect* has some good suggestions for covering companies differently, including writing about the median wage of its employees and about whether a company offers retirement plans and sick days, which would be of value to people looking for jobs.[27]

Find solutions. Most business owners know the problems they face, whether it's hiring experienced workers or paying for workers' compensation insurance. The more stories written about how to solve issues facing businesses and consumers, the more readers will come to the media for that information.

Above all, find stories about people—whether a business owner or someone making the minimum wage—to tell the bigger story about an issue or topic. People love to read about other people, even in business stories.

Keep it simple. The more you can explain a complex business topic in a way that the average consumer or businessperson can understand, the more likely the story will help.

Business news doesn't have to be full of numbers and terms. And it's not always negative, and it's not always positive. It's simply news and information that a businessperson or a consumer needs to improve their situation.

A BETTER RELATIONSHIP

Businesses and other entities attempt to "control" what is reported in the media through the interviews and information they provide to journalists. Economist Joseph Stiglitz argues that many business reporters depend on their sources, so they have to please them. In addition, journalists often write the story that their sources want them to write to gain or maintain access; as a result, many business reporters come "to think like the business he covers."[28]

The solution, according to Jesse Eisinger of ProPublica, is less "hero worship" coverage of executives. He notes that political reporting often sees two sides to an issue, a tactic not often found in business journalism. Business reporting needs to become less reliant on company access and more dependent on public records and other sources of information as the basis of stories.[29] London School of Economics research confirms that business journalists rely too heavily on "access reporting," which impacts their ability to fulfill the role of acting as a guardian for the less powerful.[30] While this may require more work on the part of the reporters, it would lead to more vigorous reporting that would benefit society.

While some business journalism could benefit from less access, business executives and owners could also try to be more accessible and actually help reporters working in stories. For example, when a *Business Insider* journalist began working on a story about how Expensify CEO David Barrett sent out an e-mail to company employees just before the 2020 presidential election stating that voting against Democratic candidate Joe Biden was a "vote against democracy," the reporter asked the company to talk to employees about the topic. The CEO sent the request to his entire staff, saying that they were free to "provide a candid, honest statement on your take on the preparation" of the article.[31] Unfortunately, such cooperation is the exception and not the standard.

Former *Wall Street Journal* reporter Paul Glader, who now teaches at King's College in New York, suggests that one solution is for business reporters to develop a skill to determine when a company or industry is in trouble, such as by looking at whether a company's inventory is rising, which indicates its products are not selling well.[32] The issue with that solution is that many media organizations don't have enough journalists to allow some staff to work on long-term stories while others cover daily news.

Here's at least one way that companies can be more open and accessible to business reporters: public companies can allow journalists to ask questions to executives on their quarterly earnings conference calls and other calls with analysts and investors. And private companies can set aside at least one day a quarter to make its executives accessible to talk to reporters for stories. This would be a start. Some companies already invite new reporters to spend off-the-record time with their leaders to gain a better understanding of the business. Why not continue those meetings on a regular basis?

MORE TRAINING

Business journalism needs more opportunities for its practitioners to improve their skills and knowledge as the business and financial world becomes more complex. Recently the Booth School of Business at the University of Chicago began offering a ten-week program for up-and-coming business journalists with the aim of shaping the next generation of leaders in business reporting. Students audit classes, participate in events, collaborate with peers, and socialize with the university's scholars.[33]

The Wharton School at the University of Pennsylvania offers a shorter program for business journalists as well as one-day seminars across the country throughout the year. Recent seminars have been held on topics ranging from Federal Reserve Board policy to funding and scaling start-ups. The University of South Carolina recently hired a former *Wall Street Journal* journalist to start a business journalism program, and the International Center for Journalists has been holding business and personal finance workshops for Hispanic journalists. In addition, the Dow Jones News Fund has an internship program for college students interested in careers in business journalism. And the Donald W. Reynolds National

Center for Business Journalism has many online training sessions for new and seasoned business reporters.

More such training efforts need to be implemented in business journalism for the field to improve. Economist Joseph Stiglitz writes that "there needs to be more independent financing of investigative and analytic reporting, with a recognition that reporting on economics is different from reporting on finance or business, and that such reporting requires specialized training."[34]

There's so much more than can be done in training existing business journalists, particularly those who didn't take business or business journalism courses while in college. It's time for media organizations to spend money on such training, and it's time for journalists writing about business and the economy to seek out such training, whether it's taking classes at night or on the weekend or even going back to school full time. But media companies should take the lead here and emphasize training around business, finance, and the economy. The *Financial Times*, for example, has begun giving accounting seminars to some of its reporters and hiring writers with financial-sector expertise.[35]

Here's an idea: have local business executives come into the newsroom on a regular basis to talk about how companies operate, and about stories that would help them run their operations more effectively.

MORE FUNDING

While traditional media such as daily newspapers have cut the financial resources devoted to business journalism, other media organizations—and investors—have added funding to business and economics news outlets in recent years. Such funding, which lags the financial backing of other industries, could be expanded. Here are some examples to demonstrate that putting money into business news organizations has actually paid off.

Business news streaming channel *Cheddar* raised $22 million in funding in 2018. That's on top of the $32 million it raised in three previous rounds. The company, which broadcasts online through venues such as YouTube, projected revenue of $18 million in 2018, up from $11.3 million in 2017.[36] The operation, which targets millennials as its core audience, was valued at $160 million in 2018, reports Benjamin Mullin of the *Wall Street Journal*.[37] It was later sold in 2019 for $200 million. The investors earned their money back, and more, by investing in business journalism that focused on a niche audience, a key point.

Other business news outlets have raised money from investors who see their potential. In 2013 New York–based IAC (the former InterActive-Corp), which owns multiple websites, acquired the personal finance news site *Investopedia* for $80 million. The business has increased its revenue to approximately $35 million in 2018, up from $11 million in 2015, and has doubled its monthly users to 30 million, according to CEO David Siegel.[38] Business news site *Benzinga* announced in 2016 that it had closed on a $3 million round of financing that allowed it to expand. It hired data scientists, reporters, editors, and developers, and its content is now syndicated on seventy websites, including *Yahoo Finance* and MSN.[39] In 2015 personal finance news and information website NerdWallet raised $64 million in outside funding.[40]

The *Atlantic* launched business news site *Quartz* in 2013, building it from scratch. The site became profitable in 2016, reporting a profit of more than $1 million from revenue topping $30 million, a 60 percent increase over the previous year.[41] The success came from focusing primarily on digital advertising revenue. In 2018 the *Atlantic* agreed to sell *Quartz* to a Japanese company for between $75 million and $110 million, depending on its financial performance. The website is now owned by its management.

LEARN FROM EACH OTHER

David Callaway, the former CEO of *The Street* and former editor-in-chief of *MarketWatch*, who wrote the foreword for this book, suggests that smaller business news outlets should look to form partnerships with start-up digital newsrooms such as ProPublica or Hechinger Report to add depth to their coverage and to handle more complex stories. Newsrooms learn techniques and strategies from other newsrooms, he says.[42]

Larger business news organizations such as the Wall Street Journal, Bloomberg, and Reuters could create joint ventures with smaller news organizations to help boost investigative business reporting. Many of the niche websites mentioned earlier in this book have a depth and breadth to the coverage of specific industries that no longer exist in other media. The Center for Cooperative Media at Montclair State University's School of Communication and Media has discovered that such collaborations have become more common in mainstream journalism. They also allow media organizations to share the cost of in-depth journalism.

Remember the *Charlotte Ledger* and its coverage of how the pandemic was affecting Black and Hispanic consumers? That story was reported as a collaboration among NPR station WFAE; the *Charlotte Ledger*; *Qcity Metro*, which covers the Black community; and *La Noticia*, the Hispanic newspaper in Charlotte. It was supported by funds from Facebook, the North Carolina Local News Lab Fund, Google, and WFAE members.

In Europe a collaborative network of journalists covering housing called the Housing Project includes a newsletter, a Twitter account, and an online library of information and data. It has a mailing list of 210 members. Such a network could easily be copied in the United States across multiple business and economics news topics.[43]

Many mainstream news organizations argue they don't have the funding to provide business news as thoroughly as they once did. But they can collaborate with other news organizations and share the content. American City Business Journals has struck a deal with The Financial Times allowing it to use some of the FT's content. The arrangement allows Charlotte-based ACBJ to publish a few pieces of Financial Times content every day on the 40 local business journal sites.[44]

FOCUS ON CONSUMERS

Steve Schifferes of City University of London correctly argues that two different audiences have developed for business news. One is the specialist audience of investors and executives that the business reporter at bigger media organizations usually write for. The second—and much bigger audience—is a generalist audience with "much more limited understanding of economic and financial issues."[45] It is the latter audience that is often ignored when it comes to business news coverage from the major players in the field.

Allen Wastler, former managing editor of the websites for CNBC and CNN Money, suggests that business news organizations think of small business coverage in a way that could be more appealing to consumers: "Taking a cue, some business news outfits call their small business sections something along the lines of 'entrepreneurship' or 'enterprise' or such. But it's not about changing labels. It's about changing the coverage approach.

Maybe instead of lumping all small businesses together, it should be more about industry verticals: retailers, restaurants, etc. Or perhaps divided by business models: product-based vs. service based, for example."[46]

Some business and personal finance news organizations are attempting to provide more consumer-focused news. Notable examples include NerdWallet, CNBC's Make It, and Penny Hoarder as well as *Tarbell*, an online news site that investigates the health care industry from a consumer perspective.

Consumers need economics news. They need to understand what is happening in their local economy and how it affects them and their ability to spend money. While some ways to do that are provided earlier in this chapter, there are plenty more ways to provide that news. A news outlet could perform a valuable service to its consumers by comparing the prices of a variety of products at local grocery stores. It could check complaints with state regulators to see what barber shops and beauty salons have sanitary violations or have paid fines. And it could regularly publish the inspection reports of restaurants. Yes, this type of story takes more time than what is usually covered—time usually available only to business reporters at the larger news organizations covered in chapter 3. But the coverage is immensely valuable to small business owners and consumers.

SUSTAINABLE BUSINESS MODELS

While the larger business news organizations such as the Wall Street Journal have a sustainable business model, other companies such as Bloomberg L.P. and Reuters rely on nonjournalism operations to fund their media business. And there is no tried-and-true business model for coverage that's oriented toward the public.

Some business models have shown promise, such as the newsletter format. *Quartz* relied almost solely on digital advertising in its beginning and was able to become profitable within four years. Its business news coverage often goes against the conventional wisdom or finds a unique angle not covered by other media.

Business Insider, founded in 2008, was sold to German-based media company Axel Springer in 2015 for $343 million and has found a niche in targeting millennial readers who consider other business news outlets too stale and boring. It has hired dozens of business reporters and editors in the past few years. Tech news site *The Information*, which is profitable, has more than ten thousand subscribers paying $399 a year because it focuses on breaking stories and doesn't cover every tidbit of news. Farhad Manjoo of the *New York Times* writes that *The Information* is successful because it offers readers "quality instead of volume," publishing two to three stories a day.[47]

Other media organizations are exploring interesting potential revenue streams. Personal finance news company Investopedia launched an online video class series. Video courses are part of an attempt to diversify its revenue away from advertising for the first time in the company's twenty-year history. The Investopedia Academy reported $5 million in revenue in 2018, four times the total it earned in 2017.[48] Business news site *Quartz* has generated revenue from newsletters and its mobile app, which has been downloaded 1 million times. *Business Insider* created a research arm that sells detailed reports on companies and industries.

American City Business Journals, a leader in charging for most of its content online, now has a goal of services providing one-third of its revenue by 2023. Most of its forty-plus papers around the country host dozens of events each year where readers are charged to attend, and the company recently began charging companies $250 to include a listing in one of its papers' "People on the Move" section.[49]

The bigger business model issue is with daily newspapers and other local news outlets, which have all but given up on providing business and economics news. Newsletters such as the *Charlotte Ledger* look like they could fill that void. E-mail newsletters focused on business news in towns and cities could sprout and multiply during the next decade. So could newsletters focused on specific industries.

Despite the obstacles that have caused the problems with business journalism, I'm optimistic about the future of business journalism, both for Wall Street and for Main Street. Critics and pundits have been predicting the demise of journalism through various formats for decades. Television was supposed to be the death knell for radio, and both were supposed to kill newspapers. The internet spelled the demise of all three.

But media have always morphed and adapted. It's time for business journalism to do the same. There are 30 million business owners and more than 300 million consumers in this country who all want business news that suits their needs. Let's put Main Street on equal footing with those on Wall Street.

APPENDIX
TIMELINE

This timeline looks at the major events in business journalism over the past decade. It shows how the field has evolved into providing more news and information for a small audience focused on Wall Street and big companies and fewer stories that are of interest to smaller businesses, employees, and consumers who are the economic drivers in many towns and cities.

JUNE 2011

- *Riverside* [California] *Press-Enterprise* closes its weekly business publication.
- *Charlotte Observer* cuts stock listings.
- *Capital Regional Business Journal* in Wisconsin ceases publication.
- Ogden, Utah, daily newspaper kills its business magazine.
- *Des Moines Register* lays off its agriculture reporter.

JULY 2011

- *Denver Post* cuts stock and mutual fund listings.
- CNBC's *Nightly Business Report* lays off managing editor and executive vice president.
- Pew Research Center study finds that front-page business news stories at the *Wall Street Journal* declined by a third since being acquired by Rupert Murdoch.
- American City Business Journals cuts print editions of *Mass High Tech*.
- *Los Angeles Times* lays off assistant business editor.

AUGUST 2011

- *Nightly Business Report* opens Houston bureau.

SEPTEMBER 2011

- AOL terminates *TechCrunch* founder after he starts a venture capital fund.

- *Law360* opens Los Angeles and Chicago bureaus.
- Bloomberg completes deal to acquire Bureau of National Affairs, now known as Bloomberg Industry Group.

OCTOBER 2011
- *Financial Times* closes its Tilt website.

NOVEMBER 2011
- Tech news site *The Verge* launches.
- CNBC spoofed on *Saturday Night Live*.
- *Nightly Business Report* sold for second time in fifteen months.

DECEMBER 2011
- Federal Reserve chairman pens letter criticizing Bloomberg News.
- *Tampa Tribune* lays off business editor.
- Reuters makes four layoffs in restructuring.
- *Indianapolis Business Journal* columnist accused of running Ponzi scheme.

JANUARY 2012
- The *Columbian* newspaper in Washington state drops business section.

FEBRUARY 2012
- The Aon company blocks journalists from attending its annual meeting.
- Media organizations fight with business groups who want to create a secret court in Delaware.

MARCH 2012
- *Vancouver Sun* business columnist loses defamation case.
- LexisNexis acquires *Law360* news site.
- *Denver Post* lays off business columnist.
- Bloomberg Television cuts thirty staffers.

APRIL 2012
- Fake Bank of America news release sent to Dow Jones Newswires and the *Wall Street Journal*.

MAY 2012
- One of Greece's largest banks sues Reuters and a reporter.
- Business journalist creates nonprofit to do investigative reporting.

JUNE 2012

- *Wall Street Journal* editor resigns after acknowledging ethics violation.
- New Orleans *Times-Picayune* lays off business editor, business reporter.
- *Birmingham News* lays off business editor and two business reporters.
- *Smart Money* to halt print publication.
- Groupon bans business media from annual meeting.

JULY 2012

- *Hudson Valley Business Journal* ends twenty-six-year print run.
- *Wall Street Journal* intern fired for faking quotes.

AUGUST 2012

- *Toronto Star* mistakenly reports that a business has closed.

SEPTEMBER 2012

- Coal company sues reporter alleging libel.
- *The Street* acquires *The Deal* magazine.
- Financial news site *Quartz* launched by the *Atlantic.*

OCTOBER 2012

- Relativity Media CEO asks *The New Yorker* to retract article about his management style.
- Dominion Energy refuses to talk to *Virginia-Pilot* reporter who covers it.

NOVEMBER 2012

- *Bloomberg BusinessWeek* criticized for poll on attractive B-school students.
- *Idaho Stateman* cuts stand-alone business section.
- Multiple business media report Google acquisition of Wi-Fi operator based on fake news release.

DECEMBER 2012

- *Nightly Business Report* lays off seven, closes Chicago bureau.
- Securities and Exchange Commission charges *The Street* with accounting fraud.

JANUARY 2013

- Fort Worth daily newspaper lays off consumer watchdog columnist.
- CNET parent CBS Corporation forces tech news site to withdraw award from *The Dish* because of litigation between the two companies.

- Reuters lays off nine editorial staffers.
- *Corporate Report Wisconsin* magazine closes after twenty-eight years.
- *Financial Times* announces plans to cut thirty-five jobs.
- Associated Press reporter duped by fake LinkedIn account.

FEBRUARY 2013

- *MarketWatch* lays off nine editorial staffers.
- Marketing company apologizes for having employees pose as home buyers on TV newscasts.
- Casino owner Sheldon Adelson sues *Wall Street Journal* alleging libel.

MARCH 2013

- *Black Enterprise* cuts its yearly issues to ten from twelve.

APRIL 2013

- Amazon founder Jeff Bezos invests in *Business Insider*.
- Reuters publishes obituary of investor George Soros, who hadn't died.
- Reuters fires editor indicted on hacking charges.
- Retailer Target begins selling products endorsed by *Wired* magazine.

MAY 2013

- *Bloomberg News* reporters accused of spying on executives using terminal.
- *BuzzFeed* launches business news section.

JUNE 2013

- Zynga blocks reporters from attending annual meeting.

JULY 2013

- Saudi prince alleges *Forbes* has defamed his country.
- *Salt Lake Tribune* business editor is laid off.
- The *Oklahoman* cuts Money & Markets page.

AUGUST 2013

- Cleveland *Plain Dealer* cuts stand-alone business section.
- *Wired* uses reporters to produce sponsored content.
- CNET sells reporter's review to company as an ad.

SEPTEMBER 2013

- *Time* and CNN agree to end *CNN Money* joint venture.
- Reuters cancels Next, its website for consumers.

OCTOBER 2013

- *Chicago Sun-Times* halts publication of print business magazine *Grid*.
- Fake news release is published on Dow Jones Newswires.
- *Vancouver Sun* cuts its Monday business section.

NOVEMBER 2013

- *Bloomberg News* lays off fifty journalists.

DECEMBER 2013

- Tech news site *The Information* launched by former *Wall Street Journal* reporter.
- *Canadian Business* and *Profit* magazines merge publications.
- Bloomberg editor in chief reaffirms ban on covering itself.
- Reuters cuts forty-five editorial jobs.

JANUARY 2014

- Tech journalists Kara Swisher and Walt Mossberg leave *Wall Street Journal* to start tech news site *Recode*.
- *Orange County Register* lays off investigative business reporter.
- Dow Jones & Company CEO departs amid revenue decline.
- Bloomberg News wins lawsuit over publishing transcript of a company's conference call.

FEBRUARY 2014

- *Seeking Alpha* removes stories with fake bylines.

MARCH 2014

- *Business Insider* raises $12 million from investors.
- The Dolan Company, parent of business newspapers, files for Chapter 11 bankruptcy reorganization.
- E. W. Scripps Company purchases *Kitsap Peninsula Business Journal* in Washington state.
- Bloomberg News accused of spiking stories in China, and some staff quit as a result.

APRIL 2014

- American City Business Journals launches *Bizwomen* news site.

MAY 2014

- *Fortune* journalist says he was offered shares in an upcoming tech initial public offering.
- McDonald's blocks media from attending its annual meeting.

JUNE 2014

- *Wall Street Journal* removes articles from archives written by freelance writer who accepted gifts.
- Associated Press announces it will begin producing earnings stories using technology.

JULY 2014

- *Wall Street Journal* lays of more than twenty editorial staffers.
- Court dismisses case against *Seeking Alpha* asking it to disclose anonymous writer.
- New York *Daily News* lays off two business journalists.

AUGUST 2014

- Bloomberg News lays off fourteen journalists in Washington bureau.
- Politicians complain about Securities and Exchange Commission leaks to business reporters.

SEPTEMBER 2014

- Asian investors close deal to purchase *Forbes* magazine.
- Memphis *Commercial Appeal* cuts stand-alone business news section.
- Koch Industries complains reporter only used 5 percent of its responses.

OCTOBER 2014

- CNN cancels its *CNN Money* show.

NOVEMBER 2014

- Wall Street Journal ends its radio network, which ran across the country.
- CNBC lays off eight website staffers.
- Uber executive suggests investigating reporters who write negative stories about the company.

- Bloomberg News mandates that enterprise stories should include at least one female source.

DECEMBER 2014

- Washington Post moves its *Capitol Business* publication content to inside main newspaper.

JANUARY 2015

- CNBC begins moving some stories behind a paywall.
- Judge fines whistleblowers for speaking to media about fraud at banks.
- *Business Insider* gets $25 million in funding from investors.
- *Wall Street Journal* ends its Sunday section, which appeared in newspapers across the country.

FEBRUARY 2015

- *Crain's New York Business* lays off 40 percent of editorial staff.
- *Idaho Statesman* drops stock market report from the daily newspaper.
- Little Rock daily newspaper cuts printed stock listings.
- Lumber Liquidators stock plunges after CEO mentions upcoming *60 Minutes* show.
- Online subscribers top 500,000 for *Financial Times*.

MARCH 2015

- Tech news site *Gigaom* closes.

APRIL 2015

- *Seeking Alpha* launches a premium service.
- *BuzzFeed News* removes articles after advertiser complains.

MAY 2015

- *American Lawyer* parent lays off sixty-one employees.
- *Forbes* sells majority stake in *RealClearPolitics*.
- Personal finance news site NerdWallet raises $64 million from investors.
- Vox Media acquires tech news site *Recode*.

JUNE 2015

- *Consumer Reports* lays off seventeen staffers, closes *ShopSmart* magazine.

- *Wall Street Journal* lays off bulk of personal finance staff.
- Pittsburgh hospital bans sale of local newspaper in gift shop after coverage.
- *Tampa Tribune* lays off business editor for second time in five years.

JULY 2015

- *Kansas City (MO) Star* dissolves business news desk.
- Fake *Bloomberg News* story reports that Twitter is being sold.
- San Diego business newspaper announces it will close after 129 years.
- McGraw-Hill acquires business newsletter publisher SNL Financial.
- LexisNexis buys regulatory news wire MLex for an undisclosed amount.

AUGUST 2015

- Pearson sells stake in the *Economist* for $730 million.
- *Boston Globe* launches *STAT* to cover health care.

SEPTEMBER 2015

- *Bloomberg News* lays off fifty-five editorial staffers.
- *Wall Street Journal* launches service covering central banks that costs $2,000.
- Vanguard fires employee who spoke to *The Street* journalist.
- Massey Energy sues Bloomberg over leaked documents.
- German media company buys 88 percent stake in *Business Insider* for $343 million.

OCTOBER 2015

- *Forbes* publishes profile of fictional businessman.

NOVEMBER 2015

- Fourteen journalists leave *Bloomberg Markets* magazine.
- Nikkei completes acquisition of *Financial Times*.

DECEMBER 2015

- *American Banker* stops daily print edition.
- Business newspapers owned by the Dolan Company sold for $35 million.
- Twitter deletes two tweets from business reporter at the request of Bank of America.

JANUARY 2016

- Personal finance news site *Grow* launches.
- *Chicago Tribune* cuts Monday business section.
- Journalist stands by story removed from *Atlanta Business Chronicle* site.

FEBRUARY 2016

- Business news channel *Cheddar* launches, aimed at eighteen- to thirty-four-year-old market.

MARCH 2016

- *Investor's Business Daily* becomes a weekly and cut twenty news jobs.
- *Wall Street Week* moves to Fox Business Network.
- *International Business Times* lays off at least fifteen editorial employees.

APRIL 2016

- *Tulsa World* moves its business news to inside its local news section.
- *Huffington Post* kills story on Uber after founder joins its board.

MAY 2016

- Real estate news site *Bisnow* sold for $50 million.
- Hedge fund operator files libel and defamation suit against Bloomberg News.

JUNE 2016

- *Consumer Reports* accepts buyout offers from fifty employees.
- The *Columbian* newspaper in Vancouver, Washington, lays off business editor.
- Environmental group buys ads in *Wall Street Journal* criticizing its editorial page.
- *International Business Times* lays off at least fourteen editorial staffers.

JULY 2016

- Tech editor and tech reporter laid off at *Newsweek*.
- WeWork files lawsuit against ex-employee for giving financial information to Bloomberg News.
- *Market News International* lays off seventeen editorial staffers.
- Department of Homeland Security attempts to take two cell phones from *Wall Street Journal* reporter.

AUGUST 2016

- North Dakota paper *Bismarck Tribune* cuts printed stock listings.
- Crain Communications sells *Business Insurance* for an undisclosed amount.

SEPTEMBER 2016

- Business news channel *Cheddar* raises $8 million.

OCTOBER 2016

- Rogers Communications stops printing copies of *MoneySense* and *Canadian Business.*
- Bloomberg Television moves to twenty-four-hour schedule.
- *The Street* cuts five editorial staffers.
- *Harvard Business Review* announces it will cut print issues from ten to six in 2017.

NOVEMBER 2016

- American City Business Journals closes *Upstart Business Journal.*
- Layoffs at Bloomberg News total thirty journalists.
- *MarketWatch* lays off five editorial staffers.

DECEMBER 2016

- *Roanoke Business* magazine ceases publication.
- *STAT News* launches $299/year subscription plan.
- Bloomberg ends publication of *Bloomberg Pursuits.*

JANUARY 2017

- *New London Day* in Connecticut cuts stand-alone business section.
- *Wall Street Journal* settles libel suit with billionaire Sheldon Adelson with no money changing hands.
- *Entrepreneur* cuts to print issues from schedule.

FEBRUARY 2017

- *The Street* lays off ten editorial staffers.
- *Financial Times* cuts twenty editorial jobs.
- *Milwaukee Journal Sentinel* cuts stock listings, stand-alone business section.

MARCH 2017

- Angry CEO tweets sex phone hotline phone number to reporter asking for an interview.
- JetSmarter sends agreement to business journalists in attempt to get them to cover company uncritically.
- Dow Jones launches personal finance site *Moneyish*.
- Hedge fund granted injunction preventing Reuters story.

APRIL 2017

- *Richmond Times-Dispatch* cuts stand-alone business section and lays off deputy business editor.
- Securities and Exchange Commission files charges against writers paid to pump stock prices on business news websites.
- *SmartCEO* magazine closes after fifteen years.
- Personal finance site NerdWallet lays off forty.

MAY 2017

- *Paste* magazine ends business news section.
- Coal company files defamation suit against the *New York Times*.
- Sears CEO blames business media for company woes.
- Google fires employees for leaking to tech reporters.

JUNE 2017

- *Fortune* and *Money* magazines cut editorial staffers.
- *Las Vegas Business Press* ends print publication after thirty-four years.
- *Bloomberg Businessweek* content goes behind paywall.
- *Bloomberg News* lays off half-dozen staffers.
- *New York Times* ends Haggler consumer column.

JULY 2017

- Business owner sues *Crain's Chicago Business*, alleging defamation.
- American City Business Journals papers begin charging for "People on the Move" items.
- Immigration bond company sues *BuzzFeed News*, alleging defamation.
- Business journalist joins Experian to add personal finance content to its website.

AUGUST 2017

- ABC settles defamation lawsuit filed by South Dakota meat producer for $177 million.
- DoubleLine Capital attacks *Wall Street Journal* reporters on Twitter for unpublished article.

SEPTEMBER 2017

- *USA Today* lays off two reporters from Money desk.
- *Wall Street Journal* ends Europe print edition.

OCTOBER 2017

- Time Inc. cuts *Fortune* issues to twelve from sixteen.
- *Arkansas Democrat-Gazette* cuts Monday business news section.
- Investment adviser TD Ameritrade launches a financial news network.
- *Consumer Reports* shuts Consumerist website.

NOVEMBER 2017

- Walt Disney Company bans *Los Angeles Times* reporters from movie previews because of negative business-related stories.
- *Business Insider* rolls out paid content site.
- Personal finance site NerdWallet lays off fifty-three staffers.
- *Forbes* cuts its print editions to 10/year.
- HQ Trivia CEO threatens to fire reporter for talking to reporter.

DECEMBER 2017

- *The Street* lays off ten editorial staffers.
- *Mashable* lays off two business reporters.
- Software company sues tech news site *Ars Technica*, claiming defamation.

JANUARY 2018

- The Raleigh *News & Observer* drops the last of its printed stock listings.
- Market News International lays off reporters, its third layoff in eighteen months.
- Morgan Stanley fires executive after he harassed Reuters reporter.
- *Florida Times-Union* in Jacksonville cuts two business reporters.

FEBRUARY 2018

- *Wired* magazine adds a paywall.
- Canadian government tells companies involved in its fighter jet purchases not to talk to journalists.
- Forbes acquires *The Memo* to expand European editorial.
- *Omaha World-Herald* cuts two business reporters and stand-alone business section.

MARCH 2018

- *Columbus Dispatch* moves business news into its metro and state section.
- Business news channel raises $22 million in funding.
- *Institutional Investor* ends print edition.

APRIL 2018

- Goodyear Tire & Rubber asks judge to call reporter and ask him not to publish documents.
- Apple warns employees to stop leaking information to media.
- The Raleigh *News & Observer* drops Sunday Work & Money section.
- *Sacramento Bee* lays off two business reporters.
- Student loan company creates fake expert quoted in CNBC and *Washington Post* stories.

MAY 2018

- Bloomberg launches a paywall to its website starting at $34.99 per month.
- Equifax Inc. bars reporters from annual meeting.
- Harley-Davidson bars reporters from annual meeting.
- Tesla Motors CEO Elon Musk criticizes coverage of his company.

JUNE 2018

- Canadian Broadcasting Corporation ends *On the Money* show.
- *Central Valley Business Journal* in California shuts down after twenty-eight years.

JULY 2018

- Business news site *Quartz* is sold by the *Atlantic* to Japanese company.
- Personal finance journalist Jean Chatzky acquires personal finance site *DailyWorth*.

- *Forbes* removes column arguing Amazon should take over libraries.
- Crain Communications sells *InvestmentNews* for $27.1 million.

AUGUST 2018
- *Investopedia* lays off one-third of its staff.

SEPTEMBER 2018
- *Grand Rapids Business Journal* sold to private company.
- Craig Newmark provides $20 million to tech news startup *The Markup*.

OCTOBER 2018
- *Minnesota Business* magazine ceases operations.
- Biotech investor sues health care industry site *STAT*.
- Amazon pulls ads from Bloomberg over China hack story.
- Bloomberg BNA lays off forty-six staffers.

NOVEMBER 2018
- Tech news site *Recode* folded into *Vox*.
- *USA Today* lays off two staffers from its Money desk.
- *Fortune* magazine sold to Asian businessman for $150 million.

DECEMBER 2018
- *The Street* sells The Deal and BoardEx for $87.3 million.
- Personal finance site NerdWallet discontinues investigations team, cuts four positions.
- *Yahoo Finance* launches premium subscription service.
- Securities and Exchange Commission charges former *Money* journalist for running a Ponzi scheme.
- *Consumer Reports* starts a show on Telemundo.

JANUARY 2019
- *Dallas Morning News* lays off two business reporters, cuts stand-alone business news section.
- *Financial Times* publishes story on fake BlackRock CEO letter.
- *Indianapolis Star* drops two business columnists.
- *San Francisco Chronicle* publishes story on fake press release.
- Condé Nast launches *Vogue Business*.

FEBRUARY 2019

- *Corpus Christi Business News* becomes online-only publication.
- *Capitol Forum* sues Bloomberg, alleging improper use of its content.
- Personal finance site *The Billfold* shuts down.
- Kiplinger sold to publishers of *The Week* for undisclosed amount.

MARCH 2019

- Reuters cuts twenty-five jobs in its Paris bureau.
- *Sacramento Business Journal* reporter arrested covering a protest.
- Personal finance site The Penny Hoarder cuts editorial staff.
- Wirecard sues *Financial Times* over its coverage. Company later collapses.

APRIL 2019

- British Airways stops offering *Financial Times* on flights after critical articles.
- *Money* announces it will stop printing magazine after failed sale.
- Bloomberg adds luxury real estate listings to its website.
- Business news channel *Cheddar* is sold for $200 million to Altice USA.

MAY 2019

- Parent of Dealreporter and Mergermarket sold for $1.7 billion.
- *Quartz* rolls out a metered paywall.
- CBC announces plans to launch new weekly business show in Canada.
- *Fortune* announces it is raising its price.

JUNE 2019

- *Consumer Reports* receives $6 million gift from Craig Newmark.
- Kiplinger acquires some of *Money*'s subscribers.
- *Yahoo Finance* launches subscription service for investors starting at $34.99 per month.
- *CNET* closes its quarterly print magazine.
- *Quartz* lays off business-side employees.

JULY 2019

- *Entrepreneur* lays off four editorial staffers in a move to digital.
- *Forbes* adds ten editorial staffers.
- Retailer Staples Inc. launches its own magazine.
- *Forbes* removes article about disgraced money manager Jeffrey Epstein.

AUGUST 2019

- Newspaper company GateHouse Media and the Midwest Center for Investigative Reporting partner to create agricultural news.
- Financial news site *The Street* is sold for $16.5 million to Maven.
- American City Business Journals buys majority stake in business data company.
- *Financial Times* invests in the *Business of Fashion*.
- A market-research firm working for Facebook offers to pay journalists hundreds of dollars share their thoughts about social media.
- Reports disclose that fictitious personal finance expert called "Patricia Russell" convinced multiple business journalists to include her in stories.

SEPTEMBER 2019

- *Consumers Digest* sued by freelancers owed payment.
- Kiplinger lays off eleven staffers as part of a reorganization.
- Medium launches business magazine *Marker*.
- *BuzzFeed News* files documents alleging Tesla CEO Elon Musk is intimidating one of its reporters.
- *Fortune* magazine hires twelve new editorial staffers.

OCTOBER 2019

- Bloomberg Law retracts article about Labor Department official.
- Meredith Corporation sells personal finance magazine *Money* to digital advertising firm.

NOVEMBER 2019

- Canadian-based tech news site The Logic raises $1.8 million.
- *Business People–Vermont* magazine closes its doors.
- McClatchy ends Saturday publication of its daily newspapers.

DECEMBER 2019

- CNBC ends *Nightly Business Report* show on public television.
- An Arizona business owner grabs an *Arizona Republic* reporter's cellphone, which was recording the conversation, during an interview.
- Bloomberg Media acquires *CityLab* and lays off staffers.

JANUARY 2020

- Two television stations form editorial partnership with *Dayton Business Journal*.
- Chicago radio station severs ties with *Crain's Chicago Business* over a story about its parent.
- *Buffalo Law Journal* merges with *Buffalo Business First*.
- Quibi CEO Meg Whitman apologizes for comparing biz journalists to sexual predators.
- Tech news site *dot.LA* launches.

FEBRUARY 2020

- *Hollywood Reporter* cuts editorial staff.
- Chinese government revokes press credentials of *Wall Street Journal* reporters.

MARCH 2020

- *Fortune* magazine launches a paywall.
- *Los Angeles Times* merges its business news section with main news section.

APRIL 2020

- *Bellingham Business Journal* in Washington state closes.
- Cleveland *Plain Dealer* lays off its business news desk.
- Parent of *American Banker*, Bond Buyer lays off twenty-seven staffers.
- *Reading Eagle* newspaper in Pennsylvania puts Business Weekly inside the paper instead of a pull-out section.
- Tech news site *GeekWire* cuts five staff positions.
- *Fortune* magazine lays off thirty-five staffers.
- Tech news site *Protocol* lays off thirteen editorial staffers.
- Business news channel *Cheddar* closes its Los Angeles studio and makes layoffs.

MAY 2020

- Vancouver, Washington, *Columbian* eliminates daily business page and Sunday business section.
- *Hollywood Reporter* faces questions about ownership interference in coverage.

- *Wired* magazine lays off at least three editorial staffers, including transportation editor.
- Business news site *Quartz* lays off at least thirty-five editorial staffers.
- Local TV station runs segment produced by Amazon touting its efforts to keep warehouse workers safe.

JUNE 2020

- Indictment alleges lobbyist paid writer to promote bitcoin in publications such as *Investor's Business Daily*.

JULY 2020

- *Wall Street Journal* staffers ask for changes in race policy and business coverage.

AUGUST 2020

- Subscriptions to Dow Jones & Company products hit 3.8 million.
- Fake news story sends railroad stock soaring.

SEPTEMBER 2020

- *Vogue Business* launches subscriptions starting at $154 a year.
- Red Ventures agrees to acquire tech news site *CNET* for $500 million.
- Tech news site *Digital Trends* lays off thirteen editorial staffers.

OCTOBER 2020

- Tesla drops its public relations department.
- *Business Insider* buys a majority stake in *Morning Brew*.
- *MarketWatch* adds a paywall around its content.

NOVEMBER 2020

- BridgeTower Media business newspapers sold to private equity firm.

NOTES

INTRODUCTION

1. Juliann Francis, Zoom conversation with author, October 27, 2020.

2. Francis.

3. Penelope Muse Abernathy, *News Deserts and Ghost Newspapers: Will Local News Survive?* (Chapel Hill: University of North Carolina Press, 2020), 12–14.

4. Francis, Zoom.

5. Alan M. Jacobs, J. Scott Matthews, Timothy Hicks and Eric Merkley, "Whose News? Class-Biased Economic Reporting in the United States," Washington Center for Equitable Growth, March 3, 2020, https://equitablegrowth.org/working-papers/whose-news-class-biased-economic-reporting-in-the-united-states/.

6. Chris Roush, "Omaha Daily Loses Two Biz Reporters, Standalone Biz Section," *TalkingBizNews*, February 20, 2018, https://talkingbiznews.com/they-talk-biz-news/omaha-world-herald-loses-two-biz-reporters-standalone-biz-section/.

7. Chuck Melvin, "The Journal Sentinel's Business Section Is Changing," *Milwaukee Journal Sentinel*, February 25, 2017, https://www.jsonline.com/story/money/business/2017/02/25/journalism-evolves-newspapers-must-adjust/98361498/.

8. US Bureau of Labor Statistics, "Job Growth at Small Businesses, 1992–2013," *Economics Daily*, May 12, 2014, https://www.bls.gov/opub/ted/2014/ted_20140512.htm.

9. Francis, Zoom.

10. Chris Roush, "How a Lack of Business Coverage Is Hurting Our State," *WRAL-TechWire*, August 16, 2017, https://www.wraltechwire.com/2017/08/16/how-a-lack-of-business-coverage-is-hurting-our-state/16884279/#2AT7COApZwobwbVY.99.

11. Mary Jane Pardue, "Most Business Editors Find Journalism Graduates Still Unprepared," *Journalism & Mass Communication Educator* 69, no. 1 (March 2014): 49–60, https://doi.org/10.1177/1077695813506989.

12. Ben Popken, "SEC Cracks Down on Fake Stock News," *NBC News*, April 11, 2017, https://www.nbcnews.com/business/markets/sec-cracks-down-fake-stock-news-n745141.

13. Jack Loechner, "Fake News OK for Some," *MediaPost*, July 26, 2018, https://www.mediapost.com/publications/article/322551/fake-news-ok-for-some.html.

14. Steven Pearlstein, " 'No Comment': The Death of Business Reporting," *Washington Post*, July 26, 2018, https://www.washingtonpost.com/business/no-comment-the-death-of-business-reporting/2018/07/06/4fbca852-7e31-11e8-bb6b-c1cb691f1402_story.html.

15. Matthew Herper, "Elizabeth Holmes' Superpower," *Forbes*, May 31, 2018, https://www.forbes.com/sites/matthewherper/2018/05/31/elizabeth-holmes-super power /?sh=7b3dd2c519ef.

16. Ryan Felton, "Goodyear Asked a Judge to Call Jalopnik and Request We Not Publish Documents on Its Dangerous RV Tire," *Jalopnik*, April 10, 2018, https://jalop nik.com/goodyear-asked-a-judge-to-call-jalopnik-and-request-we-1825120219.

17. Erik Wemple, "Disney Declines to Participate in L.A. Times Movie Preview over Stories on Company's Anaheim Dealings," *Washington Post*, November 3, 2017, https://www.washingtonpost.com/blogs/erik-wemple/wp/2017/11/03/disney-de clined-to-participate-in-l-a-times-movie-preview-over-stories-on-companys-anaheim -dealings/.

18. Tracy Rucinski, "Sears CEO Lampert Blames Company's Woes on 'Irrespon-sible' Media," Reuters, May 11, 2017, https://www.reuters.com/article/us-sears-share holders-idUSKBN1862R2.

19. Dean Starkman, "A Narrowed Gaze: How the Business Press Forgot the Rest of Us," *Columbia Journalism Review*, January/February 2012, https://archives.cjr.org/cover _story/a_narrowed_gaze.php.

CHAPTER 1. A SYMBIOTIC RELATIONSHIP

1. David Forsyth, *The Business Press in America: 1750–1865* (Philadelphia: Chilton, 1964), 12.

2. Forsyth, 11.

3. "Introduction of Paper Money in China," *Jeremy Norman's History of Informa-tion*, accessed May 3, 2021, https://historyofinformation.com/index.php?cat=4 9#en try_201.

4. Randall L. Pouwels, *The African and Middle Eastern World, 600–1500* (Oxford: Oxford University Press, 2005), 139.

5. "The History of Accounting—from Record Keeping to Artificial Intelligence," *Medius*, August 29, 2020, https://www.medius.com/blog/history-of-accounting/.

6. George Matthews, *News and Rumor in Renaissance Europe: The Fugger Newslet-ters* (New York: Capricorn, 1959), 19–20.

7. Greg Steinmetz, *The Richest Man Who Ever Lived: The Life and Times of Jacob Fugger* (New York: Simon & Schuster, 2016), 15.

8. Alfred Chandler Jr. and James Cortada, *A Nation Transformed by Information: How Information Has Shaped the United States from Colonial Times to Present* (Oxford: Oxford University Press, 2003).

9. Rictor Norton, *Early Eighteenth-Century Newspaper Reports*, available at https://grubstreet.rictornorton.co.uk/.

10. Norton.

11. Norton.

12. Alfred D. Chandler, "Henry Varnum Poor: Editor of the American Railroad Journal" (master's thesis, University of North Carolina, 1951), 8.

13. Gerald Baldasty, *The Commercialization of News in the Nineteenth Century* (Madison: University of Wisconsin Press, 1992), 153.

14. Alfred P. Sloan Jr., "My Years with General Motors," *Fortune*, September 1963.

15. L. M. Simons, "Follow the Money," *American Journalism Review*, November 1999, 56.

16. Norman Solomon, "Money Makes Headlines in Today's News Coverage," *Nieman Reports*, Summer 2002, 17.

17. "The Quality of Business Journalism in America," Louis Harris Poll (Boston: John Hancock Financial Services, 1992), 3.

18. Mike Haggerty and Wallace Rasmussen, *The Headline vs. the Bottom Line: Mutual Distrust between Business and the News Media* (Nashville: The First Amendment Center, Freedom Forum Institute, 1994), 20.

19. "Business Journalism Surveys," a Selzer & Co. poll (Reston, VA: American Press Institute, 2002), 2.

20. Maha Rafi Atal, "The Cultural and Economic Power of Advertisers in the Business Press," *Journalism* (November 2017): 1–18.

21. Haggerty and Rasmussen, *The Headline vs. The Bottom Line*, 16.

22. Grant Hannis, "Taking Care of Business: Equipping Students to Become Business Journalists," *Journalism & Mass Communication Educator* 71, no. 3 (Fall 2016): 344–59.

23. Paul C. Tetlock, "Giving Content to Investor Sentiment: The Role of Media in the Stock Market," *Journal of Finance* 62, no. 3 (June 2007): 1139–68.

24. Craig Carroll, "How the Mass Media Influence Perceptions of Corporate Reputation: Exploring Agenda-Setting Effects within Business News Coverage" (PhD diss., University of Texas, 2004), https://repositories.lib.utexas.edu/bitstream/handle/2152/2153/carrollce30855.pdf?sequence=2&isAllowed=y.

25. Wang Ying, Zhang Tianzhen, and Song Jiameng, "Effects Financial Media Have on Firm Value and Suggestions for Investor Relations Media Strategy," paper presented at 2018 International Conference on Advances in Social Sciences and Sustainable Development, May 2018, available at https://www.atlantis-press.com/proceedings/asssd-18/25894426.

26. Felix Meschke, "CEO Interviews on CNBC," presentation at AFA 2003 Washington, DC, meetings, June 2004, http://dx.doi.org/10.2139/ssrn.302602.

27. Alexander Dyck and Luigi Zingales, "The Media and Asset Prices," working paper, Harvard Business School, August 2003, http://www.anderson.ucla.edu/faculty_pages/romain.wacziarg/mediapapers/DyckZingales.pdf.

28. Yi Jin, "Agenda-Setting Effects of Television News Coverage on Perceptions of Corporate Reputation" (master's thesis, University of Missouri-Columbia, 2008), 52.

29. James D. Westphal and David L. Deephouse, "Avoiding Bad Press: Interpersonal Influence in Relations between CEOs and Journalists and the Consequences for Press Reporting about Firms and Their Leadership," *Organization Science* 22, no. 4 (September 2010): 1061–86.

30. Westphal and Deephouse, 1068.

31. Gregory Miller, "The Press as a Watchdog for Accounting Fraud," *Journal of Accounting Research* 44, no. 5 (October 2006): 1001–33, https://doi.org/10.1111/j.1475-679X.2006.00224.x.

32. James Taylor, "White-Collar Crime and the Law in Nineteenth-Century Britain," *Business History* 60, no. 3 (September 2018): 343–60, https://www.tandfonline.com/doi/abs/10.1080/00076791.2017.1339691?journalCode=fbsh20.

33. Daniel Riffe and Bill Reeder, "Most Rely on Newspapers for Local Business News," *Newspaper Research Journal* 28, no. 2 (Spring 2007): 82–98.

34. Dukas Linden Public Relations, "As Financial Media Consumption Rises, US Investors Want More Positive News of Business Recovery Plans," May 5, 2020, https://www.dlpr.com/blog_posts/as-financial-media-consumption-rises-u-s-investors-want-more-positive-news-of-business-recovery-plans/.

35. Tomasz Piotr Wisniewski and Brendan Lambe, "The Role of Media in the Credit Crunch: The Case of the Banking Sector," *Journal of Economic Behavior & Organization* 85 (January 2013): 163–75.

36. Nicholas Guest, "Do Journalists Help Investors Analyze Firms' Earnings News?" (PhD diss., Massachusetts Institute of Technology Sloan School of Management, 2017), 30.

37. Samuel B. Bonsall, Jeremiah Green, and Karl A. Muller, "Market Uncertainty and the Importance of Media Coverage at Earnings Announcements," *Journal of Accounting & Economics*, September 25, 2019, https://ssrn.com/abstract=3459543.

38. Dealbook, "Taking Stock of Jim Cramer's Picks," *New York Times*, May 20, 2009, https://dealbook.nytimes.com/2009/05/20/taking-stock-of-jim-cramers-picks/.

39. Steven Goldberg, "Jim Cramer's Stock Picks Stink," *Kiplinger Personal Finance*, May 18, 2016, https://www.kiplinger.com/article/investing/t052-c007-s001-jim-cramer-s-stock-picks-stink.html.

40. Andrew Hill, "Column Inches Aid Share Prices," *The Financial Times*, May 20, 2015, https://www.ft.com/content/9ebe01e8-fb22-11e4-9aed-00144feab7de.

41. Lily H. Fang, Joel Peress, and Lu Zheng, "Does Media Coverage of Stocks Affect Mutual Funds' Trading and Performance?," *Review of Financial Studies* 27, no. 12 (December 2014): 3441–66, https://doi.org/10.1093/rfs/hhu056.

42. Francesco Marconi, "Study: News Automation by AP Increases Trading in Financial Markets," Associated Press, December 8, 2016, https://insights.ap.org/industry-trends/study-news-automation-by-ap-increases-trading-in-financial-markets.

43. Chen-Hui Wu and Chan-Jane Lin, "The Impact of Media Coverage on Investor Trading Behavior and Stock Returns," *Pacific-Basin Finance Journal* 43 (2017): 151–72.

44. Joanna Strycharz, Nadine Strauss, and Damian Trilling, "The Role of Media Coverage in Explaining Stock Market Fluctuations: Insights for Strategic Financial Communication," *International Journal of Strategic Communication* 12, no. 1 (2018): 67–85, https://dx.doi.org/10.1080/1553118X.2017.1378220.

45. Bonsall, Green, and Miller, "Market Uncertainty and the Importance of Media Coverage," 2.

46. Leland Bybee, Bryan T. Kelly, Asaf Manela, and Dacheng Xiu, "The Structure of Economic News," January 1, 2020, http://dx.doi.org/10.2139/ssrn.3446225.

47. Adam Hale Shapiro and Daniel J. Wilson, "What's in the News? A New

Economic Indicator," *FRBSF Economic Letter*, April 10, 2017, https://www.frbsf.org /economic-research/publications/economic-letter/2017/april/measuring-econom ic-sentiment-in-news/.

48. Matthew Johnson, "Regulation by Shaming: Deterrence Effects of Publicizing Violations of Workplace Safety and Health Laws," *American Economic Review* 110 (6): 1866–904.

CHAPTER 2. THE BUSINESS MODEL FAILURE

1. Martha Woodham, "Daily Papers See Circulation Slip," *Atlanta Business Chronicle*, November 29, 1999, https://www.bizjournals.com/atlanta/stories/1999/11/29 /story7.html.

2. Penelope Muse Abernathy, "Vanishing Readers and Journalists," University of North Carolina Hussman School of Journalism and Media, accessed December 12, 2020, https://www.usnewsdeserts.com/reports/news-deserts-and-ghost-newspa pers-will-local-news-survive/the-news-landscape-in-2020-transformed-and-dimin ished/vanishing-readers-and-journalists/.

3. "AJC Editor Explains Business Section Changes," *Talking Biz News*, March 8, 2009, https://talkingbiznews.com/they-talk-biz-news/ajc-editor-explains-business -section-changes/.

4. "How the Media Have Depicted the Economic Crisis during Obama's Presidency," Pew Research Center, October 5, 2009, https://www.journalism.org/2009 /10/05/covering-great-recession/.

5. Richard Perez-Pena, "Study Says Reporting on Economy Was Narrow," *New York Times*, October 5, 2009, https://www.nytimes.com/2009/10/05/business/me dia/05pew.html.

6. Lucy Sutherland, "The Marginalizing of Business News at Small and Mid-Sized American Dailies" (master's thesis, Emerson College, 2004).

7. Asher Schechter, "Business Journalism Fails Spectacularly in Holding the Powerful to Account," ProMarket, a publication of The Stigler Center at the University of Chicago Booth School of Business, May 30, 2017, https://promarket.org/2017/05/30 /business-journalism-fails-spectacularly-holding-powerful-account/.

8. Nadine Strauss, "Financial Journalism in Today's High-Frequency News and Information Era," *Journalism* 20, no. 2 (2019): 274–91, doi:10.1177/1464884917753556.

9. Craig Ey, "Business and the Media," *Philadelphia Business Journal*, February 11, 2011, https://www.bizjournals.com/philadelphia/print-edition/2011/02/04/busi ness-and-the-media.html.

10. Howard R. Gold, "Ten Years after the Financial Crisis, Business Journalism Awaits Its Reckoning," *Columbia Journalism Review*, September 17, 2018, https:// www.cjr.org/business_of_news/ten-years-financial-crisis-business-journalism.php.

11. Amy Zhang, "NYU Hosts Lecture for Wall Street Journal Editor," *Washington Square News*, September 25, 2013, https://nyunews.com/2013/09/25/wsj/.

12. Elizabeth Grieco, "Fast Facts about the Newspaper Industry's Financial Struggles as McClatchy Files for Bankruptcy," Pew Research Center, February 14, 2020,

https://www.pewresearch.org/fact-tank/2020/02/14/fast-facts-about-the-newspa per-industrys-financial-struggles/.

13. Elizabeth Grieco, "US Newspapers Have Shed Half of Their Newsroom Employees since 2008," Pew Research Center, April 20, 2020, https://www.pewresearc h.org/fact-tank/2020/04/20/u-s-newsroom-employment-has-dropped-by-a-quarter -since-2008/.

14. J. Clara Chan, "US Newsrooms Lost a Record 16,160 Jobs in 2020, Study Finds," *The Wrap*, January 7, 2020, https://www.thewrap.com/2020-newsroom-lay offs-data/.

15. Michael Barthel, "5 Key Takeaways about the State of the News Media in 2018," Pew Research Center, July 23, 2019, https://www.pewresearch.org/fact-tank /2019/07/23/key-takeaways-state-of-the-news-media-2018/.

16. Barthel.

17. Abernathy, "Vanishing Readers and Journalists."

18. John Gramlich, "19 Striking Findings from 2019," Pew Research Center, December 13, 2019, https://www.pewresearch.org/fact-tank/2019/12/13/19-striking -findings-from-2019/.

19. Brad Adgate, "Newspaper Revenue Drops as Local News Interest Rises amid Coronavirus," *Forbes*, April 13, 2020, https://www.forbes.com/sites/bradadgate /2020/04/13/newspapers-are-struggling-with-coronavirus/?sh=14d731f739ef.

20. Julie Posetti, Emily Bell, and Pete Brown, "Journalism and the Pandemic Survey," International Center for Journalists, July 2020, https://www.icfj.org/our -work/journalism-and-pandemic-survey.

21. "American Views 2020: Trust, Media and Democracy," Gallup and the John S. and James L. Knight Foundation, November 9, 2020, https://knightfoundation.org /wp-content/uploads/2020/08/American-Views-2020-Trust-Media-and-Democracy .pdf.

22. Megan Brenan, "Americans Remain Distrustful of Mass Media," Gallup, September 30, 2020, https://news.gallup.com/poll/321116/americans-remain-dis trustful-mass-media.aspx.

23. Megan Brenan and Helen Stubbs, "News Media Viewed as Biased but Crucial to Democracy," Gallup, August 4, 2020, https://news.gallup.com/poll/316574 /news-media-viewed-biased-crucial-democracy.aspx.

24. James McCarthy, "Why Do Business Reporters Hate Business?," *National Review*, November 30, 2020, https://www.nationalreview.com/2020/11/why-do-busi ness-reporters-hate-business/.

25. James Berger, "This Is the Media's Real Bias—Pro-Business, Pro-Corporate, Pro-CEO," *Salon*, October 30, 2015, https://www.salon.com/2015/10/30/this_is_the _medias_real_bias_pro_business_pro_corporate_pro_ceo/.

26. Liz Ryan, "The Nasty Bias in Business Journalism," *Huffington Post*, December 15, 2012, https://www.huffpost.com/entry/nasty-bias-business-journalism _b_1963044.

27. Tomi Nokelainen and Juho Kanniainen, "Coverage Bias in Business News:

Evidence and Methodological Implications," *Management Research Review* 41, no. 4 (2018): 487–503, https://doi.org/10.1108/MRR-02-2017-0048.

28. Chris Roush, "Ex-Fox Business Anchor Claims Anti-Business Bias in Media," *Talking Biz News*, September 15, 2014, https://talkingbiznews.com/they-talk-biz-news/ex-fox-business-anchor-claims-anti-business-bias-in-media/.

29. Chris Roush, "Media Bias Hurts Understanding of the Economy," *Talking Biz News*, June 13, 2007, https://talkingbiznews.com/they-talk-biz-news/media-bias-hurts-understanding-of-the-economy/.

30. Alan M. Jacobs, J. Scott Matthews, Timothy Hicks, and Eric Merkley, "Whose News? Class-Biased Economic Reporting in the United States," Washington Center for Equitable Growth, March 3, 2020, https://equitablegrowth.org/working-papers/whose-news-class-biased-economic-reporting-in-the-united-states/.

31. "Accuracy and Bias in the News Media," Gallup Inc. and the John S. and James L. Knight Foundation, June 20, 2018, https://knightfoundation.org/reports/perceived-accuracy-and-bias-in-the-news-media/.

32. Jon Christian, "One of the Web's Most Prolific Online Marketing Writers Has Been Promoting His Clients in Articles for Forbes, Entrepreneur, and Inc. Magazine," *BuzzFeed News*, July 2, 2018, https://www.buzzfeednews.com/article/jonchristian/jayson-demers-audienceboom-forbes-entrepreneur-pay-for-play#.bqAOyPPdv.

33. US Small Business Administration Office of Advocacy, "Small Businesses Generate 44 Percent of US Economic Activity," January 30, 2019, https://advocacy.sba.gov/2019/01/30/small-businesses-generate-44-percent-of-u-s-economic-activity/.

34. George McKerrow, telephone interview, December 7, 2020.

35. Sougata Mukherjee, "Buoyed by Area's Economic Drivers, TBJ Hits News Milestone," *Triangle Business Journal*, January 30, 2020, https://www.bizjournals.com/triangle/news/2020/01/30/editors-notebookbuoyed-by-areas-economic-drivers.html?iana.

36. Lesley Weidenbener, "Greg Morris to Retire as Publisher of IBJ, Indiana Lawyer," *Indianapolis Business Journal*, December 11, 2020, https://www.ibj.com/articles/greg-morris-to-retire-as-publisher-of-ibj-indiana-lawyer.

37. "Willingness to Pay for News Online," Boston Consulting Group, November 2009, https://la-rem.com/wp-content/uploads/2013/12/BCG-Monde.pdf.

38. Richard Fletcher, "Paying for News and the Limits of Subscription," Reuters Institute for the Study of Journalism, https://www.digitalnewsreport.org/survey/2019/paying-for-news-and-the-limits-of-subscription/.

39. Rob Salkowitz, "Survey: US Consumers Love Online News but Won't Pay for It," *Forbes*, February 18, 2020, https://www.forbes.com/sites/robsalkowitz/2020/02/18/survey-us-consumers-love-online-news-but-wont-pay-for-it/?sh=288c745c1083.

CHAPTER 3. THE DOMINATORS

1. Lionel Barber, "Too Big to Fail: The Future of Financial Journalism," speech delivered at City University, November 22, 2018, https://aboutus.ft.com/en-gb/announcements/too-big-to-fail-the-future-of-financial-journalism/.

2. "Award-Winning Seamless Newsroom," *Bloomberg News*, accessed November 25, 2020, https://www.bloombergmedia.com/talent/.

3. "Bloomberg vs. Capital IQ, vs. FactSet vs. Thomson Reuters Eikon," Wall Street Prep, https://www.wallstreetprep.com/knowledge/bloomberg-vs-capital-iq-vs-factset-vs-thomson-reuters-eikon/.

4. "Sign Up for a Wall Street Journal Subscription," *Wall Street Journal*, accessed November 25, 2020, https://store.wsj.com/shop/us/us/wsjusns20a/?inttracking Code=aaqwzr8c&icid=WSJ_ON_PHP_ACQ_NA&n2IKsaD9=n2IKsaD9&P g9aWOPT=Pg9aWOPT&Cp5dKJWb=Cp5dKJWb&APCc9OU1=APCc9OU1.

5. "Bloomberg vs. Capital IQ."

6. Lucia Moses, "Bloomberg and Reuters: The Future of News," *Adweek*, April 2, 2012, https://www.adweek.com/digital/bloomberg-and-reuters-future-news-139320/.

7. "FT Tops One Million Paying Readers," *Financial Times*, April 1, 2019, https://aboutus.ft.com/en-gb/announcements/ft-tops-one-million-paying-readers/.

8. "Make Sense of a Disrupted World," *Financial Times*, https://subs.ft.com/spa3_uk3m?segmentId=6ef08f79-bae9-bfdb-a1af-17ce5e3dea7c&utm_us=JJYAAR&ds_medium=cpc&ds_rl=1266218&gclid=CjoKCQiA2uH-BRCCARI sAEeef3mkz7sZhbY7tcdVfOfU9VxX1ZMj_L3sejqCAOKkoxsyIN6IG0ZZTOAaAt 2LEALw_wcB&gclsrc=aw.ds.

9. "Subscribe to CNBC Pro," CNBC, accessed November 25, 2020, https://www.cnbc.com/application/pro/.

10. Tracy M. Cook, "How Much US Newspapers Charge for Digital Subscriptions," American Press Institute, February 14, 2018, https://www.americanpressinstitute.org/publications/reports/digital-subscription-pricing/.

11. "Paying for News: Why People Subscribe and What It Says about the Future of Journalism," American Press Institute, May 2, 2017, https://www.americanpressinstitute.org/publications/reports/survey-research/paying-for-news/.

12. Richard Fletcher, "How and Why People Are Paying for Online News," Reuters Institute for the Study of Journalism, https://www.digitalnewsreport.org/survey/2020/how-and-why-people-are-paying-for-online-news/.

13. "News and Research," *Bloomberg News*, accessed November 25, 2020, https://www.bloomberg.com/company/news-and-research/.

14. "News and Research."

15. Daniel Kadlec, "How Bloomberg Pressures Editors; They Can't Pay for the Machine—but They Can Get It for Credit," *Columbia Journalism Review* 36, no. 3 (1997): 39.

16. Chris Roush, "Bloomberg Maintains Market Share Lead over Reuters," *Talking Biz News*, March 28, 2019, https://talkingbiznews.com/they-talk-biz-news/bloomberg-maintains-market-share-lead-over-reuters/.

17. "Average Household Income of a Bloomberg Pursuits Reader: $575,000," *Capital New York*, June 8, 2015.

18. Chris Roush, "CEO Sees International Potential with Dow Jones Properties," *Talking Biz News*, August 9, 2019, https://talkingbiznews.com/they-talk-biz-news/ceo-sees-international-potential-with-dow-jones-properties/.

19. "WSJ.com Audience Profile," *Wall Street Journal*, accessed November 26, 2020, https://images.dowjones.com/wp-content/uploads/sites/183/2018/05/09164150/WSJ.com-Audience-Profile.pdf.

20. Federal Reserve System Board of Governors, 2019 Survey of Consumer Finances, https://www.federalreserve.gov/econres/scfindex.htm.

21. Bryan Borzykowski, "This Is How Much to Pay Yourself if You Run Your Own Business," *CNBC*, February 29, 2020, https://www.cnbc.com/2020/02/28/this-is-how-much-to-pay-yourself-as-a-business-owner.html.

22. Peter Spiegel, "Leading the FT's News Operation across North America—and Plans for Growth in the 'Land of Opportunity,'" interview by Paul Blanchard, *Media Masters*, April 9, 2020, audio, 10:43, https://www.mediamasters.fm/peter-spiegel/.

23. Spiegel.

24. Roger Yu and Nathan Bomey, "Japanese Publisher Nikkei to Buy Financial Times," *USA Today*, July 23, 2015, https://www.usatoday.com/story/money/2015/07/23/financial-times-newspaper-up-sale-owner-says/30556369/.

25. Angela Haggerty, "Financial Times Kicks Off Trials to Sell Advertisers 'Blocks of Time' to Tackle Industry's Viewability Issue," *The Drum*, May 22, 2014, https://www.thedrum.com/news/2014/05/22/financial-times-kicks-trials-sell-advertisers-blocks-time-tackle-industry-s.

26. Tim Bradshaw, "The Business of Fashion Strikes Deal with the Financial Times," *Financial Times*, August 15, 2019, https://www.ft.com/content/94962380-bf4f-11e9-89e2-41e555e96722.

27. "Financial Times Acquires Majority Stake in TNW," *Financial Times*, March 5, 2019, https://aboutus.ft.com/en-gb/announcements/financial-times-acquires-majority-stake-in-tnw/.

28. "FT Knowledge Builder Tool Helps Readers Quantify Topic Expertise," *Financial Times*, November 29, 2018, https://aboutus.ft.com/en-gb/announcements/ft-knowledge-builder-tool-helps-readers-quantify-topic-expertise/.

29. Lucinda Southern, "'Long-Term Planning': The Financial Times Now Has 1M Paying Readers," *Digiday*, April 1, 2019, https://digiday.com/media/long-term-planning-ft-now-1-million-paying-readers/.

30. Freddy Mayhew, "News Publishers Hit New Online Records with Coronavirus Coverage," *Press Gazette* [UK], April 7, 2020, https://www.pressgazette.co.uk/ft-and-reach-titles-hit-new-online-records-with-coronavirus-coverage/.

31. Melissa Mittelman, "Blackstone to Buy Thomson Reuters Unit in a $20 Billion Deal," *Bloomberg News*, January 30, 2018, https://www.bloomberg.com/news/articles/2018-01-30/blackstone-to-acquire-thomson-reuters-unit-in-20-billion-deal.

32. Josh London, "Introducing Reuters Professional: Global Intelligences Powering Smart Decisions," Reuters, November 10, 2020, https://www.reuters.com/article/rpb-reutersprofessional/introducing-reuters-professional-global-intelligence-powering-smart-decisions-idUSKBN27Q2B7.

33. Chris Roush, "Reuters News Reports Flat Revenue, Expected to Lose Revenue from Cancelled Events," *Talking Biz News*, May 9, 2020, https://talkingbiznews.com

/they-talk-biz-news/reuters-news-reports-flat-revenue-expected-to-lose-revenue
-from-cancelled-events/.

34. "Thomson Reuters Acquires FC Business Intelligence," Thomson Reuters, October 4, 2019, https://www.thomsonreuters.com/en/press-releases/2019/october /thomson-reuters-acquires-fc-business-intelligence.html.

35. "Reuters: The Facts," Thomson Reuters, accessed November 26, 2020, https://www.thomsonreuters.com/content/dam/openweb/documents/pdf/reu ters-news-agency/fact-sheet/reuters-fact-sheet.pdf.

36. "Network Profile," National Media Spots Inc., accessed November 26, 2020, https://www.nationalmediaspots.com/network-demographics/CNBC.pdf.

37. "Comcast Reports 2nd Quarter 2021 Results," Comcast Corporation, July 29, 2021, https://www.cmcsa.com/news-releases/news-release-details/comcast-reports -2nd-quarter-2021-results.

38. Brian Flood, "Fox Business Beats CNBC over Full Week for First Time Ever," The Wrap, September 20, 2016, https://www.thewrap.com/fox-business-beats-cnbc -week-tv-ratings/.

39. Chris Roush, "CNBC's Jay Yarow Is Business Journalist of the Year," Talking Biz News, December 15, 2017, https://talkingbiznews.com/we-talk-biz-news/cnbcs -jay-yarow-is-business-journalist-of-the-year/.

40. Chris Roush, "CNBC Claims No. 1 Spot among Biz News Sites," Talking Biz News, April 15, 2020, https://talkingbiznews.com/they-talk-biz-news/cnbc-claims-no-1 -spot-among-biz-news-sites/.

41. "Premium Subscriptions," The Street, accessed November 26, 2020, https:// subscription.thestreet.com/compare-all-subscriptions.

42. "Manage Your Portfolio with Seeking Alpha," Seeking Alpha, accessed November 26, 2020, https://seekingalpha.com/subscriptions.

43. "IBD Digital + Weekly Print Combo," Investor's Business Daily, accessed November 26, 2020, https://www.investors.com/product/ibd-digital-weekly-print/.

44. Daniel Fisher, "In or Out of Bankruptcy, Reorg Research Is Watching," Forbes, June 1, 2016, https://www.forbes.com/sites/danielfisher/2016/06/01/in-or -out-of-bankrtuptcy-reorg-is-watching/?sh=599e7fa1785c.

CHAPTER 4. THE PUBLIC RELATIONS FACTOR

1. Duncan Hood, "The Story Behind Our Tim Hortons Cover Story," Globe and Mail, February 22, 2017, https://www.theglobeandmail.com/report-on-business /rob-magazine/the-story-behind-our-tim-hortons-cover-story/article34103827/.

2. Hood.

3. Alexandra Tanzi and Shelly Hagan, "Public Relations Jobs Boom as Buffett Sees Newspapers Dying," Bloomberg News, April 27, 2019, https://www.bloomberg .com/news/articles/2019-04-27/public-relations-jobs-boom-as-buffett-sees-newspa pers-dying.

4. Elizabeth Grieco, "US Newspapers Have Shed Half of Their Newsroom Employees since 2008," Pew Research Center, April 20, 2020, https://www.pewresearch

.org/fact-tank/2020/04/20/u-s-newsroom-employment-has-dropped-by-a-quarter
-since-2008/.

5. "Public Relations Specialists Job Outlook," US Bureau of Labor Statistics, accessed December 1, 2010, https://www.bls.gov/ooh/media-and-communication/pub
lic-relations-specialists.htm#tab-6.

6. "Reporters, Correspondents, and Broadcast News Analysts Job Outlook," US
Bureau of Labor Statistics, accessed December 1, 2020, https://www.bls.gov/ooh/me
dia-and-communication/reporters-correspondents-and-broadcast-news-analysts.ht
m#tab-6.

7. Alex T. Williams, "The Growing Pay Gap between Journalism and Public Relations," Pew Research Center, August 11, 2014, https://www.pewresearch.org/fact
-tank/2014/08/11/the-growing-pay-gap-between-journalism-and-public-relations/.

8. Chris Roush, "Q&A: KQED's Jamali Talks about Covering PG&E," *Talking Biz
News*, July 23, 2020, https://talkingbiznews.com/highlighted-news/qa-kqeds-jamali
-talks-about-covering-pge/.

9. Chris Roush, "Utility Refuses to Talk to Newspaper," *Talking Biz News*, October 4, 2012, https://talkingbiznews.com/they-talk-biz-news/utility-refuses-to-talk
-to-newspaper/.

10. Chris Roush, "When Merrill Lynch Tried to Bribe Charles Gasparino," *Talking
Biz News*, May 21, 2015, https://talkingbiznews.com/they-talk-biz-news/when-mer
rill-lynch-tried-to-bribe-charles-gasparino/.

11. Rod Meloni, "The GM Recall: Damage Control on Steroids," *ClickonDetroit*,
March 18, 2014, https://www.clickondetroit.com/news/2014/03/18/the-gm-recall
-damage-control-on-steroids/.

12. Chris Roush, "Bloomberg Reporter Gets Last Laugh with Wal-Mart's PR Person," *Talking Biz News*, September 16, 2014, https://talkingbiznews.com/they-talk
-biz-news/bloomberg-reporter-gets-last-laugh-with-wal-marts-pr-person/.

13. Dan Beyers, "Editor's Note: Looking for the Clues to the Next Big Story,"
Washington Post, May 4, 2014, https://www.washingtonpost.com/business/capital
business/editors-note-looking-for-the-clues-to-the-next-big-story/2014/05/02/c5
1a3006-cfb7-11e3-937f-d3026234b51c_story.html.

14. Beyers.

15. Paul Waldie, "The Real Threats to Journalism in Canada," TEDx, filmed April
14, 2016, at Queens University, Kingston, Ontario, Canada, video, 10:14, https://www
.youtube.com/watch?v=N9j4MnsH-9Y&feature=emb_logo.

16. Jack Shafer, "Jeff Bezos Has Two Words for You: 'No Comment,'" Reuters,
August 19, 2013, http://blogs.reuters.com/jackshafer/2013/08/19/jeff-bezos-has-two
-words-for-you-no-comment/.

17. Harvey Radin, "Why Are We Hearing 'No Comment' So Often from Newsmakers," *Times of San Diego*, April 9, 2017, https://timesofsandiego.com/opinion
/2017/04/09/why-are-we-hearing-no-comment-so-often-from-newsmakers/.

18. Steven Pearlstein, "'No Comment': The Death of Business Reporting,"
Washington Post, July 6, 2018, https://www.washingtonpost.com/business/no-com

ment-the-death-of-business-reporting/2018/07/06/4fbca852-7e31-11e8-bb6b
-c1cb691f1402_story.html.

19. Pearlstein.

20. Julia Angwin, "The Scourge of 'On Background' in Silicon Valley," *The Markup*, October 3, 2020, https://www.getrevue.co/profile/themarkup/issues/the
-scourge-of-on-background-in-silicon-valley-281176.

21. Angwin.

22. Herb Greenberg, "Kors Calls Speculation 'False and Unfounded,'" *The Street*, July 21, 2014, https://www.thestreet.com/jim-cramer/greenberg-kors-calls-allega
tions-false-and-unfounded-12779340.

23. Rick Barrett, "Harley-Davidson Shareholders Ask Questions, but Media Kept Out of Annual Meeting," *Milwaukee Journal Sentinel*, May 10, 2018, https://
www.jsonline.com/story/money/business/2018/05/10/harley-davidson-sharehold
ers-ask-questions-media-kept-out-meeting/600370002/.

24. M. G. Siegler, "Facebook PR: Tonight We Dine in Hell!," *TechCrunch*, June 17, 2011, https://techcrunch.com/2011/06/17/we-will-fight-in-the-shade/.

25. Jacob Silverman, "Spies, Lies, and Stonewalling: What It's like to Report on Facebook," *Columbia Journalism Review*, July 1, 2020, https://www.cjr.org/special_re
port/reporting-on-facebook.php.

26. Alex Kantrowitz, "Why People Can't Stand Tech Journalists: An Interview with Casey Newton," *OneZero*, August 21, 2020, https://onezero.medium.com/why
-people-cant-stand-tech-journalists-an-interview-with-casey-newton-b5ab0826bc2a.

27. Jenny Gold, "Reporter's Notebook: The Tale of Theranos and the Mysterious Fire Alarm," California Healthline, March 21, 2018, https://californiahealthline.org
/news/reporters-notebook-the-tale-of-theranos-and-the-mysterious-fire-alarm/.

28. Gold.

29. Sophie Kleeman, "Microsoft Keeps Dossiers on Journalists and Sent Us One by Accident," *Gizmodo*, August 3, 2016, https://gizmodo.com/microsoft-keeps-dos
siers-on-journalists-and-sent-us-one-1784741210.

30. Gretchen Morgenson, "After 20 Years of Financial Turmoil, a Columnist's Last Shot," *New York Times*, November 10, 2017, https://www.nytimes.com/2017/11/10
/business/after-20-years-of-financial-turmoil-a-columnists-last-shot.html.

31. Morgenson.

32. Ansgar Zerfass and Muschda Sherzada, "Corporate Communications from the CEO's Perspective: How Top Executives Conceptualize and Value Strategic Communication," *Corporate Communications: An International Journal* 20, no. 3 (2015): 291–309.

33. David Carr, "A Glimpse of Murdoch Unbound," *New York Times*, January 29, 2012, https://www.nytimes.com/2012/01/30/business/media/twitter-gives-glimpse
-into-rupert-murdochs-mind.html.

34. Shannon Bowen, "'We Are Professional Manipulators'—PR Pros, Are We Lying to Ourselves?," *PRWeek*, August 12, 2015, https://www.prweek.com/article
/1359922/we-professional-manipulators-pr-pros-lying-ourselves.

35. Dan Bauman and Chris Quintana, "Drew Cloud Is a Well-Known Expert on Student Loans. One Problem: He's Not Real," *Chronicle of Higher Education*, April 24, 2018, https://www.chronicle.com/article/drew-cloud-is-a-well-known-expert-on-stu dent-loans-one-problem-hes-not-real/.

36. Dana Melius, "Can We Talk? About 'Fake News?,'" *St. Peter* [Minnesota] *Herald*, September 28, 2018, https://www.southernminn.com/st_peter_herald/opinion /article_b75b5de7-7dfe-5627-98cc-548c451fc02c.html.

37. Yvonne Zacharias, "Monsanto Accused of Discrediting Singer Neil Young and Reuters Writer," *Talking Biz News*, August 12, 2019, https://talkingbiznews.com /we-talk-biz-news/monsanto-accused-of-discrediting-singer-neil-young-and-reu ters-writer/.

38. Carey Gillam, "How Monsanto Manipulates Journalists and Academics," *Guardian*, June 2, 2019, https://www.theguardian.com/commentisfree/2019/jun/02 /monsanto-manipulates-journalists-academics.

39. Allen Wastler, "PR Pitch: We'll Pay You to Mention Our Clients," *CNBC*, September 11, 2014, https://www.cnbc.com/2014/09/11/pr-pitch-well-pay-you-to-men tion-our-clientscommentary.html.

40. Chris Roush, "Fortune Journalist Offered Shares in IPO," *Talking Biz News*, May 8, 2014, https://talkingbiznews.com/they-talk-biz-news/fortune-journalist-of fered-shares-in-ipo/.

41. Kavita Kumar, "Memphis Paper Takes Schnucks to Task for Denying Kroger Sale in Works," *St. Louis Post-Dispatch*, September 7, 2011, https://www.stltoday.com /business/local/memphis-paper-takes-schnucks-to-task-for-denying-kroger-sale-in -works/article_89bde408-d96f-11e0-94ca-0014abcf6878.html.

42. Kumar.

43. Kumar.

44. Ansgar Zerfass, Dejan Verčič, and Markus Wiesenberg, "Managing CEO Communication and Positioning," *Journal of Communication Management* 20, no. 1 (2016): 37–55.

CHAPTER 5. THE CEO CAN DO BETTER

1. Justin Bariso, "Elon Musk Had a Hilarious Response to a Reporter's Request for an Interview," *Inc.*, April 2, 2018, https://www.inc.com/justin-bariso /elon-musk-had-a-hilarious-response-to-a-reporters-request-for-an-interview-emo tional-intelligence.html?sr_share=twitter&cid=sf01001.

2. Doha Madani and Nick Visser, "What You Need to Know about Zuckerberg's Media Blitz," *Huffington Post*, March 21, 2018, https://www.huffpost.com/entry /mark-zuckerberg-cnn-apology-cambridge-analytica_n_5ab30119e4b054d118df8495.

3. Olivia Barrow, "Why You Should Get to Know the Humans at Your Local News Outlets," *LinkedIn*, October 8, 2015, https://www.linkedin.com/pulse/why-you -should-get-know-humans-your-local-news-outlets-olivia-barrow/?trk=hp-feed-arti cle-title-publish.

4. Barrow.

5. Rakesh Khurana, "The Curse of the Superstar CEO," *Harvard Business Review*, September 2002, https://hbr.org/2002/09/the-curse-of-the-superstar-ceo.

6. James E. Arnold, "Communications and Strategy: The CEO Gets (and Gives) the Message," *Public Relations Quarterly* 33 (Summer 1988): 5–13.

7. Ansgar Zerfass and Muschda Sherzada, "Corporate Communications from the CEO's Perspective: How Top Executives Conceptualize and Value Strategic Communication," *Corporate Communications: An International Journal* 20, no. 3 (2015): 291–309.

8. Mike Haggerty and Wallace Rasmussen, *The Headline vs. the Bottom Line: Mutual Distrust between Business and the News Media* (Nashville: The Freedom Forum First Amendment Center, 1994), 1.

9. Haggerty and Rasmussen, 1.

10. Quoted in Steve Weinberg, *Taking on the Trust: The Epic Battle of Ida Tarbell and John D. Rockefeller* (New York: Norton, 2008), 225.

11. Alan R. Raucher, *Public Relations and Business: 1900–1929* (Baltimore: Johns Hopkins Press, 1968), 140.

12. R. D. Reynolds, "The 1906 Campaign to Sway Muckraking Periodicals," *Journalism Quarterly* 56, no. 4 (Fall 1979): 513–20.

13. Stewart Pinkerton, *The Fall of the House of Forbes: The Inside Story of the Collapse of a Media Empire* (New York: St. Martin's Press, 2011), 73.

14. Chris Roush, *Profits and Losses: Business Journalism and Its Role in Society* (Portland, OR: Marion Street Press, 2011), 90–95.

15. Roush, 90–95.

16. Elizabeth L. Stevens, "Making Bill," *Brill's Content*, September 1998, 100–114.

17. Virgil Scudder and Ken Scudder, *World Class Communication: How Great CEOs Win with the Public, Shareholders, Employees and the Media* (New York: Wiley, 2012), 85.

18. Zerfass and Sherzada, "Corporate Communications from the CEO's Perspective," 291–309.

19. "Final Rule: Selective Disclosure and Insider Trading," Securities and Exchange Commission, October 23, 2000, https://www.sec.gov/rules/final/33-7881.htm.

20. Christopher D. Allen, "CEO Speeches: From Nightmare to Opportunity," *Public Relations Quarterly* 8, no. 1 (Summer 1994): 25–27.

21. Scudder and Scudder, "World Class Communication," 291–309.

22. Guy Shani and James Westphal, "Avoiding Bad Press: Interpersonal Influence in Relations between CEOs and Journalists and the Consequences for Press Reporting about Firms and Their Leadership," *Organization Science* 22, no. 4 (2011): 1061–86.

23. Andrew C. Call, Scott A. Emett, Eldar Maksymov, and Nathan Y. Sharp, "Meet the Press: Survey Evidence on Financial Journalists as Information Intermediaries" (November 2018; rev. February 2020), https://dx.doi.org/10.2139/ssrn.3279453.

24. Conor Dougherty, "Try to Interview Google's Co-Founder. It's Emasculating,"

New York Times, January 27, 2016, https://www.nytimes.com/2016/01/27/insider /try-to-interview-googles-chief-executive-its-emasculating.html?_r=0.

25. Guy Kohut and Albert Segars, "The President's Letter to Stockholders: An Examination of Corporate Communication Strategy," *Journal of Business Communication* 29, no. 1 (Winter 1992): 7–19.

26. Carol Loomis, "The Sinking of Bethlehem Steel: A Hundred Years Ago One of the 500's Legendary Names Was Born. Its Decline and Ultimate Death Took Nearly Half That Long," *Fortune*, April 5, 2014, http://archive.fortune.com/magazines/for tune/fortune_archive/2004/04/05/366339/index.htm.

27. Rob Copeland, "Google's Sundar Pichai Is a Really Nice Guy. Is That Enough?," *Wall Street Journal*, September 11, 2020, https://www.wsj.com/articles/googles-sund ar-pichai-is-a-really-nice-guy-is-that-enough-11599848504.

28. Vivek Wadhwa, "Come Clean When Things Go Wrong," *Wall Street Journal*, December 12, 2013, https://www.wsj.com/articles/BL-232B-2108.

29. Wadhwa.

30. Zerfass and Sherzada, "Corporate Communications from the CEO's Perspective," 291–309.

31. Meg Garner, "Business Journalists and How They Use Twitter," *Talking Biz News*, January 6, 2016, http://talkingbiznews.com/2/twitter-wins/.

32. Richard Vidgen, Julian Mark Sims, and Phillip Powell, "Do CEO Bloggers Build Community?," *Journal of Communication Management* 17, no. 4 (2013): 364–85.

33. Wan-Hsiu Sunny Tsai and Linjuan Rita Men, "Social CEOs: The Effects of CEOs' Communication Styles and Parasocial Interaction on Social Networking Sites," *New Media & Society* 19, no. 11 (2017): 1848–67.

34. Caroline O'Donovan, "Hootsuite CEO Directs Comment-Seeking Reporter to Phone Sex Line," *BuzzFeed News*, February 28, 2017, https://www.buzzfeednews .com/article/carolineodonovan/hootsuite-ceo-tweeted-a-sex-hotline-number-at-re porter#.rtJnxqaell.

35. Andrew Phelps, "Chesapeake Energy Fights Bad PR by Buying Promoted Tweets on Twitter," Nieman Lab, June 28, 2011, https://www.niemanlab.org/2011/06 /chesapeake-energy-fights-bad-pr-by-buying-promoted-tweets-on-twitter/.

36. Chris Roush, "Business Journalism, Investors and Twitter," *Talking Biz News*, June 7, 2011, https://talkingbiznews.com/they-talk-biz-news/business-journalism-in vestors-and-twitter/.

37. Lionel Barber, "Too Big to Fail: FT Editor Lionel Barber on the Future of Financial Journalism," *Financial Times*, November 23, 2018, https://www.ft.com/con tent/d2a3e50e-ef07-11e8-89c8-d36339d835c0.

38. Chris Roush, "The Information: Why Did Company CEO Lie to Us?," *Talking Biz News*, January 25, 2020, https://talkingbiznews.com/they-talk-biz-news/the-in formation-why-did-company-ceo-lie-to-us/.

39. Gregor Halff, "The Presentation of CEOs in Economic Downturn," *Corporate Reputation Review* 16, no. 3 (2013): 234–43.

40. James Westphal and David Deephouse, "Avoiding Bad Press: Interpersonal

Influence in Relations between CEOs and Journalists and the Consequences for Press Reporting about Firms and Their Leadership," *Organization Science* 22, no. 4 (2011): 1061–86.

41. William Holstein, "What a Declining Business Media Means to CEOs," *Strategy+Business*, September 28, 2009, https://www.strategy-business.com/article/000 03?gko=83b3c.

CHAPTER 6. SOCIETAL CHANGES AND ECONOMIC FORCES

1. "Fortune 500: 1955–2005," *CNN Money*, n.d., accessed January 8, 2021, https://money.cnn.com/magazines/fortune/fortune500_archive/full/1955/401.html.

2. US Census Bureau, "2007 SUSB Annual Data Tables by Establishment Industry," n.d., accessed January 6, 2021, https://www.census.gov/data/tables/2007/econ/susb/2007-susb-annual.html.

3. US Census Bureau, "2017 SUSB Annual Data Tables by Establishment Industry," n.d., accessed January 6, 2021, https://www.census.gov/data/tables/2007/econ/susb/2007-susb-annual.htmlhttps://www.census.gov/data/tables/2017/econ/susb/2017-susb-annual.html.

4. US Census Bureau, "2007 SUSB Annual Data Tables by Establishment Industry"; and US Census Bureau, "2017 SUSB Annual Data Tables by Establishment Industry."

5. US Bureau of Labor Statistics, "Job Growth at Small Businesses, 1992–2013," *Economics Daily*, May 12, 2014, https://www.bls.gov/opub/ted/2014/ted_20140512.htm.

6. George McKerrow, telephone interview with author, December 7, 2020.

7. Andrew Flowers, "Big Business Is Getting Bigger," *FiveThirtyEight*, May 18, 2015, https://fivethirtyeight.com/features/big-business-is-getting-bigger/.

8. Christopher Mims, "Why Do the Biggest Companies Keep Getting Bigger? It's How They Spend on Tech," *Wall Street Journal*, July 26, 2018, https://www.wsj.com/articles/why-do-the-biggest-companies-keep-getting-bigger-its-how-they-spend-on-tech-1532610001.

9. Vijay Govindarajan, Baruch Lev, Anup Srivastava, and Luminita Enache, "The Gap between Large and Small Companies Is Growing. Why?," *Harvard Business Review*, August 16, 2019, https://hbr.org/2019/08/the-gap-between-large-and-small-companies-is-growing-why.

10. David McLaughlin, "The Big Keep Getting Bigger in the Pandemic-Rearranged Economy," *Bloomberg Businessweek*, May 3, 2020, https://www.bloomberg.com/news/articles/2020-05-03/the-big-keep-getting-bigger-in-the-pandemic-rearranged-economy.

11. David Dayen, "After the Crisis, Big Business Could Get Even Bigger," *American Prospect*, May 19, 2020, https://prospect.org/coronavirus/after-the-crisis-big-business-could-get-even-bigger/.

12. US Small Business Administration Office of Advocacy, "Small Businesses

Generate 44 Percent of US Economic Activity," January 30, 2019, https://advocacy
.sba.gov/2019/01/30/small-businesses-generate-44-percent-of-u-s-economic-activ
ity/.

13. Lydia Saad, "What Percentage of Americans Own Stock?," Gallup, September
13, 2019, https://news.gallup.com/poll/266807/percentage-americans-owns-stock
.aspx.

14. Justin McCarthy, "Stock Investments Lose Some Luster after COVID-19
Sell-Off," Gallup, April 24, 2020, https://news.gallup.com/poll/309233/stock-invest
ments-lose-luster-covid-sell-off.aspx.

15. Steven M. Rosenthal and Theo Burke, "Who Owns US Stock? Foreigners and
Rich Americans," Tax Policy Center, October 20, 2020, https://www.taxpolicycenter
.org/taxvox/who-owns-us-stock-foreigners-and-rich-americans.

16. Robin Wigglesworth, "How America's 1% Came to Dominate Equity Ownership," *Financial Times*, February 10, 2020, https://www.ft.com/content/2501e154
-4789-11ea-aeb3-955839e06441.

17. B. Ravikumar, "How Has Stock Ownership Trended in the Past Few Decades?," Federal Reserve Bank of St. Louis, April 9, 2018, https://www.stlouisfed.org
/on-the-economy/2018/april/stock-ownership-trended-past-few-decades.

18. Patricia Cohen, "We All Have a Stake in the Stock Market, Right? Guess
Again," *New York Times*, February 8, 2018, https://www.nytimes.com/2018/02/08
/business/economy/stocks-economy.html.

19. US Census Bureau, "Quarterly Residential Vacancies and Homeownership,
Third Quarter 2020," October 27, 2020, https://www.census.gov/housing/hvs/files
/currenthvspress.pdf.

20. Laurie Goodman, Christopher Mayer, and Christopher R. Hayes, "To Explain
Changes in the Homeownership Rate, Look beyond Demographic Trends," Urban
Institute, March 6, 2018, https://www.urban.org/urban-wire/explain-changes-home
ownership-rate-look-beyond-demographic-trends.

21. US Census Bureau, "Quarterly Residential Vacancies and Homeownership,
Third Quarter 2020."

22. Jenny Schuetz, "Who Is the New Face of American Homeownership?,"
Brookings Institution, October 9, 2017, https://www.brookings.edu/blog/the-ave
nue/2017/10/09/who-is-the-new-face-of-american-homeownership/.

23. Monique Morrissey, "The State of American Retirement Savings," Economic Policy Institute, December 10, 2019, https://www.epi.org/publication/the
-state-of-american-retirement-savings/.

24. US Bureau of Labor Statistics, "National Compensation Survey: Employee
Benefits in the United States, March 2018," September 2018, https://www.bls.gov
/ncs/ebs/benefits/2018/employee-benefits-in-the-united-states-march-2018.pdf.

25. Federal Reserve System Board of Governors, "Report on the Economic
Well-Being of US Households in 2018," May 2019, https://www.federalreserve.gov
/publications/2019-economic-well-being-of-us-households-in-2018-retirement.htm.

26. US Census Bureau, "Census 2000 Shows America's Diversity," March 12,

2001, https://www.census.gov/newsroom/releases/archives/census_2000/cb01cn61
.html.

27. Kaiser Family Foundation, "Distribution of US Population by Race/Ethnicity:
2010 and 2050," March 18, 2013, https://www.kff.org/racial-equity-and-health-policy
/slide/distribution-of-u-s-population-by-raceethnicity-2010-and-2050/.

28. "Male Journalists Dominate the News," *Economist*, March 25, 2019, https://
www.economist.com/graphic-detail/2019/03/25/male-journalists-dominate
-the-news.

29. Chris Roush, "Gizmodo's Narisetti Explains How to Have a Diverse Newsroom," *Talking Biz News*, May 26, 2017, https://talkingbiznews.com/we-talk-biz
-news/gizmodos-narisetti-explains-how-to-have-a-diverse-newsroom/.

30. "Newsroom Diversity Survey," American Society of News Editors (2016), accessed January 6, 2020, https://www.asne.org/newsroom_diversitysurvey.

31. "The Status of Women in the US Media 2016," Women's Media Center
(2017), accessed January 6, 2020, http://www.womensmediacenter.com/reports/sta
tus-of-women-in-us-media.

32. "The Status of Women in the US Media 2016."

33. Tamil Nadu, "Diverse Workforce Key for Success of Newsrooms," *Hindu*, May
12, 2018, https://www.thehindu.com/news/national/tamil-nadu/diverse-workforce
-key-for-success-of-newsrooms/article23858482.ece.

34. Sherrell Dorsey, "Black Tech News Coverage Struggles to Find a Home in
Mainstream Newsrooms," *Columbia Journalism Review*, July 8, 2019, https://www.cjr
.org/analysis/black-media-tech-coverage.php.

35. US Census Bureau, "Annual Business Survey Release Provides Data on
Minority- and Women-Owned Businesses," May 19, 2020, https://www.census.gov
/newsroom/press-releases/2020/annual-business-survey-data.html.

36. Sifan Liu and Joseph Parilla, "Businesses Owned by Women and Minorities
Have Grown. Will COVID-19 Undo That?," Brookings Institution, April 14, 2020,
https://www.brookings.edu/research/businesses-owned-by-women-and-minorities
-have-grown-will-covid-19-undo-that/.

37. US Bureau of Labor Statistics, "National Longitudinal Surveys," accessed January 6, 2021, https://www.bls.gov/nls/questions-and-answers.htm#anch41.

38. Jeffrey R. Young, "How Many Times Will People Change Jobs? The Myth of
the Endlessly-Job-Hopping Millennial," *EdSurge*, July 20, 2017, https://www.edsurge
.com/news/2017-07-20-how-many-times-will-people-change-jobs-the-myth-of-the
-endlessly-job-hopping-millennial.

39. US Bureau of Labor Statistics, "Employee Tenure in 2020," September 22,
2020, https://www.bls.gov/news.release/pdf/tenure.pdf.

40. Guy Berger, "Will This Year's College Grades Job-Hop More than Previous
Grads?" *LinkedIn* (official blog), April 12, 2016, https://blog.linkedin.com/2016/04/12
/will-this-year_s-college-grads-job-hop-more-than-previous-grads.

41. Valeria Bolden-Barrett, "Employee Loyalty Is Down—and Weak Company
Culture Is to Blame," *HR Dive*, February 26, 2019, https://www.hrdive.com/news
/employee-loyalty-is-down-and-weak-company-culture-is-to-blame/549061/.

42. Federal Reserve Bank of Atlanta, "Wage Growth Tracker," accessed January 8, 2021, https://www.frbatlanta.org/chcs/wage-growth-tracker.

43. ADP Research Institute, "Workforce Vitality Report," October 2020, accessed January 8, 2021, https://workforcereport.adp.com/.

44. Jonathan Yoe, "Why Are Older People Working Longer?," US Bureau of Labor Statistics, July 2019, https://www.bls.gov/opub/mlr/2019/beyond-bls/why-are-older -people-working-longer.htm.

45. Pew Research Center, "Social Media Fact Sheet," June 12, 2019, https://www .pewresearch.org/internet/fact-sheet/social-media/.

46. Amy Mitchell, Mark Jurkowitz, J. Baxter Oliphant, and Elisa Shearer, "Americans Who Mainly Get Their News on Social Media Are Less Engaged, Less Knowledgeable," Pew Research Center, July 30, 2020, https://www.journalism.org/2020/07/30 /americans-who-mainly-get-their-news-on-social-media-are-less-engaged-less -knowledgeable/.

47. Amy Mitchell, Mark Jurkowitz, J. Baxter Oliphant, and Elisa Shearer, "Appendix: Knowledge Questions Used for Average Correct Responses," Pew Research Center, July 30, 2020, https://www.journalism.org/2020/07/30/appendix-knowl edge-questions-used-for-average-correct-responses/.

48. Mitchell, Jurkowitz, Oliphant, and Shearer, "Appendix."

49. Jack Morse, "Half of US Adults Don't Know That Facebook Does Not Do Original News Reporting," Mashable, December 8, 2020, https://mashable.com/arti cle/american-adults-pew-survey-facebook-original-news-reporting/.

50. Caroline Binham, "Companies Fear Rise of Fake News and Social Media Rumours," Financial Times, September 29, 2019, https://www.ft.com/content/4241a2f6 -e080-11e9-9743-db5a370481bc.

51. "Don't Let Confirmation Bias Narrow Your Perspective," News Literacy Project, n.d., https://newslit.org/tips-tools/dont-let-confirmation-bias-narrow-your-per spective/.

52. Gordon Scott, "Confirmation Bias," Investopedia, August 2, 2019, https:// www.investopedia.com/terms/c/confirmation-bias.asp.

53. Lionel Barber, "Too Big to Fail: The Future of Financial Journalism," Financial Times, November 25, 2018, https://aboutus.ft.com/en-gb/announcements/too-big-to -fail-the-future-of-financial-journalism/.

CHAPTER 7. POLITICAL POLARIZATION

1. Melanie Sill, e-mail with the author, February 5, 2021.

2. Mark Jurkowitz, Amy Mitchell, Elisa Sherer, and Mason Walker, "Democrats Report Much Higher Levels of Trust in a Number of News Sources than Republications," Pew Research Center, January 24, 2020, https://www.journalism.org /2020/01/24/democrats-report-much-higher-levels-of-trust-in-a-number-of-news -sources-than-republicans/.

3. Frank Newport, "The Impact of Increased Political Polarization," Gallup, December 5, 2019, https://news.gallup.com/opinion/polling-matters/268982/im pact-increased-political-polarization.aspx.

4. Darrell M. West and Beth Stone, "Nudging News Producers and Consumers toward More Thoughtful, Less Polarized Discourse," Center for Effective Public Management at Brookings, February 2014, https://www.brookings.edu/wp-content/up loads/2016/06/West-Stone_Nudging-News-Consumers-and-Producers.pdf.

5. West and Stone.

6. Mark Jurkowitz, Amy Mitchell, Elisa Sherer, and Mason Walker, "US Media Polarization and the 2020 Election: A Nation Divided," Pew Research Center, January 24, 2020, https://www.journalism.org/2020/01/24/u-s-media-polarization-and-the -2020-election-a-nation-divided/.

7. Sidney Fussell, "It's Hard to Escape Facebook's Vortex of Polarization," *Wired*, October 30, 2020, https://www.wired.com/story/facebook-vortex-political-polarization/.

8. Rani Molla, "Social Media Is Making a Bad Political Situation Worse," *Vox*, November 10, 2020, https://www.vox.com/recode/21534345/polarization-election-social -media-filter-bubble.

9. Megan Brenan, "Americans' Trust in Mass Media Edges Down to 41%," Gallup, September 26, 2019, https://news.gallup.com/poll/267047/americans-trust-mass -media-edges-down.aspx.

10. Zaid Jilani and Jeremy Adam Smith, "What Is the Trust Cost of Polarization in America?," *Greater Good Magazine*, March 4, 2019, https://greatergood.berkeley.edu /article/item/what_is_the_true_cost_of_polarization_in_america.

11. Eitan Goldman, Nandina Gupta, and Ryan D. Israelsen, "Political Polarization in Financial News," February 13, 2020, https://ssrn.com/abstract=3537841.

12. Vishal P. Baloria and Jonas Heese, "The Effects of Media Slant on Firm Behavior," *Journal of Financial Economics*, August 17, 2017, Harvard Business School Accounting & Management Unit Working Paper No. 18-015, http://dx.doi.org/10.2139 /ssrn.3021229.

13. Lucia Moses, "Study Shows How Left/Right Sites Politicize the News," *Digiday*, April 12, 2017, https://digiday.com/media/study-shows-leftright-sites-politicize-news/.

14. Stephen Hiltner, "Andrew Ross Sorkin on the Origins, and the Future, of Dealbook," *New York Times*, December 20, 2017, https://www.nytimes.com/2017/12/20 /insider/andrew-ross-sorkin-dealbook-origins.html.

15. Margaret Sullivan, *Ghosting the News: Local Journalism and the Crisis of American Democracy* (New York: Columbia Global Reports, 2020), 20–22.

16. Lee Drutman, *The Business of America Is Lobbying: How Corporations Became Politicized and Politics Became More Corporate* (New York: Oxford University Press, 2015), excerpted April 25, 2015, at https://www.businessinsider.com/how-corpora tions-turned-into-political-beasts-2015-4.

17. Sara Fischer, "News about News Dominates Election," *Axios*, November 3, 2020, https://www.axios.com/cable-news-disinformation-fake-news-bias-e155967b -cd0f-4c46-bfad-1c3ba92a6a9e.html.

18. Diana Owen, "The New Media's Role in Politics," *OpenMind*, n.d., accessed February 15, 2021, https://www.bbvaopenmind.com/en/articles/the-new-media-s-role-in -politics/.

19. Barry Ritholtz, "What Happens When Business and Politics Mix," *Bloomberg Opinion*, March 6, 2018, https://www.bloomberg.com/opinion/articles/2018-03-06/what-happens-when-business-and-politics-mix.

20. Neal Rothschild, Sara Fischer, and Stef W. Kight, "A Nation of News Consumption Hypocrites," *Axios*, June 11, 2019, https://www.axios.com/news-consumption-read-topics-56467fe6-81bd-4ae5-9173-cdff9865deda.html.

21. John V. Duca and Jason L. Saving, "Income Inequality, Media Fragmentation and Increased Political Polarization," *Contemporary Economic Policy* 35, no. 2 (August 2016): 392–413, https://onlinelibrary.wiley.com/doi/abs/10.1111/coep.12191.

22. R. Kelly Garrett, Brian E. Weeks, and Rachel L. Nelo, "Driving a Wedge between Evidence and Beliefs: How Online Ideological News Exposure Promotes Political Misperceptions," *Journal of Computer-Mediated Communication* 21, no. 5 (August 2016): 331–48, https://onlinelibrary.wiley.com/doi/full/10.1111/jcc4.12164.

23. Jiyoung Han, "Conflict Framing of the News and Group Polarization" (PhD diss., University of Minnesota, 2016), https://conservancy.umn.edu/handle/11299/181736.

24. Richard Fletcher, Alessio Cornia, and Rasmua Kleis Nielsen, "How Polarized Are Online and Offline News Audiences? A Comparative Analysis of Twelve Countries," *International Journal of Press/Politics* 25, no. 2 (April 2020): 169–95, https://doi.org/10.1177/1940161219892768.

25. Ezra Klein, "Why the Media Is So Polarized—and How It Polarizes Us," *Vox*, January 28, 2020, https://www.vox.com/2020/1/28/21077888/why-were-polarized-media-book-ezra-news.

26. Joshua P. Darr, Johanna Dunaway, and Matthew P. Hitt, "Want to Reduce Political Polarization? Save Your Local Newspaper," *Nieman Lab*, February 11, 2019, https://www.niemanlab.org/2019/02/want-to-reduce-political-polarization-save-your-local-newspaper/.

27. Dante Chinni, and Sally Bronston, "Despite Attacks on the Press, Public Supports Watchdog Role," *NBC News*, July 9, 2017, https://www.nbcnews.com/politics/white-house/despite-attacks-press-public-supports-watchdog-role-n781046.

28. Pierre Lemieux, "The Political Firm," Library of Economics and Liberty, January 8, 2018, https://www.econlib.org/archives/2018/01/the_political_f.html.

29. Todd Schaefer, "Left and Right: Era of the Politicization of Business," *Daily Record* [Ellensburg, WA], September 11, 2018, https://www.dailyrecordnews.com/opinion/editorial/left-and-right-era-of-the-politicization-of-business/article_8253694b-4571-5247-81ec-63be810f4a19.html.

30. Christopher Mims, "Why Social Media Is So Good at Polarizing Us," *Wall Street Journal*, October 19, 2020, https://www.wsj.com/articles/why-social-media-is-so-good-at-polarizing-us-11603105204.

31. Damon Centola, "Why Social Media Makes Us More Polarized and How to Fix It," *Scientific American*, October 15, 2020, https://www.scientificamerican.com/article/why-social-media-makes-us-more-polarized-and-how-to-fix-it/.

32. Greg St. Martin, "Study Finds 'Modest Correlation" between Journalists' Social Networks and Ideology of Their News Content," *News@Northeastern*, August 18,

2017, https://news.northeastern.edu/2017/08/18/study-finds-modest-correlation-between-journalists-social-networks-and-ideology-of-their-news-content/.

33. Terry Lee, "The Global Rise of 'Fake News' and the Threat to Democratic Elections in the USA," *Public Administration and Policy: An Asia-Pacific Journal* 22, no. 1 (July 2019): 15–24, https://doi.org/10.1108/PAP-04-2019-0008.

34. Maxwell Tani, "How Fox Business Is Beating CNBC by Embracing Politics," *Business Insider*, October 17, 2017, https://www.businessinsider.com/fox-business-beating-cnbc-embracing-politics-2017-10.

35. Michael Grynbaum, "Fox Business Benches Trish Regan after Outcry over Coronavirus Comments," *New York Times*, March 13, 2020, https://www.nytimes.com/2020/03/13/business/media/trish-regan-fox-hiatus.html.

36. Jack Shafer, "Bloomberg Government as DC's Daily Racing Form," *Slate*, November 18, 2010, https://slate.com/news-and-politics/2010/11/in-the-casino-that-is-washington-every-investor-and-businessman-needs-a-tip-sheet.html.

37. "Why Axios?," *Axios*, accessed February 18, 2021, https://www.axios.com/advertise/.

38. "About CQ Roll Call," *CQ Roll Call*, accessed February 18, 2021, https://cqrollcall.com/about-cq-roll-call/.

39. Helen Stubbs, "Americans Feel Overwhelmed by the News. Here's How They Adapt," Knight Foundation, September 28, 2020, https://knightfoundation.org/articles/americans-feel-overwhelmed-by-the-news-heres-how-they-adapt/.

40. Richard Tofel, "Less on Politics, More on How Government Works (or Doesn't)," Nieman Lab, n.d., accessed February 17, 2021, https://www.niemanlab.org/2020/12/less-on-politics-more-on-how-government-works-or-doesnt/.

41. West and Stone, "Nudging News Producers and Consumers."

CHAPTER 8. THE STOCK MARKET IS OVERCOVERED

1. Teresa Ghilarducci, "Most Americans Don't Have a Real Stake in the Stock Market," *Forbes*, August 31, 2020, https://www.forbes.com/sites/teresaghilarducci/2020/08/31/most-americans-dont-have-a-real-stake-in-the-stock-market/?sh=108a1dc61154.

2. Ghilarducci.

3. Annie Nova, "Who Benefits When the Stock Market Goes Up? Probably Not You," *CNBC*, June 12, 2020, https://www.cnbc.com/2020/06/12/heres-who-benefits-when-the-stock-market-goes-up.html.

4. Jack Murtha, "Why Stock Market Reporting Should Be Treated with Caution," *Columba Journalism Review*, August 25, 2015, https://www.cjr.org/analysis/stock_market_reporting.php.

5. Chris Roush, "Report: Only Half of Investors Trust the Financial Media," *Talking Biz News*, December 21, 2018, https://talkingbiznews.com/they-talk-biz-news/report-only-half-of-investors-trust-the-financial-media/.

6. Sean McElwee, "What if We Reported on Poverty the Way We Report on the Stock Market?," *Talking Points Memo*, August 25, 2015, https://talkingpointsmemo.com/cafe/media-bias-rich-and-famous-stock-market-poverty.

7. Chris Roush, "Professor Studies Stock Price Changes and Business Journalism," *Talking Biz News*, April 26, 2014, https://talkingbiznews.com/they-talk-biz-news/professor-studies-stock-price-changes-and-business-journalism/.

8. James Deporre, "'Up Is Good and Down Is Bad' Works for the Media but Not for Traders," *Real Money*, January 23, 2019, https://realmoney.thestreet.com/investing/stocks/up-is-good-and-down-is-bad-works-for-the-media-but-not-for-traders-14842837.

9. Stefan Theil, "The Media and Markets: How Systematic Misreporting Inflates Bubbles, Deepens Downturns and Distorts Economic Reality," Shorenstein Center on Media, Politics and Public Policy Discussion Paper Series, #D-86 (June 2014), https://dash.harvard.edu/bitstream/handle/1/12872174/d86-theil.pdf?sequence=1&isAllowed=y.

10. Theil.

11. Tyler Clifford, "Jim Cramer Blames Bears, Media for the Public's Low Interest in Stocks," *CNBC*, December 5, 2019, https://www.cnbc.com/2019/12/05/jim-cramer-blames-bears-media-for-the-publics-low-interest-in-stocks.html.

12. Andrew Call, Scott Emett, Eldar Maksymov, and Nathan Sharp, "Meet the Press: Survey Evidence on Financial Journalists as Information Intermediaries," November 2018; rev. February 2020, https://dx.doi.org/10.2139/ssrn.3279453.

13. Theil, "Media and Markets."

14. Murtha, "Why Stock Market Reporting Should Be Treated with Caution."

15. Felix Salmon, "Ban Daily Stock Market Reports," *Splinter News*, August 31, 2015, https://splinternews.com/ban-daily-stock-market-reports-1793850395.

16. Felix Salmon, "CNN Reliable Sources," interview by Howard Kurtz, *CNN Reliable Sources*, August 14, 2011, http://transcripts.cnn.com/TRANSCRIPTS/1108/14/rs.01.html.

17. Nir Kaissar, "I Ran the Numbers Again. Stocks Are Not the Economy," *Bloomberg Opinion*, October 27, 2020, https://www.bloomberg.com/opinion/articles/2020-10-27/stock-market-is-not-the-economy-by-any-yardstick?sref=jO7iaJLA.

18. Matt Phillips, "Repeat after Me: The Markets Are Not the Economy," *New York Times*, May 10, 2020, https://www.nytimes.com/2020/05/10/business/stock-market-economy-coronavirus.html.

19. Phillips.

20. "Total Market Value of US Stock Market," Siblis Research, n.d., accessed December 28, 2020, https://siblisresearch.com/data/us-stock-market-value/#:~:text=The%20total%20market%20capitalization%20of,about%20OTC%20markets%20from%20here.

21. Steven Melendez, "Bond Market Size vs. Stock Market Size," *Zacks Research*, March 6, 2019, https://finance.zacks.com/bond-market-size-vs-stock-market-size-5863.html.

22. "Commodity Trading: Backbone of the Global Economy," Comdex Official, April 25, 2019, https://medium.com/@comdexofficial/commodity-trading-backbone-of-the-global-economy-131c78f12989#:~:text=The%20market%20size%20of%20the,around%20%2420%20trillion%20a%20year.

23. "Foreign Exchange Turnover in April 2019," Bank for International Settlements, accessed December 28, 2020, https://www.bis.org/statistics/rpfx19_fx.htm#:~:text=Trading%20in%20FX%20markets%20reached,%245.1%20trillion%20three%20years%20earlier.&text=Growth%20of%20FX%20derivatives%20trading,of%2088%25%20of%20all%20trades.

24. Scott Wapner, interview by Jeffrey Sherman, *Doubleline*, April 27, 2018, https://doubleline.com/podcast/s3-e9-scott-wapner-cnbc-fast-money-halftime-report-the-sherman-show/.

25. A. J. Katz, "5 Questions with . . . Scott Wapner," *TVNewser.com*, October 22, 2016, https://www.adweek.com/tvnewser/5-questions-with-scott-wapner/308675/.

26. Lionel Barber, "Too Big to Fail," *Financial Times*, November 23, 2018, https://www.ft.com/content/d2a3e50e-ef07-11e8-89c8-d36339d835c0.

27. Theil, "Media and Markets."

28. Jana Schilder, "TV, Websites Keep Investors Tuned In," *Toronto Star*, October 21, 2009, https://www.thestar.com/business/personal_finance/2009/10/21/tv_websites_keep_investors_tuned_in.html.

29. Michael Hiltzik, "Market 'Turmoil' and the Problem of CNBC," *Los Angeles Times*, August 24, 2015, https://www.latimes.com/business/hiltzik/la-fi-mh-market-turmoil-and-the-problem-of-cnbc-20150824-column.html.

30. Vitaliy Katsenelson, "Why Stock Investors Shouldn't Watch Business TV," *LinkedIn*, April 15, 2019, https://www.linkedin.com/pulse/why-stock-investors-shouldnt-watch-business-tv-katsenelson-cfa/?trk=eml-email_feed_ecosystem_digest_01-recommended_articles-6-Unknown&midToken=AQGu1KyxPMkkrA&fromEmail=fromEmail&ut=0B2tNn5ZrOBoI1.

31. Harold Pollack, "The Best Investing Advice Has Always Been Too Boring for TV," *Atlantic*, January 7, 2016, https://www.theatlantic.com/business/archive/2016/01/best-investing-advice-boring/423054/.

32. Chuck Jaffe, "This Is the Right Way to Make Sense of the Stock Tips You Hear on TV," *MarketWatch*, May 23, 2016, https://www.marketwatch.com/story/this-is-the-right-way-to-make-sense-of-the-stock-tips-you-hear-on-tv-2016-05-23.

33. David Jackson, "Conversation with Seeking Alpha Founder & CEO David Jackson," interview by Zach Abramowitz, *Zach Talks*, https://www.replyall.me/zach-talks/conversation-with-seeking-alpha-founder-ceo-david-jackson/.

34. Siraj Datoo, "Zero Hedge Permanently Suspended from Twitter for 'Harassment,'" *Bloomberg News*, January 31, 2020, https://www.bloomberg.com/news/articles/2020-02-01/zero-hedge-permanently-suspended-from-twitter-for-harassment.

35. "About Us," Benzinga.com, accessed December 28, 2020, https://www.benzinga.com/about.

36. "The Motley Fool's Investing Style," *Motley Fool*, n.d., accessed December 28, 2020, https://support.fool.com/hc/en-us/articles/360036177414-The-Motley-Fool-s-investing-style.

37. Theil, "Media and Markets."

38. Chris Roush and Bill Cloud, *The Financial Writer's Stylebook: 1,100 Business Terms Defined and Rated* (Portland, OR: Marion Street Press, 2010), 106–7.

39. Theil, "Media and Markets."

40. Chris Roush, "The Financial Media and Investment Advice," *Talking Biz News*, May 6, 2014, https://talkingbiznews.com/we-talk-biz-news/the-financial-media-and-investment-advice/.

CHAPTER 9. FAILING EMPLOYEES AND CONSUMERS

1. "Labor Unions in the 60s," History Central, accessed January 29, 2021, https://www.historycentral.com/sixty/Economics/Laborunion.html#:~:text=While%20 31.5%25%20of%20workers%20were,continued%20to%20fall%20since%20 then.

2. US Bureau of Labor Statistics, "Union Members—2020," January 22, 2021, https://www.bls.gov/news.release/pdf/union2.pdf.

3. Lawrence Mishel and Julia Wolfe, "CEO Compensation Has Grown 940% since 1978," Economic Policy Institute, August 14, 2019, https://www.epi.org/publication/ceo-compensation-2018/.

4. Jeffrey Madrick, "Credulity in Business Journalism: A History of the Business Press since the 1970s," American Academy of Arts & Sciences, n.d., accessed January 29, 2021, https://www.amacad.org/sites/default/files/academy/pdfs/credulity.pdf.

5. Nadine Strauss, "Financial Journalism in Today's High-Frequency News and Information Era," *Journalism* 20, no. 2 (2018): 274–91, https://journals.sagepub.com/doi/full/10.1177/1464884917753556.

6. Helaine Olen, *Pound Foolish: Exposing the Dark Side of the Personal Finance History* (New York: Portfolio, 2012), 11.

7. Taylor Leet-Otley, "Professor's Bookshelf: Steven Greenhouse," *Wesleyan Argus*, September 15, 2014, http://wesleyanargus.com/2014/09/15/professors-bookshelf-steven-greenhouse/?utm_source=rss&utm_medium=rss&utm_campaign=professors-bookshelf-steven-greenhouse.

8. Christopher Martin, "Why Analyzing Labor Coverage Is Important," *TalkingBizNews*, April 3, 2013, https://talkingbiznews.com/we-talk-biz-news/why-analyzing-labor-coverage-is-important/.

9. Andrew Stevens and Charles Smith, "The Importance of 'Beat" Reporting," *Saskatoon StarPhoenix*, February 13, 2020, https://thestarphoenix.com/opinion/letters/opinion-the-importance-of-beat-reporting.

10. Christopher Martin, "How Writing of the Working Class Has Hurt the Mainstream Media," *Nieman Reports*, August 27, 2019, https://niemanreports.org/articles/how-writing-off-the-working-class-has-hurt-the-mainstream-media/.

11. "The Impact of Raising the Minimum Wage to $15 by 2025, by Congressional District," Economic Policy Institute, January 28, 2021.

12. Christopher Martin, *Framed! Labor and the Corporate Media* (Ithaca, NY: Cornell University Press, 2004), 65.

13. Timothy Noah, "Does the Media Care about Labor Anymore?," *Politico Magazine*, December 4, 2014, https://www.politico.com/magazine/story/2014/12/labor-coverage-decline-113320#ixzz3LbvxDbRT.

14. Chris Roush, "When Labor and the Biz Media Meet," *TalkingBizNews*, De-

cember 11, 2013, https://talkingbiznews.com/they-talk-biz-news/when-labor-and-the
-biz-media-meet/.

15. Micah Uetricht, "Steven Greenhouse on Keeping the Labor Beat Alive," *In
These Times*, February 15, 2015, https://inthesetimes.com/article/keeping-the-labor
-beat-alive.

16. David Uberti, "The Labor Beat Is Dead; Long Live the Labor Beat," *Columbia
Journalism Review*, March 12, 2015, https://www.cjr.org/analysis/when_longtime_la
bor_reporter_steven.php.

17. Abe Streep, "An American Jobs Crisis with Few Reporters to Cover It," *New
York Times*, May 27, 2020, https://www.nytimes.com/interactive/2020/05/27/maga
zine/coronavirus-colorado-unemployment-jobs.html?auth=login-google.

18. Luke Ottenhof, "America's Labor Crisis Hit a Depleted Beat," *Columbia Journalism Review*, June 1, 2020, https://www.cjr.org/united_states_project/labor-report
ing-pandemic-crisis.php.

19. Ottenhof.

20. Ottenhof.

21. Noam Scheiber, "Labor and Technology Reporting: Two Concentric Circles,"
New York Times, July 11, 2018, https://www.nytimes.com/2018/07/11/insider/work
place-technology-hype-reporting.html.

22. Stevens and Smith, "Importance of 'Beat' Reporting."

23. Christopher Martin, *No Longer Newsworthy: How the Mainstream Media Abandoned the Working Class* (Ithaca, NY: ILR Press, 2019), 69.

24. Martin, 122.

25. Steven Greenhouse, "Through the Working Class," *Columbia Journalism Review*, Winter 2019, https://www.cjr.org/special_report/through-the-working-class.php.

26. Liz Ryan, "The Nasty Bias in Business Journalism," *Huffington Post*, December 15, 2012, https://www.huffpost.com/entry/nasty-bias-business-journalism_b
_1963044.

27. "Reuters Launches 'The Great Reboot,' a Section Dedicated to the Future
of the Workplace," Reuters, September 29, 2020, https://www.reuters.com/article
/rpb-thegreatreboot/reuters-launches-the-great-reboot-a-section-dedicated-to-the-fu
ture-of-the-workplace-idUKKBN26K2BX.

28. Martin, *No Longer Newsworthy*, 68.

29. Juliana Menasce Horowitz, Ruth Igielnik, and Rakesh Kochhar, "Trends in
Income and Wealth Inequality," Pew Research Center, January 9, 2020, https://www
.pewsocialtrends.org/2020/01/09/trends-in-income-and-wealth-inequality/.

30. Katherine Schaeffer, "6 Facts about Economic Inequality in the US," Pew
Research Center, February 7, 2020, https://www.pewresearch.org/fact-tank/2020
/02/07/6-facts-about-economic-inequality-in-the-u-s/.

31. Juliana Menasce Horowitz, Ruth Igielnik, and Rakesh Kochhar, "Most Americans Say There Is Too Much Economic Inequality in the US, but Fewer than Half
Call It a Top Priority," Pew Research Center, January 9, 2020, https://www.pewsocial
trends.org/2020/01/09/most-americans-say-there-is-too-much-economic-inequali
ty-in-the-u-s-but-fewer-than-half-call-it-a-top-priority/.

32. H. Roger Segelken, "Economic Mobility: The (Illusory) American Dream," *Cornell Chronicle*, February 3, 2015, https://news.cornell.edu/stories/2015/02/eco nomic-mobility-illusory-american-dream.

33. Alicia Adamczyk, "Inequality Has Been Building for Decades in the US, but Experts Say the Pandemic 'Ripped It Open,'" *CNBC*, October 23, 2020, https://www .cnbc.com/2020/10/23/coronavirus-is-exacerbating-economic-inequality-in-the-us .html.

34. Greg Iacurci, "US Is Worst among Developed Nations for Worker Benefits," *CNBC*, February 4, 2021, https://www.cnbc.com/2021/02/04/us-is-worst-among -rich-nations-for-worker-benefits.html?fbclid=IwAR37J5b271mW3pP50WB Z2YMG0HdN17z_VexJp6cvsZig31WxL4blXBseSho.

35. Andrea Grisold and Hendrik Theine, "How Come We Know? The Media Coverage of Economic Inequality," *International Journal of Communication* 11 (2017): 4265–84.

36. Josh Bivens, "Inequality Is Slowing US Economic Growth," Economic Policy Institute, December 12, 2017, https://www.epi.org/publication/secular-stagnation/.

37. Dan Froomkin, "It Can't Happen Here," *Nieman Reports*, Winter 2013, https:// niemanreports.org/articles/it-cant-happen-here-2/.

38. Denise-Marie Ordway and Heather Bryant, "Covering Poverty: What to Avoid and How to Get It Right," Shorenstein Center on Media, Politics and Public Policy, September 4, 2018, https://journalistsresource.org/tip-sheets/covering-poverty -avoid-get-right/.

39. Sarah Jones, "The Great Remove: How Journalism Got So Out of Touch with the People It Covers," *Columbia Journalism Review*, Spring/Summer 2018, https:// www.cjr.org/special_report/journalism-class.php.

40. Stuart M. Butler and Jonathan Grabinsky, "Tackling the Legacy of Persistent Urban Inequality and Concentered Poverty," Brookings Institution, November 16, 2020, https://www.brookings.edu/blog/up-front/2020/11/16/tackling-the-legacy-of -persistent-urban-inequality-and-concentrated-poverty/.

41. Kristin Wong, "Does Personal Finance Still Work in Our Changing Economy?," *New York Times*, January 23, 2020, https://www.nytimes.com/2020/01/23 /smarter-living/does-personal-finance-still-work-in-our-changing-economy.html.

42. Chuck Jaffe, "Money Magazine's Demise Puts Consumers on Alert," *Quincy Patriot Ledger*, April 16, 2019, https://www.enterprisenews.com/unknown/20190426 /wealth-health-money-magazines-demise-puts-consumers-on-alert.

43. Ralph Nader, "Degrading Newspapers' Business Sections," Common Dreams, April 6, 2018, https://www.commondreams.org/views/2018/04/06/degrad ing-newspapers-business-sections.

44. Anandi Mani, Sendhil Mullainathan, Eldar Shafir, and Jiaying Zhao, "Poverty Impedes Cognitive Function," *Science*, August 30, 2013, 976–80, https://scholar.har vard.edu/files/sendhil/files/976.full_.pdf.

45. Maria LaMagna, "Low-Income Families Are Getting Terrible Financial Advice Online," *MarketWatch*, April 3, 2018, https://www.marketwatch.com/story/low -income-families-are-getting-terrible-financial-advice-online-2018-04-02.

CHAPTER 10. HEALTH CARE COVERAGE IS SICK

1. Andy Miller, Zoom interview with author, January 11, 2021.

2. Andy Miller, Zoom interview.

3. "National Health Expenditure Data," Centers for Medicare & Medicaid Services, n.d., https://www.cms.gov/Research-Statistics-Data-and-Systems/Statistics-Trends-and-Reports/NationalHealthExpendData/NHE-Fact-Sheet, accessed January 20, 2021.

4. "National Health Expenditure Data."

5. "National Health Expenditure Data."

6. "National Health Expenditure Data."

7. Kaiser Family Foundation, "How Much Does the US Spend on Health and How Has It Changed?," May 1, 2012, https://www.kff.org/report-section/health-care-costs-a-primer-2012-report/.

8. Wendell Potter, phone interview with author, December 1, 2020.

9. Chris Roush, "Hartford Courant Insurance Reporter Levick Leaves Paper," *TalkingBizNews*, July 31, 2009, https://talkingbiznews.com/they-talk-biz-news/hartford-courant-insurance-reporter-levick-leaves-paper/.

10. Alan L. Otten, "The Influence of the Mass Media on Health Policy," *Health Affairs* 11, no. 4 (Winter 1992): 111–18, https://www.healthaffairs.org/doi/full/10.1377/hlthaff.11.4.111.

11. Sarah E. Gollust, Erika Franklin Fowler, and Jeff Niederdeppe, "Television News Coverage of Public Health Issues and Implications for Public Health Policy and Practice," *Annual Review of Public Health* 40 (2019): 167–85, https://www.annualreviews.org/doi/pdf/10.1146/annurev-publhealth-040218-044017.

12. "Poor Coverage of Health Care by the Corporate Media: How Can the Electorate Be Informed?," Physicians for a National Health Program, n.d., accessed January 15, 2021, https://pnhp.org/2016/05/27/poor-coverage-of-health-care-by-the-corporate-media-how-can-the-electorate-be-informed/.

13. "As Economic Concerns Recede, Environmental Protection Rises on Public's Policy Agenda," Pew Research Center, February 13, 2020, https://www.pewresearch.org/politics/2020/02/13/as-economic-concerns-recede-environmental-protection-rises-on-the-publics-policy-agenda/.

14. Hannah Fingerhut, "Is Treatment of Minorities a Key Election Issue? Views Differ by Race, Party," Pew Research Center, July 13, 2016, https://www.pewresearch.org/fact-tank/2016/07/13/partisan-racial-divides-exist-over-how-important-treatment-of-minorities-is-as-a-voting-issue/.

15. Gary Schwitzer, "Transparency by Drug Companies, Scrutiny by Journalists, Vital in Vaccine News," *HealthNewsReview*, November 9, 2020, https://www.healthnewsreview.org/2020/11/transparency-by-drug-companies-scrutiny-by-journalists-vital-in-vaccine-news/.

16. Maggie Mahar, "How the Media Covers Health Care," *HealthBeatBog*, November 30, 2007, https://healthbeatblog.com/2007/11/how-the-media-c/.

17. Mahar.

18. "Health," Living Facts, n.d., accessed January 16, 2021, https://www.living facts.org/en/topics/health.

19. "Health Spending Growth Has Outpaced Growth of the US Economy," *HealthSystemTracker*, n.d., accessed January 16, 2020, https://www.healthsystem tracker.org/chart-collection/u-s-spending-healthcare-changed-time/#item-usspend ingovertime_4.

20. US Bureau of Labor Statistics, "Consumer Price Index Summary," January 13, 2021, https://www.bls.gov/news.release/cpi.nro.htm.

21. Ryan Nunn, Jana Parsons, and Jay Shambaugh, "A Dozen Facts about the Economics of the US Health-Care System," Brookings Institution, March 10, 2020, https://www.brookings.edu/research/a-dozen-facts-about-the-economics-of-the-u-s -health-care-system/.

22. Megan Leonhardt, "Nearly 1 in 4 Americans Are Skipping Medical Care Because of the Cost," *CNBC*, March 12, 2020, https://www.cnbc.com/2020/03/11/near ly-1-in-4-americans-are-skipping-medical-care-because-of-the-cost.html.

23. Kaiser Family Foundation, "Poll: Nearly 1 in 4 Americans Taking Prescription Drugs Say It's Difficult to Afford Their Medicines," March 1, 2019, https:// www.kff.org/health-costs/press-release/poll-nearly-1-in-4-americans-taking-prescrip tion-drugs-say-its-difficult-to-afford-medicines-including-larger-shares-with-low-in comes/.

24. "Bill of the Month," *Kaiser Health News*, n.d., accessed January 16, 2021, https://khn.org/news/tag/bill-of-the-month/.

25. Wendi C. Thomas, "What It Looks like When a Hospital We Investigated Erases $11.9 Million in Medical Debt," *ProPublica*, December 24, 2019, https://www .propublica.org/article/what-it-looks-like-when-a-hospital-we-investigated-erases -millions-in-medical-debt; and Venessa Wong, "34 Devastating Stories about How People Are Still Crushed by Medical Debt," *BuzzFeed*, January 17, 2019, https://www .buzzfeednews.com/article/venessawong/34-heart-wrenching-stories-about-what -struggling-with.

26. Katherine Keisler-Starkey and Lisa N. Bunch, "Health Insurance Coverage in the United States: 2019," US Census Bureau, September 15, 2020, https://www .census.gov/library/publications/2020/demo/p60-271.html.

27. Zack Cooper, Amanda E. Kowalski, Eleanor N. Powell, and Jennifer Wu, "Politics and Health Care Spending in the United States," National Bureau of Economic Research, September 2020, https://www.nber.org/papers/w23748.

28. Julie Rovner, "The Complicated, Political, Expensive, Seemingly Eternal US Healthcare Debate Explained," *BMJ*, October 10, 2019, https://doi.org/10.1136/bmj .l5885.

29. "Core Topic: Health Reform," Association of Health Care Journalists, n.d., accessed January 17, 2021, https://healthjournalism.org/core-topic.php?id=1&page =overview.

30. Bradley Jones, "Increasing Share of Americans Favor a Single Government Program to Provide Health Care Coverage," Pew Research Center, September 29, 2020,

https://www.pewresearch.org/fact-tank/2020/09/29/increasing-share-of-amer icans-favor-a-single-government-program-to-provide-health-care-coverage/.

31. Amina Dunn, "Democrats Differ over Best Way to Provide Health Coverage for All Americans," Pew Research Center, July 26, 2019, https://www.pewresearch .org/fact-tank/2019/07/26/democrats-differ-over-best-way-to-provide-health-cover age-for-all-americans/.

32. "Congress, Budget Deals and Hospital Funding—How Politics Are Affecting Health Care Spending," Yale University School of Medicine, November 17, 2017, https://medicine.yale.edu/news-article/16204/.

33. Samantha Liss, "Buoyed by Bailout Funds, All Major For-Profit Hospital Chains Reported Increased Profits in Q2," HealthcareDive, August 10, 2020, https:// www.healthcaredive.com/news/buoyed-by-bailout-funds-all-major-for-profit-hospi tal-chains-reported-incr/583091/.

34. Daniel McDermott, Lina Stolyar, Cynthia Cox, Robin Rudowitz, Rachel Garfield, Jeannie Fuglestein Biniek, and Tricia Neuman, "Health Insurer Financial Performance through September 2020," Kaiser Family Foundation, December 16, 2020, https://www.kff.org/private-insurance/issue-brief/health-insurer-financial-perfor mance-through-september-2020/.

35. American Association for the Advancement of Science, "New Research Reveals Pharma Companies Are More Profitable than Most S&P 500 Companies," EurekAlert!, March 3, 2020, https://www.eurekalert.org/pub_releases/2020-03/bu-n rr022720.php.

36. Adam Johnson, "Top Health Insurers Report Billions in Profit during the Pandemic," QuoteWizard, August 26, 2020, https://quotewizard.com/news/posts /health-insurers-record-profits-during-pandemic.

37. Reed Abelson, "Major US Health Insurers Report Big Profits, Benefitting from the Pandemic," New York Times, August 5, 2020, https://www.nytimes.com /2020/08/05/health/covid-insurance-profits.html.

38. Wendell Potter, telephone interview.

39. David Allison, "Piedmont Healthcare Plans Expansion at Athens Hospital," Atlanta Business Chronicle, January 14, 2021, https://www.bizjournals.com/atlanta /news/2021/01/14/piedmont-healthcare-expansion-athens-regional.html.

40. US Bureau of Labor Statistics, The Economics Daily, "Number of Hospitals and Hospital Employment in Each State in 2019," accessed January 31, 2021, https:// www.bls.gov/opub/ted/2020/number-of-hospitals-and-hospital-employment-in -each-state-in-2019.htm.

41. Wendell Potter, phone interview.

42. US Bureau of Labor Statistics, "Average Employee Medical Premium $6,797 for Family Coverage in 2020," October 2, 2020, https://www.bls.gov/opub/ted/2020 /average-employee-medical-premium-6797-dollars-for-family-coverage-in-2020 .htm.

43. Rachel Layne, "Many Small-Business Employees May Be Close to Losing Health Insurance," Working Knowledge (Harvard Business School), September 17, 2020,

https://hbswk.hbs.edu/item/many-small-business-workers-may-be-close-to-los ing-health-insurance.

44. Robert King, "Survey Funds Nearly Half of Americans Having Health Insurance Troubles," *FierceHealthcare*, August 19, 2020, https://www.fiercehealthcare .com/payer/survey-finds-nearly-half-americans-having-insurance-coverage -troubles.

45. US Bureau of Labor Statistics, "Average Employee Medical Premium."

46. Robert King, "Nearly 8M Americans in Danger of Losing Job-Based Insurance, Commonwealth Fund Analysis Finds," *FierceHealthcare*, October 7, 2020, https://www.fiercehealthcare.com/payer/nearly-8-million-americans-danger-los ing-job-based-insurance-commonwealth-fund-analysis-finds.

47. US Bureau of Labor Statistics, "77 Percent of Private Industry Workers in Medical Care Plans with Two Networks in 2018," July 26, 2019, https://www.bls.gov /opub/ted/2019/77-percent-of-private-industry-workers-in-medical-care-plans-with -two-networks-in-2018.htm.

48. Julie Leask, Claire Hooker, and Catherine King, "Media Coverage of Health Issues and How to Work More Effectively with Journalists: A Qualitative Study," *BMC Public Health* 10, no. 535 (2010), https://doi.org/10.1186/1471-2458-10-535.

49. "KHN Ethics Guidelines," *Kaiser Health News*, n.d., accessed January 17, 2021, https://khn.org/ethics-guidelines/.

50. "About Us," *STAT News*, accessed January 17, 2021, https://www.statnews .com/about/.

CHAPTER 11. USING TECHNOLOGY TO IMPROVE COVERAGE

1. David Skerrett, "The State of Artificial Intelligence around the Globe," *EContentMag*, Summer 2018, 14–15.

2. Michael Casey, "Without Stronger Transparency, More Financial Crises Looms," Committee to Protect Journalists, February 2014, https://cpj.org/2014/02 /attacks-on-the-press-transparency-finance.php.

3. Gina Chua, telephone interview, July 18, 2018.

4. Chua, telephone interview.

5. Chua, telephone interview.

6. Chua, telephone interview.

7. Francesco Marconi, "Study: News Automation by AP Increases Trading in Financial Markets," Associated Press, December 8, 2016, https://insights.ap.org/in dustry-trends/study-news-automation-by-ap-increases-trading-in-financial-markets.

8. Max Frumes, "Financial Journalism in the Age of Elon Musk's Dystopia," *LinkedIn*, October 18, 2017, https://www.linkedin.com/pulse/financial-journalism -age-elon-musks-dystopia-part-1-3-max-frumes/?published=t.

9. Ben Ashwell, "How Automated Financial News Is Changing Quarterly Earnings Coverage," *IR Magazine*, June 6, 2018, https://www.irmagazine.com/reporting /how-automated-financial-news-changing-quarterly-earnings-coverage.

10. Allan Wastler, "Business Reporter Jobs and the Threat from Machines," *Talking*

Biz News, July 20, 2015, http://talkingbiznews.com/2/biz-reporter-jobs-and-the-threat-from-machines/.

11. Joe Pinsker, "Algorithm-Generated Articles Don't Foretell the End of Journalism," *Atlantic*, June 30, 2014, https://www.theatlantic.com/business/archive/2014/06/algorithm-generated-articles-dont-foretell-the-end-of-journalism/373691/.

12. Stacey Vanek Smith, "An NPR Reporter Raced a Machine to Write a News Story. Who Won?," NPR, May 20, 2015, https://www.npr.org/sections/money/2015/05/20/406484294/an-npr-reporter-raced-a-machine-to-write-a-news-story-who-won.

13. Emily Withrow, telephone interview, July 26, 2018.

14. Tim Peterson, "Quartz Forms Quartz AI Studio with $250k Grant from Knight Foundation," *Digiday*, November 20, 2018, https://digiday.com/media/quartz-forms-quartz-ai-studio/.

15. Withrow, telephone interview.

16. Max Frumes, telephone interview, May 24, 2018.

17. Frumes, telephone interview.

18. Max Frumes, "Introducing Quant Media: Combining Predictive Technology with Business Journalism," *LinkedIn*, February 27, 2018, https://www.linkedin.com/pulse/introducing-quant-media-combining-predictive-business-max-frumes/?published=t.

19. Frumes, telephone interview.

20. Frumes, telephone interview.

21. John Micklethwait, "The Future of News: Automated, Personalized, Mobile, Paid For, and (Eventually) Less Fake. Quality Journalism Is Coming Back," *Bloomberg Businessweek*, May 3, 2018, https://www.bloomberg.com/news/articles/2018-05-03/john-micklethwait-the-future-of-news.

22. John Micklethwait, "Bloomberg to Expand Story Automation Efforts," *Talking Biz News*, April 26, 2016, https://talkingbiznews.com/they-talk-biz-news/micklethwait-bloomberg-to-expand-story-automation-efforts/.

23. Ron Day, "AI's Newest Target for Worker Displacement? Journalists," *BigThink*, May 26, 2018, https://bigthink.com/ron-day/ais-newest-target-for-worker-displacement-journalists.

CHAPTER 12. THE EDUCATION IMPERATIVE

1. Mary Jane Pardue, "Most Business Editors Find Journalism Students Still Unprepared," *Journalism and Mass Communication Educator* 69, no. 1 (Spring 2014): 49–60.

2. Maha Rafi Atal, "The Cultural and Economic Power of Advertisers in the Business Press," *Journalism*, November 2017, 1–18.

3. Allan Richards and Kathy Kirkpatrick, "The JMC Innovation Project: A Pivotal Moment for Journalism, Media and Communication Education; Assessing the State of Innovation," *Journalism & Mass Communication Educator* 73, no. 2 (Spring 2018): 136–46.

4. Kenneth R. Ahern and Denis Sosyura, "Rumor Has It: Sensationalism in Financial Media," *Review of Financial Studies* 28, no. 7 (July 2015): 2050–93.

5. Atal, "Cultural and Economic Power of Advertisers."

6. Emily Overholt, "Reynolds Foundation Establishes Business Journalism Bureau at ASU's Cronkite School," *Phoenix Business Journal*, July 30, 2014, https://www.bizjournals.com/phoenix/news/2014/07/30/reynolds-foundation-establishes-business.html.

7. Joseph Weber, "Teaching Business and Economic Journalism: Fresh Approaches," *Journalism and Mass Communication Educator* 71, no. 4 (December 2016): 1–17.

8. Trudy Lieberman, "Health Reporting: Semester-long Course on Covering the Science, Policy and Business of Health Care," Shorenstein Center on Media, Politics and Public Policy, May 3, 2012, https://journalistsresource.org/syllabi/health-reporting/.

9. James Hamilton, *FACS/FORD Study of Economic and Business Journalism for the Ford Foundation by the Foundation for American Communications* (Los Angeles: Foundation for American Communications, 1987), 1–2.

10. Louise Story, "What Business Reporters Can Get Out of an MBA," Columbia University, March 5, 2013, http://coveringbusiness.com/2013/03/04/what-business-reporters-can-get-out-of-an-mba/.

11. Menachem Wecker, "Embattled News Industry May Offer Options for MBA's," *US News & World Report*, February 15, 2012, https://www.usnews.com/education/best-graduate-schools/top-business-schools/articles/2012/02/15/embattled-news-industry-may-offer-options-for-mbas.

12. Neil Reisner, "Are Journalism Students Up to Code?," *Quill*, March/April 2014, 9, 22.

13. Grant Hannis, "Taking Care of Business: Equipping Students to Become Business Journalists," *Journalism & Mass Communication Educator* 71, no. 3 (Fall 2016): 344–59.

14. Chris Roush, "Why Journalism Schools Should Teach Tech Reporting," *Talking Biz News*, March 5, 2014, https://talkingbiznews.com/they-talk-biz-news/why-journalism-schools-should-teach-tech-reporting/.

15. Steve Weinberg, *A Journalism of Humanity: A Candid History of the World's First Journalism School* (Columbia: University of Missouri Press, 2008), xx.

16. Stephen Shepard, *Deadlines and Disruption: My Turbulent Path from Print to Digital* (New York: McGraw-Hill, 2013), 59.

17. Ahern and Sosyura. "Rumor Has It."

18. David Cuillier and Carol Schwalbe, "GIFTed Teaching: A Content Analysis of 253 Great Ideas for Teaching Awards in Journalism and Mass Communication Education," *Journalism & Mass Communication Educator* 65, no. 1 (Spring 2010): 22–39.

19. "Leading Daily Newspapers in the United States as of September 2017, by Circulation," *Statista*, n.d., https://www.statista.com/statistics/184682/us-daily-newspapers-by-circulation/.

20. Chris Roush, "Economist Sees 46 Percent Increase in US Digital Circulation," *Talking Biz News*, August 10, 2017, http://talkingbiznews.com/1/economist-sees-46-percent-increase-in-u-s-digital-circulation/.

21. Chris Roush, "Weeklies on the Rise," *Columbia Journalism Review*, January/February 2020, 10–12.

CHAPTER 13. FIXING BUSINESS JOURNALISM

1. Sean Griffey, "Growth in Digital Media—Three Strategies That Work in Any Economic Environment," *LinkedIn*, December 17, 2020, https://www.linkedin.com/pulse/growth-digital-mediathree-strategies-work-any-economic-sean-griffey/?trackingId=fGrqOAd3QxmB%2B%2FWFxybNzg%3D%3D.

2. Edmund Lee, "Axios Buys Charlotte Agenda, a Digital Start-Up, as Part of Push into Local News," *New York Times*, December 17, 2020, https://www.nytimes.com/2020/12/17/business/media/axios-local-news-charlotte-agenda.html.

3. "Charlotte Observer," McClatchy, accessed December 29, 2020, https://www.mcclatchy.com/our-impact/markets/the-charlotte-observer.

4. Tony Mecia, LinkedIn message to author, December 18, 2020.

5. Mecia, LinkedIn message.

6. Mecia, LinkedIn message.

7. Mecia, LinkedIn message.

8. Ken Doctor, "Newsonomics: Here Are 20 Epiphanies for the News Business of the 2020s," Nieman Lab, January 24, 2020, https://www.niemanlab.org/2020/01/newsonomics-here-are-20-epiphanies-for-the-news-business-of-the-2020s/.

9. Doctor, "Newsonomics."

10. US Small Business Administration Office of Advocacy, "Frequently Asked Questions," n.d., accessed December 28, 2020, https://www.sba.gov/sites/default/files/advocacy/Frequently-Asked-Questions-Small-Business-2018.pdf.

11. US Small Business Administration Office of Advocacy.

12. Sifan Liu and Joseph Parilla, "Businesses Owned by Women and Minorities Have Grown. Will COVID-19 Undo That?," Brookings Institution, April 14, 2020, https://www.brookings.edu/research/businesses-owned-by-women-and-minorities-have-grown-will-covid-19-undo-that/.

13. Chris Roush, "Minority and Independent Businesses Rate Biz Coverage," *Talking Biz News*, July 25, 2008, https://talkingbiznews.com/they-talk-biz-news/minority-and-independent-businesses-rate-biz-coverage/.

14. Chris Roush, "Female Bylines Drop at Wall Street Journal," *Talking Biz News*, March 22, 2017, https://talkingbiznews.com/they-talk-biz-news/female-bylines-drop-at-wall-street-journal/.

15. Mark Di Stefano, "The Economist's Editor Says There Aren't Enough Black People Working at the Magazine," *BuzzFeed News*, February 19, 2019, https://www.buzzfeed.com/markdistefano/the-economists-editor-says-there-arent-enough-black-people.

16. Chris Roush, "ACBJ to Address Diversity within the Company," *Talking Biz News*, July 9, 2020, https://talkingbiznews.com/they-talk-biz-news/acbj-to-address-diversity-within-the-company/.

17. Tamil Nadu, "Diverse Workforce Key for Success of Newsrooms," *Hindu*, May 12, 2018, https://www.thehindu.com/news/national/tamil-nadu/diverse-workforce-key-for-success-of-newsrooms/article23858482.ece.

18. Chris Roush, "Bloomberg Increases Percentage of Women in Content, Expands Training," *Talking Biz News*, December 10, 2018, https://talkingbiznews.com/they-talk-biz-news/bloomberg-increase-percentage-of-women-in-content-expands-training/.

19. Jim Waterson, "Financial Times Tool Warns if Articles Quote Too Many Men," *Guardian*, November 14, 2018, https://www.theguardian.com/media/2018/nov/14/financial-times-tool-warns-if-articles-quote-too-many-men.

20. Chris Roush, "Bloomberg Reporter Increases Women Quoted in Stories to 50 percent," *Talking Biz News*, December 28, 2018, https://talkingbiznews.com/they-talk-biz-news/bloomberg-reporter-increases-women-quoted-in-stories-to-50-percent/.

21. Ben Casselman tweet: "One of my goals this year was to be more aware of the diversity . . ." (@bencasselman, December 31, 2019), available at https://threadreaderapp.com/thread/1212049682991591425.html.

22. Ben Casselman tweet.

23. Sarah Paynter, Twitter message to author, December 17, 2020.

24. American Bankruptcy Institute, "Bankruptcy Statistics," accessed September 16, 2021, https://www.abi.org/newsroom/bankruptcy-statistics.

25. Chris Roush, "The Need for Better Local Economic News," *Talking Biz News*, February 6, 2014, https://talkingbiznews.com/they-talk-biz-news/the-need-for-better-local-economic-news/.

26. See www.gasbuddy.com and https://aaa.com.

27. Harold Meyerson, "How the Media Should Cover Corporations Now," *American Prospect*, August 20, 2019, https://prospect.org/blogs/tap/media-cover-corporations-now/.

28. Joseph Stiglitz, "The Media and the Crisis: An Information Theoretical Approach," in *Bad News: How America's Business Press Missed the Story of the Century*, ed. Anya Schiffrin (New York: New Press, 2011), 22–36.

29. Jesse Eisinger, e-mail message to author, June 28, 2018.

30. Tran Thy-Anh Huynh, "Why Did Our Watchdog Fail? A Counter Perspective on the Media Coverage of the 2007 Financial Crisis," London School of Economics, https://www.lse.ac.uk/media-and-communications/assets/documents/research/msc-dissertations/2015/Tran-Thuy-Anh-Huynh.pdf.

31. Melia Russell, tweet: "This was a first for me" (@meliarobin, October 29, 2020), https://twitter.com/meliarobin/status/1321840306183118849.

32. Paul Glader, "From Scapegoat to WonkBlog: The Business Press as Watch-

dog and Think Tank," *Forbes*, April 16, 2014, https://www.forbes.com/sites/berlin schoolofcreativeleadership/2014/04/16/from-scapegoat-to-wonkblog-the-role-for -the-business-press-as-watchdog-and-think-tank/?sh=43da5ee21040.

33. "Stigler Center Launches Journalists in Residence Program," University of Chicago Booth School of Business, November 7, 2016, https://www.chicagobooth .edu/research/stigler/news-and-media/stigler-center-launches-journalists-in-resi dence-program.

34. Stiglitz, "Media and the Crisis."

35. Stefan Theil, "The Media and Markets: How Systematic Misreporting Inflates Bubbles, Deepens Downturns and Distorts Economic Reality," Shorenstein Center on Media, Politics and Public Policy Discussion Paper Series, #D-86 (June 2014), https:// dash.harvard.edu/bitstream/handle/1/12872174/d86-theil.pdf?sequence=1&isAl lowed=y.

36. Benjamin Mullin, "Cheddar, the 'CNBC for Millennials,' Raises $22 Million for International Expansion," *Wall Street Journal*, March 19, 2018, https://www.wsj .com/articles/cheddar-the-cnbc-for-millennials-raises-22-million-for-internation al-expansion-1521487261.

37. Mullin.

38. David Siegel bio, *LinkedIn*, accessed December 28, 2020, https://www.linked in.com/in/davidmsiegel/.

39. Chris Roush, "Biz News Site Benzinga Closes on $3 Million Financing Round," *Talking Biz News*, September 19, 2016, https://talkingbiznews.com/they -talk-biz-news/biz-news-site-benzinga-closes-on-3-million-financing-round/.

40. Chris Roush, "Nerdwallet Raises $64 Million in Financing," *Talking Biz News*, May 19, 2015, https://talkingbiznews.com/they-talk-biz-news/nerdwallet-rais es-64-million-in-financing/.

41. Matthew Flamm, "Mobile-Focused Quartz Manages to Turn a Profit on Digital Journalism," *Crain's New York Business*, March 26, 2017, https://www.crainsnewyork .com/article/20170326/TECHNOLOGY/170329904/mobile-focused-quartz-man ages-to-turn-a-profit-on-digital-journalism-focused-on-quirky-and-smart-business -news.

42. David Callaway, e-mail correspondence with author, June 28, 2018.

43. Jose Miguel Calatayud, "Journalists across Europe Collaborate to Cover Airbnb and Other Housing Issues," *Nieman Lab*, November 17, 2020, https://nieman reports.org/articles/journalists-across-europe-collaborate-to-cover-airbnb-and-oth er-housing-issues/.

44. Chris Roush, "ACBJ Strikes Content Deal with Financial Times," *Talking Biz News*, June 19, 2017, https://talkingbiznews.com/they-talk-biz-news/acbj-strikes-con tent-deal-with-financial-times/.

45. Steve Schifferes, *The Media and Financial Crises: Comparative and Historical Perspectives* (New York: Routledge, 2015), xix.

46. Allen Wastler, "The Problem with Small Business News Coverage," *Talking*

Biz News, July 28, 2015, https://talkingbiznews.com/we-talk-biz-news/the-problem -with-small-business-news-coverage/.

47. Farhad Manjoo, "A Crazy Idea for Funding Local News: Charge People for It," *New York Times*, February 7, 2018, https://www.nytimes.com/2018/02/07/tech nology/funding-local-news-charge-people-money.html.

48. Max Willens, "How Investopedia Shifted to Subscription Revenue with Video Courses," *Digiday*, January 12, 2018, https://digiday.com/media/investopedia -shifted-subscription-revenue-video-courses/.

49. Chris Roush, "'People on the Move' Becomes ACBJ Revenue Stream," *Talking Biz News*, July 17, 2017, https://talkingbiznews.com/they-talk-biz-news/peo ple-on-the-move-becomes-acbj-revenue-stream/.

BIBLIOGRAPHY

Abernathy, Penelope Muse. *News Deserts and Ghost Newspapers: Will Local News Survive?* Chapel Hill: University of North Carolina Press, 2020.

———. "Vanishing Readers and Journalists," University of North Carolina Hussman School of Journalism and Media. Accessed December 12, 2020. https://www.usnewsdeserts.com/reports/news-deserts-and-ghost-newspapers-will-local-news-survive/the-news-landscape-in-2020-transformed-and-diminished/vanishing-readers-and-journalists/.

ADP Research Institute. "Workforce Vitality Report." October 2020. Accessed January 8, 2021. https://workforcereport.adp.com/.

Ahern, Kenneth R., and Denis Sosyura. "Rumor Has It: Sensationalism in Financial Media." *Review of Financial Studies* 28, no. 7 (July 2015): 2050–93.

Allen, Christopher D. "CEO Speeches: From Nightmare to Opportunity." *Public Relations Quarterly* 8, no. 1 (Summer 1994): 25–27.

Allison, David. "Piedmont Healthcare Plans Expansion at Athens Hospital." *Atlanta Business Chronicle*, January 14, 2021. https://www.bizjournals.com/atlanta/news/2021/01/14/piedmont-healthcare-expansion-athens-regional.html.

American Press Institute. "Paying for News: Why People Subscribe and What It Says about the Future of Journalism." Accessed May 2, 2017. https://www.americanpressinstitute.org/publications/reports/survey-research/paying-for-news/.

American Society of News Editors. "2016 Newsroom Diversity Survey." Accessed January 6, 2020. https://www.asne.org/newsroom_diversitysurvey.

Arnold, James E. "Communications and Strategy: The CEO Gets (and Gives) the Message." *Public Relations Quarterly* 33 (Summer 1988): 5–13.

Atal, Maha Rafi. "The Cultural and Economic Power of Advertisers in the Business Press." *Journalism* (November 2017): 1–18.

Baldasty, Gerald. *The Commercialization of News in the Nineteenth Century.* Madison: University of Wisconsin Press, 1992.

Baloria, Vishal, and Jonas Heese. "The Effects of Media Slant on Firm Behavior." *Journal of Financial Economics*, August 17, 2017. Harvard Business School Accounting & Management Unit Working Paper No. 18-015. http://dx.doi.org/10.2139/ssrn.3021229.

Barthel, Michael. "5 Key Takeaways about the State of the News Media in 2018." Pew Research Center, July 23, 2019. https://www.pewresearch.org/fact-tank/2019/07/23/key-takeaways-state-of-the-news-media-2018/.

Bauman, Dan, and Chris Quintana. "Drew Cloud Is a Well-Known Expert on Student Loans. One Problem: He's Not Real." *Chronicle of Higher Education*, April 24,

2018. https://www.chronicle.com/article/drew-cloud-is-a-well-known-expert-on -student-loans-one-problem-hes-not-real/.

Beal, Dave. "SABEW: From 1963 to Today and Beyond." *American History of Business Journalism,* March 2013. https://ahbj.sabew.org/story/04042013-sabew-from -1963-to-today-and-beyond/.

Bivens, Josh. "Inequality Is Slowing US Economic Growth." Economic Policy Institute, December 12, 2017. https://www.epi.org/publication/secular-stagnation/.

Bonsall, Samuel B., Jeremiah Green, and Karl A. Muller. "Market Uncertainty and the Importance of Media Coverage at Earnings Announcements." *Journal of Accounting & Economics,* September 25, 2019. https://ssrn.com/abstract=3459543.

Brenan, Megan. "Americans Remain Distrustful of Mass Media." Gallup, September 30, 2020. https://news.gallup.com/poll/321116/americans-remain-distrust ful-mass-media.aspx.

———. "Americans' Trust in Mass Media Edges Down to 41%." Gallup, September 30, 2020. https://news.gallup.com/poll/321116/americans-remain-distrust ful-mass-media.aspx.

Brenan, Megan, and Helen Stubbs. "News Media Viewed as Biased but Crucial to Democracy." Gallup, August 4, 2020. https://news.gallup.com/poll/316574 /news-media-viewed-biased-crucial-democracy.aspx.

Butler, Stuart M., and Jonathan Grabinsky. "Tackling the Legacy of Persistent Uren Inequality and Concentered Poverty." Brookings Institution, November 16, 2020. https://www.brookings.edu/blog/up-front/2020/11/16/tackling-the-legacy -of-persistent-urban-inequality-and-concentrated-poverty/.

Bybee, Leland, Bryan T. Kelly, Asaf Manela, and Dacheng Xiu. "The Structure of Economic News." January 1, 2020. http://dx.doi.org/10.2139/ssrn.3446225.

Call, Andrew, Scott Emett, Eldar Maksymov, and Nathan Sharp. "Meet the Press: Survey Evidence on Financial Journalists as Information Intermediaries." November 2018; rev. February 2020. https://dx.doi.org/10.2139/ssrn.3279453.

Carroll, Craig, "How the Mass Media Influence Perceptions of Corporate Reputation: Exploring Agenda-Setting Effects within Business News Coverage." PhD diss., University of Texas, 2004. https://repositories.lib.utexas.edu/bitstream /handle/2152/2153/carrollce30855.pdf?sequence=2&isAllowed=y.

Casey, Michael. "Without Stronger Transparency, More Financial Crises Loom." Committee to Protect Journalists, February 2014. https://cpj.org/2014/02/attacks -on-the-press-transparency-finance.php.

Center for Medicare & Medicaid Services. "National Health Expenditure Data." Accessed January 20, 2021. https://www.cms.gov/Research-Statistics-Data-and-Sys tems/Statistics-Trends-and-Reports/NationalHealthExpendData/NHE-Fact -Sheet.

Centola, Damon. "Why Social Media Makes Us More Polarized and How to Fix It." *Scientific American,* October 15, 2020. https://www.scientificamerican.com/arti cle/why-social-media-makes-us-more-polarized-and-how-to-fix-it/.

Chandler, Alfred D. "Henry Varnum Poor: Editor of the American Railroad Journal." Master's thesis, University of North Carolina, 1951.

Chandler, Alfred, Jr., and James Cortada. *A Nation Transformed by Information: How Information Has Shaped the United States from Colonial Times to Present.* Oxford: Oxford University Press, 2003.

Comcast Corporation. "Comcast Reports 3rd Quarter 2020 Results." October 29, 2020. https://www.cmcsa.com/news-releases/news-release-details/comcast-re ports-3rd-quarter-2020-results.

Comdex Official. "Commodity Trading: Backbone of the Global Economy." April 25, 2019. https://medium.com/@comdexofficial/commodity-trading-backbone -of-the-global-economy-131c78f12989#:~:text=The%20market%20size%20 of%20the,around%20%2420%20trillion%20a%20year.

Cook, Tracy M. "How Much US Newspapers Charge for Digital Subscriptions." American Press Institute, February 14, 2018. https://www.americanpressinstitute.org /publications/reports/digital-subscription-pricing/.

Cooper, Zack, Amanda E. Kowalski, Eleanor N. Powell, and Jennifer Wu. "Politics and Health Care Spending in the United States." National Bureau of Economic Research, September 2020. https://www.nber.org/papers/w23748.

Cuillier, David, and Carol Schwalbe. "GIFTed Teaching: A Content Analysis of 253 Great Ideas for Teaching Awards in Journalism and Mass Communication Education." *Journalism & Mass Communication Educator* 65, no. 1 (Spring 2010): 22–39.

Dorsey, Sherrell. "Black Tech News Coverage Struggles to Find a Home in Mainstream Newsrooms." *Columbia Journalism Review*, July 8, 2019. https://www.cjr .org/analysis/black-media-tech-coverage.php.

Drutman, Lee. *The Business of America Is Lobbying: How Corporations Became Politicized and Politics Became More Corporate.* New York: Oxford University Press, 2015. Excerpted April 25, 2015, at https://www.businessinsider.com/how-corpo rations-turned-into-political-beasts-2015-4.

Duca, John V., and Jason L. Saving. "Income Inequality, Media Fragmentation and Increased Political Polarization." *Contemporary Economic Policy* 35, no. 2 (August 2016): 392–413. https://onlinelibrary.wiley.com/doi/abs/10.1111/coep.12191.

Dunn, Amina. "Democrats Differ over Best Way to Provide Health Coverage for All Americans." Pew Research Center, July 26, 2019. https://www.pewresearch.org /fact-tank/2019/07/26/democrats-differ-over-best-way-to-provide-health-cover age-for-all-americans/.

Dyck, Alexander, and Luigi Zingales. "The Media and Asset Prices." Working paper, Harvard Business School. August 2003. http://www.anderson.ucla.edu/faculty _pages/romain.wacziarg/mediapapers/DyckZingales.pdf.

Ey, Craig. "Business and the Media." *Philadelphia Business Journal*, February 11, 2011. https://www.bizjournals.com/philadelphia/print-edition/2011/02/04/business -and-the-media.html.

Fang, Lily H., Joel Peress, and Lu Zheng. "Does Media Coverage of Stocks Affect

Mutual Funds' Trading and Performance?" *Review of Financial Studies* 27, no. 12 (December 2014): 3441–66. https://doi.org/10.1093/rfs/hhu056.

Federal Reserve System Board of Governors. "Report on the Economic Well-Being of US Households in 2018." May 2019, https://www.federalreserve.gov/publi cations/2019-economic-well-being-of-us-households-in-2018-retirement.htm.

———. 2019 Survey of Consumer Finances. Accessed December 13, 2020. https:// www.federalreserve.gov/econres/scfindex.htm.

Fingerhut, Hannah. "Is Treatment of Minorities a Key Election Issue? Views Differ by Race, Party." Pew Research Center, July 13, 2016. https://www.pewresearch.org /fact-tank/2016/07/13/partisan-racial-divides-exist-over-how-important-treat ment-of-minorities-is-as-a-voting-issue/.

Fletcher, Richard. "Paying for News and the Limits of Subscription." Reuters Insti- tute for the Study of Journalism. Accessed November 13, 2021. https://www.di gitalnewsreport.org/survey/2019/paying-for-news-and-the-limits-of-subscrip tion/.

Fletcher, Richard, Alessio Cornia, and Rasmua Kleis Nielsen. "How Polarized Are On- line and Offline News Audiences? A Comparative Analysis of Twelve Countries." *International Journal of Press/Politics* 25, no. 2 (April 2020): 169–95. https://doi .org/10.1177/1940161219892768.

Forsyth, David. *The Business Press in America: 1750–1865.* Philadelphia: Chilton, 1964.

Gallup Inc. and John S. and James L. Knight Foundation. "Accuracy and Bias in the News Media." June 20, 2018. https://knightfoundation.org/reports/perceived -accuracy-and-bias-in-the-news-media/.

———. "American Views 2020: Trust, Media and Democracy." November 9, 2020. https://knightfoundation.org/wp-content/uploads/2020/08/American-Views -2020-Trust-Media-and-Democracy.pdf.

Garrett, R. Kelly, Brian E. Weeks, and Rachel L. Nelo. "Driving a Wedge between Ev- idence and Beliefs: How Online Ideological News Exposure Promotes Political Misperceptions." *Journal of Computer-Mediated Communication* 21, no. 5 (August 2016): 331–48, https://onlinelibrary.wiley.com/doi/full/10.1111/jcc4.12164.

Gold, Howard R. "Ten Years after the Financial Crisis, Business Journalism Awaits Its Reckoning." *Columbia Journalism Review,* September 17, 2018. https://www .cjr.org/business_of_news/ten-years-financial-crisis-business-journalism.php.

Goldman, Eitan, Nandina Gupta, and Ryan D. Israelsen. "Political Polarization in Financial News." February 13, 2020. https://ssrn.com/abstract=3537841.

Gollust, Sarah, Erika Franklin Fowler, and Jeff Niederdeppe. "Television News Cov- erage of Public Health Issues and Implications for Public Health Policy and Practice." *Annual Review of Public Health* 40 (2019): 167–85. https://www.annu alreviews.org/doi/pdf/10.1146/annurev-publhealth-040218-044017.

Goodman, Laurie, Christopher Mayer, and Christopher R. Hayes. "To Explain Changes in the Homeownership Rate, Look beyond Demographic Trends." Ur- ban Institute, March 6, 2018. https://www.urban.org/urban-wire/explain-chang es-homeownership-rate-look-beyond-demographic-trends.

Govindarajan, Vijay, Baruch Lev, Anup Srivastava, and Luminita Enache. "The Gap between Large and Small Companies Is Growing. Why?" *Harvard Business Review,* August 16, 2019. https://hbr.org/2019/08/the-gap-between-large-and-small -companies-is-growing-why.

Gramlich, John. "19 Striking Findings from 2019." Pew Research Center, December 13, 2019. https://www.pewresearch.org/fact-tank/2019/12/13/19-striking-findings -from-2019/.

Greenhouse, Steven. "Through the Working Class." *Columbia Journalism Review,* Winter 2019. https://www.cjr.org/special_report/through-the-working-class.php.

Greenspan, Jacob. "How Big a Problem Is It That a Few Shareholders Own Stock in So Many Competing Companies?" *Harvard Business Review,* February 19, 2019. https://hbr.org/2019/02/how-big-a-problem-is-it-that-a-few-shareholders-own -stock-in-so-many-competing-companies.

Grieco, Elizabeth. "Fast Facts about the Newspaper Industry's Financial Struggles as McClatchy Files for Bankruptcy." Pew Research Center, February 14, 2020. https://www.pewresearch.org/fact-tank/2020/02/14/fast-facts-about-the-news paper-industrys-financial-struggles/.

———. "US Newspapers Have Shed Half of Their Newsroom Employees since 2008." Pew Research Center, April 20, 2020. https://www.pewresearch.org/fact -tank/2020/04/20/u-s-newsroom-employment-has-dropped-by-a-quarter -since-2008/.

Grisold, Andrea, and Hendrik Theine. "How Come We Know? The Media Coverage of Economic Inequality." *International Journal of Communication* 11 (2017): 4265–84.

Guest, Nicholas. "Do Journalists Help Investors Analyze Firms' Earnings News?" PhD diss., Massachusetts Institute of Technology Sloan School of Management, 2017.

Haggerty, Michael, and Wallace Rasmussen. *The Headline vs. the Bottom Line: Mutual District between Business and the News Media.* Nashville: The Freedom Forum First Amendment Center, 1994.

Halff, Gregor. "The Presentation of CEOs in Economic Downturn." *Corporate Reputation Review* 16, no. 3 (2013): 234–43.

Hamilton, James. *FACS/FORD Study of Economic and Business Journalism for the Ford Foundation by the Foundation for American Communications.* Los Angeles: Foundation for American Communications, 1987.

Han, Jiyoung. "Conflict Framing of the News and Group Polarization." PhD diss., University of Minnesota, 2016, https://conservancy.umn.edu/handle/11299/181736.

Hannis, Grant. "Taking Care of Business: Equipping Students to Become Business Journalists." *Journalism & Mass Communication Educator* 71, no. 3 (Fall 2016): 344–59.

Louis Harris Poll. "The Quality of Business Journalism in America." Boston: John Hancock Financial Services, 1992.

Horowitz, Juliana Menasce, Ruth Igielnik, and Rakesh Kochhar. "Most Americans

Say There Is Too Much Economic Inequality in the US, but Fewer than Half Call It a Top Priority." Pew Research Center, January 9, 2020. https://www.pew socialtrends.org/2020/01/09/most-americans-say-there-is-too-much-econom ic-inequality-in-the-u-s-but-fewer-than-half-call-it-a-top-priority/.

———. "Trends in Income and Wealth Inequality." Pew Research Center, January 9, 2020. https://www.pewsocialtrends.org/2020/01/09/trends-in-income-and -wealth-inequality/.

Huynh, Tran Thy-Anh. "Why Did Our Watchdog Fail? A Counter Perspective on the Media Coverage of the 2007 Financial Crisis." London School of Economics. Accessed December 1, 2020. https://www.lse.ac.uk/media-and-communications /assets/documents/research/msc-dissertations/2015/Tran-Thuy-Anh-Huynh .pdf.

Jacobs, Alan M., J. Scott Matthews, Timothy Hicks, and Eric Merkley. "Whose News? Class-Biased Economic Reporting in the United States" Washington Center for Equitable Growth, March 3, 2020. https://equitablegrowth.org/working-papers /whose-news-class-biased-economic-reporting-in-the-united-states/.

Johnson, Matthew. "Regulation by Shaming: Deterrence Effects of Publicizing Viola-tions of Workplace Safety and Health Laws." *American Economic Review* 110 (6): 1866–904.

Jones, Bradley, "Increasing Share of Americans Favor a Single Government Program to Provide Health Care Coverage." Pew Research Center, September 29, 2020. https://www.pewresearch.org/fact-tank/2020/09/29/increasing-share-of -americans-favor-a-single-government-program-to-provide-health-care-coverage/.

Jones, Sarah. "The Great Remove: How Journalism Got So Out of Touch with the Peo-ple It Covers." *Columbia Journalism Review*, Spring/Summer 2018. https://www .cjr.org/special_report/journalism-class.php.

Jurkowitz, Mark, Amy Mitchell, Elisa Sherer, and Mason Walker. "Democrats Report Much Higher Levels of Trust in a Number of News Sources than Republications." Pew Research Center, January 24, 2020. https://www.journalism.org/2020/01/24 /democrats-report-much-higher-levels-of-trust-in-a-number-of-news-sources -than-republicans/.

———. "US Media Polarization and the 2020 Election: A Nation Divided." Pew Research Center, January 24, 2020. https://www.journalism.org/2020/01/24/u-s-media -polarization-and-the-2020-election-a-nation-divided/.

Kadlec, Daniel. "How Bloomberg Pressures Editors; They Can't Pay for the Ma-chine—but They Can Get It for Credit." *Columbia Journalism Review* 36, no. 3 (1997): 39.

Kaiser Family Foundation. "Distribution of US Population by Race/Ethnicity: 2010 and 2050." March 18, 2013, https://www.kff.org/racial-equity-and-health-policy/slide /distribution-of-u-s-population-by-raceethnicity-2010-and-2050/.

———. "How Much Does the US Spend on Health and How Has It Changed?" May 1, 2012, https://www.kff.org/report-section/health-care-costs-a-primer-2012-re port/.

———. "Poll: Nearly 1 in 4 Americans Taking Prescription Drugs Say It's Difficult to Afford Their Medicines." March 1, 2019, https://www.kff.org/health-costs/press -release/poll-nearly-1-in-4-americans-taking-prescription-drugs-say-its-difficult -to-afford-medicines-including-larger-shares-with-low-incomes/.

Keisler-Starkey, Katherine, and Lisa N. Bunch. "Health Insurance Coverage in the United States: 2019." US Census Bureau, September 15, 2020. https://www.cen sus.gov/library/publications/2020/demo/p60-271.html.

Khurana, Rakesh. "The Curse of the Superstar CEO." *Harvard Business Review*, September 2002. https://hbr.org/2002/09/the-curse-of-the-superstar-ceo.

Kohut, Gary F., and Albert F. Segars. "The President's Letter to Stockholders: An Examination of Corporate Communication Strategy." *Journal of Business Communication* 29, no. 1 (Winter 1992): 7–19.

Leask, Julie, Claire Hooker, and Catherine King. "Media Coverage of Health Issues and How to Work More Effectively with Journalists: A Qualitative Study." *BMC Public Health* 10, no. 535 (2010). https://doi.org/10.1186/1471-2458-10-535.

Lee, Terry. "The Global Rise of 'Fake News' and the Threat to Democratic Elections in the USA." *Public Administration and Policy: An Asia-Pacific Journal* 22, no. 1 (July 2019): 15–24. https://doi.org/10.1108/PAP-04-2019-0008.

Lieberman, Trudy. "Health Reporting: Semester-long Course on Covering the Science, Policy and Business of Health Care." Shorenstein Center on Media, Politics and Public Policy, May 3, 2012. https://journalistsresource.org/syllabi /health-reporting/.

Liu, Sifan, and Joseph Parilla. "Businesses Owned by Women and Minorities Have Grown. Will COVID-19 undo That?" Brookings Institution, April 14, 2020. https:// www.brookings.edu/research/businesses-owned-by-women-and-minorities -have-grown-will-covid-19-undo-that/.

Madrick, Jeffrey. "Credulity in Business Journalism: A History of the Business Press since the 1970s." American Academy of Arts & Sciences. Accessed January 29, 2021. https://www.amacad.org/sites/default/files/academy/pdfs/credulity.pdf.

Martin, Christopher. *Framed! Labor and the Corporate Media*. Ithaca, NY: Cornell University Press, 2004.

———. *No Longer Newsworthy: How the Mainstream Media Abandoned the Working Class*. Ithaca, NY: ILR Press, 2019.

Matthews, George. *News and Rumor in Renaissance Europe: The Fugger Newsletters*. New York: Capricorn, 1959.

McDermott, Daniel, Lina Stolyar, Cynthia Cox, Robin Rudowitz, Rachel Garfield, Jeannie Fuglestein Biniek, and Tricia Neuman. "Health Insurer Financial Performance through September 2020," Kaiser Family Foundation, December 16, 2020. https://www.kff.org/private-insurance/issue-brief/health-insurer-financial -performance-through-september-2020/.

Meschke, Felix. "CEO Interviews on CNBC." Presentation at AFA 2003 Washington, DC, meetings. June 2004. http://dx.doi.org/10.2139/ssrn.302602.

Miller, Gregory. "The Press as a Watchdog for Accounting Fraud." *Journal of Account-*

ing Research 44, no. 5 (October 2006): 1001–33, https://doi.org/10.1111/j.1475-679X.2006.00224.x.

Mishel, Lawrence, and Julia Wolfe. "CEO Compensation Has Grown 940% since 1978." Economic Policy Institute, August 14, 2019. https://www.epi.org/publication/ceo-compensation-2018/.

Mitchell, Amy, Mark Jurkowitz, J. Baxter Oliphant, and Elisa Sheare. "Americans Who Mainly Get Their News on Social Media Are Less Engaged, Less Knowledgeable." Pew Research Center, July 30, 2020. https://www.journalism.org/2020/07/30/americans-who-mainly-get-their-news-on-social-media-are-less-engaged-less-knowledgeable/.

———. "Appendix: Knowledge Questions Used for Average Correct Responses." Pew Research Center, July 30, 2020. https://www.journalism.org/2020/07/30/appendix-knowledge-questions-used-for-average-correct-responses/.

Morrissey, Monique. "The State of American Retirement Savings." Economic Policy Institute, December 10, 2019. https://www.epi.org/publication/the-state-of-american-retirement-savings/.

Mukherjee, Sougata. "Buoyed by Area's Economic Drivers, TBJ Hits News Milestone." *Triangle Business Journal*, January 30, 2020. https://www.bizjournals.com/triangle/news/2020/01/30/editors-notebookbuoyed-by-areas-economic-drivers.html?iana.

Murtha, Jack. "Why Stock Market Reporting Should Be Treated with Caution." *Columbia Journalism Review*, August 25, 2015. https://www.cjr.org/analysis/stock_market_reporting.php.

Nokelainen, Tomi, and Juho Kanniainen. "Coverage Bias in Business News: Evidence and Methodological Implications." *Management Research Review* 41, no. 4 (2018): 487–503. https://doi.org/10.1108/MRR-02-2017-0048.

Norton, Rictor. *Early Eighteenth-Century Newspaper Reports.* Accessed November 29, 2020, https://grubstreet.rictornorton.co.uk/.

Nunn, Ryan, Jana Parsons, and Jay Shambaugh. "A Dozen Facts about the Economics of the US Health-Care System." Brookings Institution, March 10, 2020. https://www.brookings.edu/research/a-dozen-facts-about-the-economics-of-the-u-s-health-care-system/.

Olen, Helaine. *Pound Foolish: Exposing the Dark Side of the Personal Finance History.* New York: Portfolio, 2012.

Ordway, Denise-Marie, and Heather Bryant. "Covering Poverty: What to Avoid and How to Get It Right." Shorenstein Center on Media, Politics and Public Policy, September 4, 2018. https://journalistsresource.org/tip-sheets/covering-poverty-avoid-get-right/.

Otten, Alan L. "The Influence of the Mass Media on Health Policy." *Health Affairs* 11, no. 4 (Winter 1992): 111–18. https://www.healthaffairs.org/doi/full/10.1377/hlthaff.11.4.111.

Ottenhof, Luke. "America's Labor Crisis Hit a Depleted Beat." *Columbia Journalism Review*, June 1, 2020. https://www.cjr.org/united_states_project/labor-reporting-pandemic-crisis.php.

Overholt, Emily. "Reynolds Foundation Establishes Business Journalism Bureau at ASU's Cronkite School." *Phoenix Business Journal,* July 30, 2014. https://www .bizjournals.com/phoenix/news/2014/07/30/reynolds-foundation-establish es-business.html.

Pardue, Mary Jane. "Most Business Editors Find Journalism Graduates Still Unpre-pared." *Journalism & Mass Communication Educator* 69, no. 1 (March 2014): 49–60. https://doi.org/10.1177/1077695813506989.

Pew Research Center. "As Economic Concerns Recede, Environmental Protection Rises on Public's Policy Agenda." February 13, 2020. https://www.pewresearch .org/politics/2020/02/13/as-economic-concerns-recede-environmental-protec tion-rises-on-the-publics-policy-agenda/.

———. "How the Media Have Depicted the Economic Crisis during Obama's Pres-idency." October 5, 2009. https://www.journalism.org/2009/10/05/cover ing-great-recession/.

———. "Social Media Fact Sheet." June 12, 2019. https://www.pewresearch.org/inter net/fact-sheet/social-media/.

Pinkerton, Stewart. *The Fall of the House of Forbes: The Inside Story of the Collapse of a Media Empire.* New York: St. Martin's, 2011.

Posetti, Julie, Emily Bell, and Pete Brown. "Journalism and the Pandemic Survey." International Center for Journalists, July 2020. https://www.icfj.org/our-work /journalism-and-pandemic-survey.

Pouwels, Randall L. *The African and Middle Eastern World, 600–1500.* Oxford: Oxford University Press, 2005.

Raucher, Alan R. *Public Relations and Business: 1900–1929.* Baltimore: Johns Hopkins University Press, 1968.

Reynolds, R. D. "The 1906 Campaign to Sway Muckraking Periodicals." *Journalism Quarterly* 56, no. 4 (Fall 1979): 513–20.

Richards, Allan, and Kathy Kirkpatrick. "The JMC Innovation Project: A Pivotal Mo-ment for Journalism, Media and Communication Education: Assessing the State of Innovation." *Journalism & Mass Communication Educator* 73, no. 2 (Spring 2018): 136–46.

Riffe, Daniel, and Bill Reeder. "Most Rely on Newspapers for Local Business News." *Newspaper Research Journal* 28, no. 2 (Spring 2007): 82–98.

Roush, Chris. *Profits and Losses: Business Journalism and Its Role in Society.* Portland, OR: Marion Street Press, 2011.

———. "Weeklies on the Rise." *Columbia Journalism Review,* January/February 2010.

Roush, Chris, and Bill Cloud. *The Financial Writer's Stylebook: 1,100 Business Terms Defined and Rated.* Portland, OR: Marion Street Press, 2010.

Rovner, Julie. "The Complicated, Political, Expensive, Seemingly Eternal US Health-care Debate Explained." *BMJ,* October 10, 2019. https://doi.org/10.1136/bmj .l5885.

Schaeffer, Katherine. "6 Facts about Economic Inequality in the US." Pew Research Center, February 7, 2020. https://www.pewresearch.org/fact-tank/2020/02/07 /6-facts-about-economic-inequality-in-the-u-s/.

Schifferes, Steve. *The Media and Financial Crises: Comparative and Historical Perspectives*. New York: Routledge, 2015.

Schuetz, Jenny. "Who Is the New Face of American Homeownership?" Brookings Institution, October 9, 2017. https://www.brookings.edu/blog/the-avenue/2017/10/09/who-is-the-new-face-of-american-homeownership/.

Scudder, Virgil, and Ken Scudder. *World Class Communication: How Great CEOs Win with the Public, Shareholders, Employees and the Media*. New York: Wiley, 2012.

Securities and Exchange Commission. "Final Rule: Selective Disclosure and Insider Trading." October 23, 2000. https://www.sec.gov/rules/final/33-7881.htm.

Shani, Guy, and James Westphal. "Avoiding Bad Press: Interpersonal Influence in Relations between CEOs and Journalists and the Consequences for Press Reporting about Firms and Their Leadership." *Organization Science* 22, no. 4 (2011): 1061–86.

Shapiro, Adam Hale, and Daniel J. Wilson. "What's in the News? A New Economic Indicator." *FRBSF Economic Letter*, April 10, 2017. https://www.frbsf.org/economic-research/publications/economic-letter/2017/april/measuring-economic-sentiment-in-news/.

Shepard, Stephen. *Deadlines and Disruption: My Turbulent Path from Print to Digital*. New York: McGraw-Hill, 2013.

Siblis Research. "Total Market Value of US Stock Market" [Database]. Accessed December 28, 2020. https://siblisresearch.com/data/us-stock-market-value/#:~:text=The%20total%20market%20capitalization%20of,about%20OTC%20markets%20from%20ohere.

Silverman, Jacob. "Spies, Lies, and Stonewalling: What It's like to Report on Facebook." *Columbia Journalism Review*, July 1, 2020. https://www.cjr.org/special_report/reporting-on-facebook.php.

Simons, L. M. "Follow the Money." *American Journalism Review*, November 1999.

Starkman, Dean. "A Narrowed Gaze: How the Business Pres Forgot the Rest of Us." *Columbia Journalism Review*, January/February 2012. https://archives.cjr.org/cover_story/a_narrowed_gaze.php.

Steinmetz, Greg. *The Richest Man Who Ever Lived: The Life and Times of Jacob Fugger*. New York: Simon & Schuster, 2015.

Stiglitz, Joseph. "The Media and the Crisis: An Information Theoretical Approach." In *Bad News: How America's Business Press Missed the Story of the Century*. Edited by Anya Schiffrin. New York: New Press, 2011.

Strauss, Nadine. "Financial Journalism in Today's High-Frequency News and Information Era." *Journalism* 20, no. 2 (2019): 274–91. doi:10.1177/1464884917753556.

Strycharz, Joanna, Nadine Strauss, and Damian Trilling. "The Role of Media Coverage in Explaining Stock Market Fluctuations: Insights for Strategic Financial Communication." *International Journal of Strategic Communication* 12, no. 1 (2018): 67–85. https://dx.doi.org/10.1080/1553118X.2017.1378220.

Sullivan, Margaret. *Ghosting the News: Local Journalism and the Crisis of American Democracy*. New York: Columbia Global Reports, 2020.

Sutherland, Lucy. "The Marginalizing of Business News at Small and Mid-Sized American Dailies." Master's thesis, Emerson College, 2004.

Taylor, James. "White-Collar Crime and the Law in Nineteenth-Century Britain." *Business History* 60, no. 3 (September 2018): 343–60. https://www.tandfonline.com /doi/abs/10.1080/00076791.2017.1339691?journalCode=fbsh20.

Tetlock, Paul C. "Giving Content to Investor Sentiment: The Role of Media in the Stock Market." *Journal of Finance* 62, no. 3 (June 2007): 1139–68.

Theil, Stefan. "The Media and Markets: How Systematic Misreporting Inflates Bubbles, Deepens Downturns and Distorts Economic Reality." Shorenstein Center on Media, Politics and Public Policy Discussion Paper Series, June 2014. https:// dash.harvard.edu/bitstream/handle/1/12872174/d86-theil.pdf?sequence=1&is Allowed=y.

Tsai, Wan-Hsiu, and Linjuan Rita Men. "Social CEOs: The Effects of CEOs' Communication Styles and Parasocial Interaction on Social Networking Sites." *New Media & Society* 19, no. 11 (2017): 1848–67.

Uberti, David. "The Labor Beat Is Dead; Long Live the Labor Beat." *Columbia Journalism Review*, March 12, 2015. https://www.cjr.org/analysis/when_longtime_la bor_reporter_steven.php.

US Bureau of Labor Statistics. "Average Employee Medical Premium $6,797 for Family Coverage in 2020." October 2, 2020. https://www.bls.gov/opub/ted/2020 /average-employee-medical-premium-6797-dollars-for-family-cover age-in-2020.htm.

———. "Consumer Price Index Summary." January 13, 2021. https://www.bls.gov /news.release/cpi.nro.htm.

———. "Employee Tenure in 2020." September 22, 2020. https://www.bls.gov /news.release/pdf/tenure.pdf.

———. "Job Growth at Small Businesses, 1992–2013." *Economics Daily*, May 12, 2014. https://www.bls.gov/opub/ted/2014/ted_20140512.htm.

———. "National Compensation Survey: Employee Benefits in the United States, March 2018." September 2018. https://www.bls.gov/ncs/ebs/benefits/2018/em ployee-benefits-in-the-united-states-march-2018.pdf.

———. "National Longitudinal Surveys." Accessed January 6, 2021. https://www.bls .gov/nls/questions-and-answers.htm#anch41.

———. "Public Relations Specialists Job Outlook." Accessed December 1, 2010. https://www.bls.gov/ooh/media-and-communication/public-relations-special ists.htm#tab-6.

———. "Reporters, Correspondents, and Broadcast News Analysts Job Outlook." Accessed December 1, 2020. https://www.bls.gov/ooh/media-and-communica tion/reporters-correspondents-and-broadcast-news-analysts.htm#tab-6.

———. "77 Percent of Private Industry Workers in Medical Care Plans with Two Networks in 2018." July 26, 2019. https://www.bls.gov/opub/ted/2019/77-percent -of-private-industry-workers-in-medical-care-plans-with-two-networks-in-2018. htm.

————. "Union Members—2020." January 22, 2021. https://www.bls.gov/news.re lease/pdf/union2.pdf.

US Census Bureau. "Annual Business Survey Release Provides Data on Minority- and Women-Owned Businesses." May 19, 2020. https://www.census.gov/news room/press-releases/2020/annual-business-survey-data.html.

————. "Census 2000 Shows America's Diversity." March 12, 2001. https://www .census.gov/newsroom/releases/archives/census_2000/cb01cn61.html.

————. "Quarterly Residential Vacancies and Homeownership, Third Quarter 2020." October 27, 2020. https://www.census.gov/housing/hvs/files/currenth vspress.pdf.

————. "2007 SUSB Annual Data Tables by Establishment Industry." Accessed Jan- uary 6, 2021. https://www.census.gov/data/tables/2007/econ/susb/2007-susb -annual.html.

————. "2017 SUSB Annual Data Tables by Establishment Industry." Accessed Janu- ary 6, 2021. https://www.census.gov/data/tables/2017/econ/susb/2017-susb-an nual.html.

US Small Business Administration Office of Advocacy. "Frequently Asked Ques- tions." Accessed December 28, 2020. https://www.sba.gov/sites/default/files /advocacy/Frequently-Asked-Questions-Small-Business-2018.pdf.

————. "Small Businesses Generate 44 Percent of US Economic Activity." January 30, 2019. https://advocacy.sba.gov/2019/01/30/small-businesses-generate-44-per cent-of-u-s-economic-activity/.

Vidgen, Richard, Julian Sims, and Phillip Powell. "Do CEO Bloggers Build Commu- nity?" *Journal of Communication Management* 17, no. 4 (2013): 364–85.

Weber, Joseph. "Teaching Business and Economic Journalism: Fresh Approaches." *Journalism and Mass Communication Educator* 71, no. 4 (December 2016): 1–17.

Weinberg, Steve. *A Journalism of Humanity: A Candid History of the World's First Jour- nalism School.* Columbia: University of Missouri Press, 2008.

————. *Taking on the Trust: The Epic Battle of Ida Tarbell and John D. Rockefeller.* New York: Norton, 2008.

Weidenbener, Lesley. "Greg Morris to Retire as Publisher of IBJ, Indiana Lawyer." *Indianapolis Business Journal,* December 11, 2020. https://www.ibj.com/articles /greg-morris-to-retire-as-publisher-of-ibj-indiana-lawyer.

West, Darrell M., and Beth Stone. "Nudging News Producers and Consumers toward More Thoughtful, Less Polarized Discourse." Center for Effective Public Man- agement at Brookings, February 2014. https://www.brookings.edu/wp-content /uploads/2016/06/West-Stone_Nudging-News-Consumers-and-Producers.pdf.

Westphal, James D., and David L. Deephouse. "Avoiding Bad Press: Interpersonal Influence in Relations between CEOs and Journalists and the Consequences for Press Reporting about Firms and Their Leadership." *Organization Science* 22, no. 4 (September 2010): 1061–86.

Williams, Alex T. "The Growing Gap between Journalism and Public Relations." Pew Research Center, August 11, 2014. https://www.pewresearch.org/fact-tank /2014/08/11/the-growing-pay-gap-between-journalism-and-public-relations/.

Wisniewski, Tomasz Piotr, and Brendan Lambe. "The Role of Media in the Credit Crunch: The Case of the Banking Sector." *Journal of Economic Behavior & Organization* 85 (January 2013): 163–75.

Women's Media Center. 2017. "The Status of Women in the US Media 2016." Accessed January 6, 2020. http://www.womensmediacenter.com/reports/status -of-women-in-us-media.

Wu, Chen-Hui, and Chan-Jane Lin. "The Impact of Media Coverage on Investor Trading Behavior and Stock Returns." *Pacific-Basin Finance Journal* 43 (2017): 151–72.

Yi, Jin. "Agenda-Setting Effects of Television News Coverage on Perceptions of Corporate Reputation." Master's thesis, University of Missouri-Columbia, 2008.

Ying, Wang, Zhang Tianzhen, and Song Jiameng. "Effects Financial Media Have on Firm Value and Suggestions for Investor Relations Media Strategy." Paper presented at 2018 International Conference on Advances in Social Sciences and Sustainable Development, May 2018. https://www.atlantis-press.com/proceed ings/asssd-18/25894426.

Yoe, Jonathan. "Why Are Older People Working Longer?" US Bureau of Labor Statistics, July 2019. https://www.bls.gov/opub/mlr/2019/beyond-bls/why-are-older -people-working-longer.htm.

Zerfass, Ansgar, and Muschda Sherzada. "Corporate Communications from the CEO's Perspective: How Top Executives Conceptualize and Value Strategic Communication." *Corporate Communications: An International Journal* 20, no. 3 (2015): 291–309.

Zerfass, Ansgar, Dejan Vercic, and Markus Wiesenberg. "Managing CEO Communication and Positioning." *Journal of Communication Management* 20, no. 1 (2016): 37–55.

INDEX

ABOUT THE AUTHOR

Chris Roush is the dean of the School of Communications at Quinnipiac University. He previously was the Walter E. Hussman Sr. Distinguished Professor in business journalism at the University of North Carolina at Chapel Hill, where he was also senior associate dean of the School of Media and Journalism. Roush has spent his entire professional career either as a practicing business journalist or teaching business journalism. He has written or cowritten eleven books about business journalism or companies. He also founded *Talking Biz News,* which covers the world of business journalism. Roush is a board member of the Foundation for Financial Journalism. He was named the Journalism Professor of the Year in 2010 by the Association for Education in Journalism and Mass Communications and the Scripps Howard Foundation. The judges noted that Roush "has become the expert in business journalism—not just at Chapel Hill, but throughout the country and even in other parts of the world."